Directions in Psycholinguistics

DIRECTIONS IN
PSYCHOLINGUISTICS

Edited by

SHELDON ROSENBERG

GEORGE PEABODY COLLEGE FOR TEACHERS

THE MACMILLAN COMPANY, NEW YORK
COLLIER–MACMILLAN LIMITED, LONDON

401
R813

THIRD PRINTING, 1967

LIBRARY OF CONGRESS CATALOG CARD NUMBER: 65–16567

THE MACMILLAN COMPANY, NEW YORK
COLLIER-MACMILLAN CANADA, LTD., TORONTO, ONTARIO

PRINTED IN THE UNITED STATES OF AMERICA

Preface

Psycholinguistics today enjoys fresh interest and an unprecedented upsurge of research activity. Recognizing this vigor and movement, the Department of Psychology of George Peabody College for Teachers held a two-week Institute in June 1963 that was designed to introduce graduate students, faculty, and research workers interested in language to major contemporary developments in research and theory. The emphasis of the Institute was basic rather than applied, and those who participated represented such fields as psychology, linguistics, English, education, and speech pathology.

The strategy of the Institute was to present psycholinguistics in the context of the work of contemporary contributors to the field. To this end, we invited as guest lecturers a group of scientists whose work was representative of what appeared to us to be some of the major directions of contemporary thinking, and because of the strong interest expressed in the research in progress, our guest lecturers were invited to take part of their time to present formal papers dealing with their current research and theoretical efforts. The present volume is an extension of these papers, which appear here as they were revised for publication by their authors after the Institute was over. Because of the ample time allowed for revision, some authors have been able to include in their articles research not available at the time of the Institute. The papers include discussions of and references to research that have not appeared elsewhere. Some of this material is in press and some of it is available at present only in unpublished form.

In the organization of the Institute, James H. Koplin and I were responsible for the presentation of general prefatory material introducing the participants to the work of each of our guest lecturers, and the first section of this book is based in part upon some of this material.

No editorial changes were made in the content of any of the papers without permission of the author, but it was necessary in some instances to modify certain aspects of form for purposes of continuity. The Editor assumes full responsibility for such changes.

Besides myself, the contributors to this volume, and their institutional affiliations, are James H. Koplin, Charles D. Spielberger, and Jum C. Nunnally of Vanderbilt University; Sol Saporta, Arthur L. Blumenthal, Peter Lackowski, and Donald G. Reiff of The University of Washington; Neal F. Johnson of The Ohio State University; James J. Jenkins of The University of Minnesota; Benton J. Underwood of Northwestern University; Lyle V. Jones of University of North Carolina; and Joseph M. Wepman of University of Chicago. An effort such as the present one is, of course, never fully represented in terms of the contributions of those whose names appear in a final publication. I therefore would like to acknowledge particularly the contribution of Dr. Felix C. Robb, President of George Peabody College for Teachers, whose policy of support for new developments in behavioral research and education made the Institute possible. I also thank Dr. Nicholas Hobbs, Chairman of the Division of Human Development of Peabody College, for his continuous encouragement and assistance during the months of planning for the Institute and for the subsequent publication. Finally, I express my gratitude to those members of the faculties of Peabody College and Vanderbilt University who attended the proceedings. They did much to make the sessions of the Institute vital and exciting experiences for everyone concerned.

SHELDON ROSENBERG

Nashville, Tennessee
March 1965

Contents

I

INTRODUCTION

INTRODUCTION TO PSYCHOLINGUISTICS

Sheldon Rosenberg

James H. Koplin

Psycholinguistics, in spite of its youth, has become in recent years a major area of basic research and theoretical effort in psychology. Symptomatic of this growth, for example, was the publication in 1962 of the first broadly distributed psychological journal devoted entirely to work in verbal learning, verbal behavior, and psycholinguistics, *The Journal of Verbal Learning and Verbal Behavior*.[1] In addition, papers of the sort that in previous years were published in technical reports and nonpsychological publications are now appearing with greater frequency in the regular psychological journals.

The Field of Psycholinguistics

Although the field that we are concerned with is clearly not the sole province of the psychologist, the emphasis of the present volume is psychological. As Miller's (1951) review, *Language and*

---

[1] Published by the Academic Press, Inc., New York.

Communication, indicates, interest in the psychological study of language behavior is not new; the recent intensification of interest in what has come to be known as psycholinguistics can be traced at least in part to the psycholinguistics monograph (1954),[2] edited by Osgood and Sebeok. Nurtured by the work of learning theorists, communication engineers, and descriptive linguists, the monograph attempted to conceptualize the area in the context of the general study of human communication, an emphasis which Osgood (1963*a*) has reiterated in a recent review of the field. In his own words, ". . . *psycholinguistics is the science of encoding and decoding processes in individual communicators."* *Encoding* processes are involved in language production and *decoding* processes in language reception.

Judging from the behavior of psychologists, this definition is usually interpreted to include, among other things, studies of (1) the influence of verbal and nonverbal antecedent conditions upon verbal behavior and verbal learning, (2) the influence of verbal stimuli upon nonverbal behavior and learning, (3) the role of verbal mediators in behavior, (4) interrelationships among various dimensions of verbal response, (5) relationships between verbal and nonverbal response dimensions, (6) language acquisition and language development, and (7) strictly normative studies of language behavior.

Since the publication of the monograph, in addition to the review by Osgood (1963*a*) already mentioned, such works have appeared as Brown's (1958) *Words and Things;* the two volumes of papers on verbal learning and verbal behavior edited by Cofer and Musgrave (1961, 1963); Gough and Jenkins' (1963) chapter on theory in verbal learning and psycholinguistics; Miller's (1962) paper on psychology and grammar; Osgood's (1963*b*) recent attempt at rapprochement between Markov process and hierarchic sentence-to-word models of sentence encoding and decoding; the book on meaning by Osgood, Suci, and Tannenbaum (1957); a collection of readings edited by Saporta (1961); Skinner's (1957) *Verbal*

---

[2] During this year we also saw the publication of Mowrer's influential paper on language.

Behavior; and a review of research literature by Rubenstein and Aborn (1960). Recently, there has been increased interest in the development of mathematical formulations relevant to psycholinguistics, especially with respect to the problem of grammar (see, for example, Jakobson, 1961; Luce, Bush, and Galanter, 1963).

That there are differences in opinion as to the kinds of research problems psycholinguists should concern themselves with is not surprising in a field as young as this one. For example, traditional research on verbal learning may not be seen by some as contributing directly to our understanding of natural language processes. That there are areas of overlapping interest for the fields of verbal learning and psycholinguistics, however, as well as areas of separation, has been pointed out by Gough and Jenkins (1963).

The position taken in the organization of the present Institute, although not necessarily shared by all of the contributors to this volume, was that the field of verbal learning has much to contribute to our understanding of natural language behavior. For example, if there is any "psychological reality" to the linguist's (e.g., Gleason, 1961) concept of "levels of linguistic structure" (sentence, phrase, morpheme, etc.), as we suspect there is (Miller, 1962; Rosenberg and Baker, 1964), it becomes important to identify and determine the influence of verbal habits that operate at levels that include isolated words, syllables, and letter combinations. Research of the sort that is included in *Meaningfulness and Verbal Learning* (Underwood and Schulz, 1960) is representative of work at these levels. In addition, research on paired-associate learning can be viewed, in a sense, as an attempt to identify conditions that influence the establishment of sequential dependencies between verbal units or between classes of units. Studies of mediation in verbal paired-associate learning which have involved the establishment of stimulus and response equivalences have already contributed to the development of a mediational theory of grammatical phenomena (see the article by Jenkins in this volume).

Another area in which the traditional field of verbal learning may contribute to psycholinguistics is language development. Specifically, while the sentence may be at the top of the linguist's hierarchy, and while it may turn out that psychologically (at least in encoding) sentence structures determine relationships at the level of the isolated word (Miller, Galanter, and Pribram, 1960), the developmental picture is, of course, just the opposite. The sequence of relevant unit-stages suggested by the results of a number of studies (e.g., Chen and Irwin, 1946; Lewis, 1936; Shirley, 1933) is phoneme, syllable, word, phrase, sentence. This is an oversimplification, of course, and these stages overlap to a certain extent, but it is important to note that there are periods in the development of language facility during which what may be the units of verbal behavior resemble some of those that have been studied extensively in the area of verbal learning. Research relevant to unit formation, for example, in nonsense syllables (Underwood, 1964; Underwood and Schulz, 1960), may have implications for the ways in which units are formed during language acquisition.

As a final point, even if one prefers to limit his definition of psycholinguistics, it would be impossible to use rote verbal learning tasks to study, for example, the effect of variations in grammatical structure, without proper attention to the contribution of variables (e.g., word frequency, intralist similarity, method of presentation, method of testing) that have been found to be of importance by psychologists working in the area of verbal learning.

Additional discussions of the relationship between verbal learning and psycholinguistics can be found in the article by Johnson and in the article by Underwood in this volume.

Although the contribution of learning theory to the development of psycholinguistic thinking has been considerable (see, for example, Osgood, 1963a, 1963b; Skinner, 1957), another area that may not always be seen as being clearly relevant to the more general concerns of psycholinguistics is verbal conditioning. From a psychological standpoint, however, unless we can identify the variables that determine whether or not verbal behavior will be emitted and at what rate it will be emitted, knowledge of other aspects of language activity may be of limited practical significance. Spielberger, in this book, is particularly concerned with the contribution of cognitive and motivational determinants to verbal conditioning.

Current Issues in Psycholinguistics

While this volume does not pretend to cover the entire field of psycholinguistics, the articles included in it are representative of a number of the major trends in research and theory today. The discussion that follows is an attempt to conceptualize what appeared to be the most important questions of concern to the contributors.

WHAT IS THE ROLE OF LINGUISTIC SCIENCE IN THE PSYCHOLOGY OF LANGUAGE?

Jenkins points out forcefully that the work of the linguist "focuses our attention on a set of neglected problems with which the psychologist *must* cope." Jenkins asserts further that observations of language behavior "demand an account of behavior that can deal with structure, hierarchy, class, and combination."

The importance attributed to the "linguistics" in psycholinguistics takes the form of concern with (1) *the psychological implications of linguistic models of grammar*—i.e., descriptive and generative (Johnson), finite state, phrase structure and transformational (Jenkins, Johnson, Saporta *et al.*)—and with (2) *the need to discover possible behavioral correlates of linguistic structures.* Jenkins views the search for behavioral correlates of linguistic structures as a major approach to the study of the structure of language behavior, and much of the research he discusses, as well as much of the material discussed by Johnson, Rosenberg, and Saporta *et al.*, is relevant to this approach. Throughout these articles one sees the contribution of linguistic science in the form of specification of manipulable dimensions of verbal materials and in the form of hypotheses about the functional units of language behavior.

HOW IS LANGUAGE STRUCTURE ACQUIRED?

The research and theory discussed by Jenkins are directed primarily to the question of how linguistic classes and their sequential arrangements—from the level of the phoneme to the level of the sentence—are learned. A possible solution to part of this problem is offered in terms of a mediation model for the establishment of stimulus and response equivalences.

Jones and Wepman, working from the vantage point of research on language pathology, propose a conceptual scheme to account for the general development of language based upon the work of a number of investigators.

HOW ARE SENTENCES GENERATED PSYCHOLOGICALLY?

Johnson's central concern is with this very basic question. He proposes a theory of language encoding based upon Chomsky's (1957) theory of grammar and the results of research which suggest strongly that language materials might be recoded into units (describable in terms of linguistic phrase structure rules) larger than the individual word or morpheme for processing. The hierarchic structure of language, as it is revealed both linguistically and psychologically, is made a basic ingredient of the theory.

WHAT IS THE ROLE PLAYED BY PRE-ESTABLISHED VERBAL HABITS IN THE ACQUISITION AND RETENTION OF VERBAL MATERIALS?

This question is the central concern of Underwood and of Rosenberg. Underwood discusses research that has contributed to the identification of some of the verbal habits from a subject's "linguistic repertoire" that appear to influence performance in verbal learning situations. These include, for example, stimulus selection habits, item coding habits (transformations of verbal units), and second-order habits (i.e., habits that determine the class of a response, such as sequential grammatical habits and conceptual habits). Recent research on the possible role of the "linguistic repertoire" in forgetting is also evaluated.

Rosenberg discusses some of the implications of recent developments in linguistics for the area of verbal learning, and he stresses the need for research on the relationship between grammatical structure (sequential grammatical habits, grammatical form class, level of linguistic structure) and such traditional verbal learning variables as associative habit and word frequency. A series of studies is reported on in which an attempt was made to compare the effects of sequential grammatical habits with the effects of sequential associative habits upon performance in simple verbal learning situations.

Much of the work discussed by Jenkins, by Johnson, and by Nunnally, since it involves studies of the effects of pre-established (experimentally and by assessment through norms of verbal behavior) verbal habits upon subsequent verbal learning, is also relevant here.

WHAT ARE THE CONDITIONS FOR THE MODIFICATION OF VERBAL BEHAVIOR?

Experiments in verbal conditioning originated in the laboratories of psychologists who embrace stimulus-response theories. Later cognitive theorists began to attack this problem. Spielberger examines the research and theorizing that have been produced by these divergent approaches. A major point developed is that the rival theories are leading to vigorous research and sensitive experiments, but the sets of accumulating facts are *not* leading to a convergence of the points of view. This convergence is seen as one of the goals of any scientific enterprise.

He contends that basic epistemological assumptions associated with each of the theoretical positions influence the design and analysis of experiments to such a degree that comparable data will not be collected. The chief issue concerns the status of the concept "awareness" in each of the systems. Awareness is interpreted as a dependent variable by stimulus-response theorists, while cognitive investigators design their experiments using awareness as an independent variable.

Having established this position, Spielberger presents a critical review of the background of verbal conditioning research and the major techniques that have been applied. The last section of the article reports several experiments by the author and his students in which it is convincingly demonstrated that the amount of variance accounted for in verbal conditioning experiments is significantly increased if awareness is viewed as an independent variable in the design.

WHAT IS THE ROLE OF INDIVIDUAL DIFFERENCES IN VERBAL BEHAVIOR?

Everyone agrees that individual differences in verbal behavior must be important, but little successful effort has been directed toward a systematic account of this variable. Nunnally presents a general theory to embrace the effects of word usage in learning, perception, and personality.

The theoretical formulation begins with some statements about the acquisition of particular words by individuals. One of the most important parts of the theory pertains to the role that motivational states play in the words produced and the rate at which they are produced by subjects.

The essential notion is that subjects do not have a single response hierarchy to a given stimulus word. Rather they have many hierarchies related to different need states.

The next section of the article expands the application of the theory to the three problem areas mentioned above and discusses the work of the author and his associates in developing instruments to measure the individual differences in word usage of subjects. These measures are labeled "semantic habit scales."

Three experiments are cited which demonstrate the fruitfulness of the approach in studies of learning, perception, and personality variables. The article concludes with some methodological cautions that are of particular importance to investigators in this area.

WHAT CAN WE LEARN ABOUT THE GENERAL STRUCTURE OF LANGUAGE BEHAVIOR FROM A CONSIDERATION OF THE RESULTS OF RESEARCH ON LANGUAGE PATHOLOGY?

One of the major hypotheses put forth by Jones and Wepman is that the study of aphasia will lead to general principles of language organization. "By determining the communication processes that are differentially affected by brain damage, we become aware of language processes that must contribute to the language skills of a normally functioning person."

From data collected in a highly structured situation and from the grammatical analysis of free speech samples from aphasics and normal adults (along with the results of observations of language development in normal children), a conceptual model of the language processing units in normal persons is proposed.

Part of the research these authors discuss was facilitated by the development of a computer program for the analysis of the grammatical form class of words.

References

Brown, R. *Words and things.* New York: The Free Press, 1958.

Chen, H. P., and O. C. Irwin. "Infant speech vowel and consonant types." *J. Speech Disorders,* 1946, **11,** 27–29.

Chomsky, N. *Syntactic structures.* The Hague: Mouton, 1957.

Cofer, C. N., and Barbara S. Musgrave (eds.). *Verbal learning and verbal behavior.* New York: McGraw-Hill, 1961.

———, and ——— (eds.). *Verbal behavior and learning.* New York: McGraw-Hill, 1963.

Gleason, H. A. *An introduction to descriptive linguistics,* rev. ed. New York: Holt, Rinehart and Winston, 1961.

Gough, P. B., and J. J. Jenkins. "Verbal learning and psycholinguistics." In M. H. Marx (ed.). *Theories in contemporary psychology.* New York: Macmillan, 1963.

Jakobson, R. (ed.). *Structure of language and its mathematical aspects.* Proceedings of symposia in applied mathematics. Vol. XII. Providence, R.I.: American Mathematical Society, 1961.

Lewis, M. M. *Infant speech: a study of the beginnings of language.* New York: Harcourt, Brace, 1936.

Luce, R. D., R. R. Bush, and E. Galanter (eds.). *Handbook of mathematical psychology,* Vol. II. New York: Wiley, 1963.

Miller, G. A. *Language and communication.* New York: McGraw-Hill, 1951.

———. "Some psychological studies of grammar." *Amer. Psychologist,* 1962, **17,** 748–762.

———, E. Galanter, and K. H. Pribram. *Plans and the structure of behavior.* New York: Henry Holt, 1960.

Mowrer, O. H. "The psychologist looks at language." *Amer. Psychologist,* 1954, **9,** 660–694.

Osgood, C. E. "Psycholinguistics." In S. Koch (ed.). *Psychology: a study of a science,* Vol. 6. New York: McGraw-Hill, 1963*a*.

———. "On understanding and creating sentences." *Amer. Psychologist.* 1963*b*, **18,** 735–751.

———, and T. A. Sebeok (eds.). "Psycholinguistics: a survey of theory and research." *J. Abnorm. Soc. Psychol.,* 1954, **49,** Suppl. to No. 4.

———, G. J. Suci, and P. H. Tannenbaum. *The measurement of meaning.* Urbana, Ill.: University of Illinois Press, 1957.

Rosenberg, S., and Norma J. Baker. "Grammatical form class as a variable in verbal learning at three levels of linguistic structure." Paper presented at meetings of Southeastern Psychological Association, Gatlinburg, Tenn., April, 1964.

Rubenstein, H., and M. Aborn. "Psycholinguistics." *Annual Rev. Psychol.,* 1960, **11,** 291–322.

Saporta, S. *Psycholinguistics: a book of readings.* New York: Holt, Rinehart and Winston, 1961.

Shirley, M. M. "The first two years: a study of twenty-five babies. II. Intellectual development." *Inst. Child Welf. Monogr. Ser.* Minneapolis: University of Minnesota Press, 1933.

Skinner, B. F. *Verbal behavior.* New York: Appleton-Century-Crofts, 1957.

Underwood, B. J. "The representativeness of rote verbal learning." In A. W. Melton (ed.). *Categories of human learning.* New York: Academic Press, 1964.

———, and R. W. Schulz. *Meaningfulness and verbal learning.* Philadelphia: J. B. Lippincott, 1960.

II

THE PSYCHOLOGY
OF
GRAMMAR

GRAMMATICAL MODELS AND LANGUAGE LEARNING[1]

Sol Saporta, Arthur L. Blumenthal, Peter Lackowski, and Donald G. Reiff

The ultimate purposes of a series of studies currently being conducted at the University of Washington are twofold: (1) to provide behavioral correlates for three theoretical models of grammatical description, and (2) to demonstrate how in a specific language-learning situation certain models facilitate second-language acquisition.

Chomsky (1957) has demonstrated that essentially three models underlie most generative grammars: a finite-state model, a phrase-structure or immediate constituent model, and a transformational model. The first two may be illustrated by the following

[1] This article is a slightly expanded and modified version of "Grammatical models and language learning," which appeared in *Monograph series on languages and linguistics, Volume 16* (*Report of the fourteenth annual round table meeting on linguistic and language studies*), Robert J. De Pietro, ed., pp. 133–142 (1963). Portions of this article that were included in the original version are reproduced here with permission. The study is supported under contract OE–2–14–010 with the Office of Education under Title VI of the National Defense Education Act.

examples. Assume that we wish to account for the following eight sequences:

NS	NX	NXN	NXGN
GNS	GNX	GNXN	GNXGN

A finite-state model might be used to generate these sequences in a way something like the following. Given a diagram such as that in Figure 1, a sequence is produced by tracing a path from the initial point on the left to the final point on the right, always proceeding in the direction of the arrows. Having reached a certain

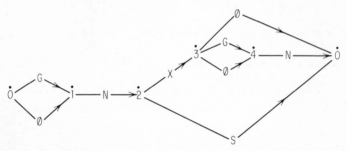

Figure 1 *Finite state grammar.* From Saporta, et al., *Monograph Series on Languages and Linguistics*, **16**, 1963, pp. 133–142. Reproduced by permission.

point in the diagram, one can proceed along any path leading from this point. Each point in the diagram is a state, and the transition from one state to another produces one of a certain set of symbols. Transition from one state to another is allowed in several ways, including zero ϕ. The initial and final states are both represented by 0. The other states are referred to as internal states. The eight sequences listed above or any list may be trivially converted into a finite-state grammar of one state as follows:

$$0 \underset{GNS}{\overset{NS}{\longleftarrow}} NX \longrightarrow 0$$

etc.

Clearly, the actual diagram is not the most efficient way of presenting the rules of combination. The description in Figure 1 can be written more concisely as follows:

011 — G	121 — N	231 — X	341 — G	401 — N
012 — φ			342 — φ	
		201 — S	301 — φ	

The first two numbers indicate the states that are connected; the third number indicates the transition between those states. Thus the sequence NXN is produced by moving from 0 to 1 producing φ, from 1 to 2 producing N, from 2 to 3 producing X, from 3 to 4 producing φ, and from 4 to 0 producing N, and so forth.

Now the same eight sequences (S) can be generated by a set of rewrite rules such as the following: where the arrow is to be read "is rewritten as," items in a column linked by a brace represent lists, one of which must be chosen, and items within angle brackets are optional.

1. $S \rightarrow A \quad B$

2. $B \rightarrow \left\{ \begin{matrix} X & \langle A \rangle \\ S & \end{matrix} \right\}$

3. $A \quad \langle G \rangle \quad N$

Such a set of rules has been referred to as a context-free phrase-structure grammar, and any finite-state grammar such as the one in Figure 1 is convertible into such a set of rewrite rules.

A phrase-structure grammar assigns to each sequence a structural description that can be represented by a branching diagram or tree. Thus the sequence NXN is represented by the following tree which reflects the application of the appropriate rules needed to derive the sequence in question:

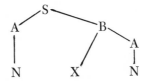

A context-sensitive phrase-structure grammar essentially consists of rules of the type $XAY \rightarrow XBY$ (that is, it rewrites only one

symbol at a time, but allows for specifying the context as part of
the condition for applying a particular rule). Figure 2 shows a
finite-state grammar and a context-free phrase-structure grammar
for a language that was used as a basis for the experiments described below. Following the grammars is a sample derivation.

A. Finite-State Grammar

011-G	121-N	231-X	341-G	451-N
012-Ø			342-Ø	
		251-S	351-Ø	
			671-G	
		561-X	672-Ø	701-N
		501-S	601-Ø	

B. Phrase-Structure Grammar

1. S → A   B   ⟨B⟩

2. B → { X – ⟨A⟩ }
       { S   }

3. A → ⟨G⟩   N

C. Sample Derivation

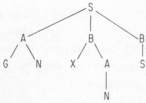

Figure 2 *Finite-state and phrase-structure grammars, with sample
derivation.* From Saporta, et al., *Monograph Series on Languages and
Linguistics*, **16**, 1963, pp. 133–142. Reproduced by permission.

A transformational grammar allows for a less restricted type of
rule permitting such operations as permutations, deletions, and
additions. A transformation operates on a given string, or on a set

of strings, with a particular structural description and yields a new string with a derived structural description.

Chomsky has pointed out the limitations of finite-state and phrase-structure grammars from the point of view of generative potential and over-all simplicity of description. That the three models are increasingly powerful seems clear. Indeed, it is apparent from a simple characterization of them that this must be the case, since a phrase-structure grammar does not preclude a finite-state type of rule, but rather adds a different type of rule as well, and similarly for a transformational grammar.

Grammatical models differ, too, in their explanatory power. Thus the ambiguity of the expression *old men and women* is demonstrated by a phrase-structure grammar which assigns to it two different structural descriptions. Similarly, the ambiguity of *the shooting of hunters* is not readily accounted for by a phrase-structure grammar but is by a grammar that includes transformational rules.

Consequently, we are not trying to provide additional evidence of a purely logical sort for what we feel has already been adequately demonstrated. Rather, we accept the proposition submitted by Chomsky and ask what kind of experimental situations can be set up which will show differences in learning behavior that correspond to the different grammatical models. Phrased in the most general terms, we are concerned with demonstrating that, all other things being equal, the learning of language can be affected by the grammatical model underlying the presentation and, of course, that the difference will be in the predicted direction.

The following grammatical drills may serve as illustrations of the different approaches:

(a) *FS* (finite state): Students are given a stem—e.g., *The man saw*—and are asked to provide appropriate items such as *John* (*The man saw John*), *him, trees, poorly* (*The man saw poorly*). The process of formulating grammatical sentences is thus viewed as a series of selections of items from some inventory, each selection of subsequent events being conditioned by antecedent events.

(b) *PS* (phrase structure): Students are presented with a particular pattern and expansions of one segment of the pattern for substitution in the appropriate position; thus, for example, with a model *The man saw John,* the student might be asked to substitute *his friend* for *John* (*The man saw his friend*), *his good friend, his very good friend,* etc. Underlying such a drill is the view that what is essentially the same pattern may be represented by different combinations of word classes, introducing a hierarchy of levels, according to which, for example, *John* and *his very good friend,* of different internal structures, may nevertheless substitute for each other in larger sequences. The two are essentially different representations of the same construction, in this case a noun phrase.

(c) *T* (transformational): Students are presented with a pattern and are required to perform a number of changes necessary to convert it into a different but related pattern. Thus, presented with a stimulus *The man saw John,* a student must make a response indicating awareness of the relationship of patterns: *Did the man see John?,* or *John was seen by the man,* etc. In addition to the hierarchical levels of PS, this drill is based on exploiting relationships between sentences.

Now the above are drills, not grammars, and the current studies are not concerned with questions of pedagogy or of certain teaching techniques. The variable we are concerned with isolating is the underlying grammatical model.

It soon became clear that there were at least two notions about which we had made assumptions but about which we had not been sufficiently explicit. Our first job then was to define what kind of behavior could appropriately be called "learning a language" and, furthermore, to determine in what sense and to what extent we could talk about "all other things (except the underlying model) being equal." The preliminary pilot studies described here are aimed at clarifying these questions.

Preliminary Studies

We assumed that we could write two grammars for the same corpus, say, a finite-state grammar and a phrase-structure grammar, and then use these grammars as a basis for presenting material to two groups of subjects.

Such a requirement seemed to provide the best kind of experimental controls, since it makes it possible in theory at least to eliminate all variables but the underlying grammatical model. But in so doing, we diluted the advantage of the phrase-structure model, since we were now restricted to using languages that could be described adequately by either generating device, and as Chomsky has pointed out, the advantage of a phrase-structure grammar is precisely that it can account for certain properties of language that cannot be handled by a simpler theory. In effect then, we were arguing that if we could demonstrate that a phrase-structure presentation could facilitate learning for languages that both models could describe, then it would follow that such a presentation would have to facilitate learning for a language that only the phrase-structure model could describe. Figure 2 shows two such grammars which are the basis for the studies described here. Each grammar is presumably the simplest one in keeping with the model, and each generated the same corpus, a total of 40 sequences of varying lengths.

In the first experiment, nonsense symbols were substituted for the terminal symbols, G being represented by #, N by □, X by ◊ , and S by /. These symbols were substituted to avoid any built-in associations that the letters might have which might prejudice the data. But this results in a rather odd use of the word "language." In fact, the sequences of nonsense symbols lack both a phonological component and a semantic component, since they are neither pronounceable nor particularly meaningful. But they do have a syntactic component, since there are clear restrictions on the combinatorial possibilities. Hence, what we are concerned with at this stage is not so much the learning of language, but the learning of syntax.

The first three experiments, which, incidentally, yielded negative results, may serve to illustrate the nature of the problem.

In the first experiment, subjects were shown each one of the 40 sequences generated by the grammars at a rate of 5 seconds each. After this, subjects saw 80 sequences composed of the same nonsense symbols. Forty of these were the same sequences as shown

before, and 40 were new arrangements of the symbols not dictated
by the grammar—that is, nongrammatical sequences. The two
groups of sequences had been randomly mixed to form a list of
80, which was then presented to each subject on a memory drum.
The subject's task was to identify those sequences that he recognized as having been shown before—that is, to distinguish grammatical from ungrammatical sequences.

The independent variable that distinguished three groups of
subjects consisted of three different systems of placing spaces between symbols within the various sequences originally shown to
the subjects. In group 1, a space appeared after each symbol, so
that only a finite-state description was immediately apparent for
a particular sequence. In group 2, a space appeared between those
symbols that were divided by the major immediate constituent
boundaries which derive from the phrase-structure grammar. In
group 3, spaces were inserted between symbols at random, using a
table of random numbers. Here the number of spaces that occurred
per sequence was equated with that in group 2. Thus, three types
of groupings of symbols were arranged on the basis of three different schemes: (1) a finite-state arrangement, (2) a phrase-
structure arrangement, and (3) a random arrangement. An analysis
of variance statistic computed for differences among the three
groups yielded no significant differences under the three conditions.

The second experiment was a replication of the first with one
change. Instead of using the four nonsense symbols as vocabulary
items, four numbers, 3, 5, 2, and 8, were used. It was hoped that
this would reduce the extreme differences among subjects in the
use of mnemonic devices. Indeed we found that although we had
tried to eliminate the phonological and semantic variables by the
use of nonsense symbols, subjects almost invariably resorted to
naming the symbols presumably in order to facilitate recall. In
any case, substituting numbers yielded no significant difference
among the groups.

We then felt that perhaps the 80-item test list might have been
inadequate. It was biased in favor of the finite-state group, since
no spacing was used on the test list. That is, on the test, the phrase-
structure group saw the same list as the finite-state group, and

the immediate constituent boundaries were not indicated on the test sequences. Therefore, it was decided to replicate experiment 2 with test lists appropriate to each group. Essentially, for the phrase-structure and random groups, spaces were maintained in the 40 test list sequences, and spaces were inserted at random in the 40 ungrammatical items within the list. The difference in the test items in experiments 2 and 3 is illustrated in Figure 3. The

A. Experiments 1, 2, 3

$$G = \# = 3$$

$$N = \square = 5$$

$$X = () = 2$$

$$S = / = 8$$

B. Experiments 2, 3

Test lists in Experiment 2	Test lists in Experiment 3		
All groups	Te Fs	PS	Random
3 5 8	3 5 8	3 5 8	3 5 8
2 8 5*	2 8 5*	2 8 5*	2 8 5*
2 3 8 5	2 3 8 5	23 8 5	2 3 85
5 2 5 2 5	5 2 5 2 5	5 25 25	5 2 525

*Ungrammatical

Figure 3 *Symbols and test lists for experiments 1, 2, and 3.* From Saporta, et al., *Monograph Series on Languages and Linguistics,* **16,** 1963, pp. 133–142. Reproduced by permission.

analysis of variance results approached, but did not reach, statistical significance.

These three pilot studies demonstrate a number of things, including the obvious fact that it is possible and almost easy to design poor experiments. It should be made explicit that the negative results reflect on the inadequacy of the experimental design and not on the proposition that a phrase-structure grammar is superior to a finite-state grammar, a proposition convincingly demonstrated on independent theoretical grounds. At best such experiments can only demonstrate that in searching for empirical evidence, there may be limitations to the kind of learning situations in which this superiority is relevant.

Implicit in the previous studies was the view that the learning of syntax was essentially the ability to distinguish grammatical from ungrammatical sequences after only one presentation. The next attempt had a different orientation.

Using the same grammars as previously, a random selection of 10 of the 40 sequences was made with the constraint that strings of all lengths be included, and this time using letters rather than nonsense symbols or numbers. Each of three groups of subjects was presented with one set of ten strings which were either (1) spaced evenly, (2) spaced according to immediate constituents, or (3) spaced randomly, with the number of spaces per sequence equaling the immediate constituent spacing. The inclusion of the third group was aimed at demonstrating that it was not merely grouping that was a factor, but the systematic grouping which characterizes immediate constituent analysis. The three lists are shown in Figure 4.

The subjects were all undergraduate students from introductory psychology courses. The three groups were of ten subjects each. The subjects were told nothing about the method of constructing the lists and were told it was important to remember the correct order of the letters without regard to the occurrence of spaces. The sequences were typed in capital letters on 3- by 5-inch cards. The subject was seated across the table from the experimenter, who laid the cards face up in front of each subject at a rate of one card every five seconds. After all ten cards in the list had been presented, the experimenter, who laid the cards on the table, picked up the deck of cards and shuffled it while the subject wrote, in any order, all the sequences he could recall. When the subject finished, the experimenter removed the response sheet and proceeded to the next trial. Ten such trials were given, and the order of the cards was varied in the same way after each trial. Response sheets were scored for the number of correct sequences recalled. The acquisition curves for the three groups are shown in Figure 5.

Finite-State	Phrase-Structure	Random
N X S	N X S	N X S
N S X N	N S XN	N S XN
N X N S	N XN S	N XN S
G N S X	GN S X	G N SX
N X N X N	N XN XN	N X NXN
G N X N G N	GN XN GN	GNX N GN
N X N X G N	N XN XGN	N XN XGN
N X G N X	N XGN X	NX GN X
G N X G N S	GN XGN S	G NX GNS
G N X G N X G N	GN XGN XGN	GNXGN XG N

Figure 4 *Finite-state, phrase-structure, and random spacing.* From Saporta, et al., *Monograph Series on Languages and Linguistics,* **16,** 1963, pp. 133–142. Reproduced by permission.

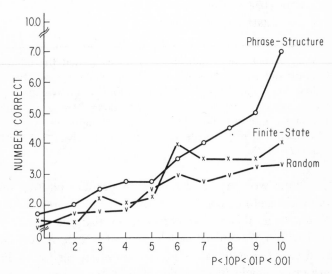

Figure 5 *Results of experiment using random, finite-state, and phrase-structure presentation.* From Saporta, et al., Monograph Series on Languages and Linguistics, **16,** 1963, pp. 133–142. Reproduced by permission.

Analyses of variance were performed for each trial. The significance of differences between group means is shown for trials 8 through 10. The acquisition of the phrase-structure group in contrast to the other groups shows how organization into immediate constituents aided recall. The lack of difference in the performances of the finite-state group and the random-spacing group suggests that mere grouping is not of itself beneficial. A summary of the statistical analysis is included as Table 1.

Table 1 *Summary of Analysis of Variance*

Source of Variation	Sum of Squares	Degrees of Freedom	Mean Square	F
A: Spacing	67	2	33.50	6.11 (P < .01)
Error (A)	148	27	5.48	
B: Trials	325	9	36.11	38.01 (P < .001)
A × B: Spacing-trials interaction	61	18	3.39	3.57 (P < .01)
Error (B)	231	243	.95	
Total	832	299		

The three significant values indicate: (1) Spacing: that the number of correct recalls differed significantly among the three groups (PS: 36.0, Finite: 28.0, Random: 24.8); (2) Trials: the group average differed from trial to trial; (3) Spacing-Trials Interaction: there is a significant difference in the rate at which the three groups improved over the ten trials. For discussion of the statistical technique involved, see Edwards (1960, pp. 227–232).

By this time we were so delighted to get any positive results that we overlooked one possible interpretation of the results. It was pointed out to us that one might consider that the groups were presented with a vocabulary of five items—G, N, S, X, and space. In such a case the systematic introduction of spaces for a phrase-structure group would increase the redundancy as opposed to the random introduction of spaces which carry more information in the sense of communication theory. However, we had explicity

told subjects not to worry about recalling position of spaces. Undoubtedly the spaces facilitate the grouping of symbols into higher-
level units, but we did not feel we had to apologize for this fact,
since it is precisely what immediate-constituent analysis purports
to do.

Current Research

Research currently underway is aimed at demonstrating that in
fact subjects differ in the strategy they use in devising a grammar
based on some sample utterances. Subjects apparently differ in the
degree to which they generalize and also in the type of model
they use.

In one experiment subjects were presented with sentences in an
artificial language of the form AB, BA where A and B are classes
of words. After they had learned a sample of sentences thoroughly,
they were called upon to use what was learned to cope with new
sentences. Their behavior with new sentences suggests that essentially three techniques are possible and indeed used: learning by
rote, learning by means of word positions in the sentence, or learning by inferring word classes and rules for their combination. It is
hypothesized that subjects who learn by rote memorization do
poorly on all new sentences. Subjects who have learned that certain
words occur in certain positions have difficulty with new sentences
where the order is reversed. Subjects who "abstract" classes and
grammatical relations have less difficulty with all new sentences.

In a second study, subjects were presented with sentences of the
forms AB, BA, and CAB. Now there are a number of ways of
learning these sentences, each of which is logically compatible with
the data but which differs in its consequences. Thus, for example,
if a subject formulates a rule, "Sentences are one of three types:
AB, BA, or CAB," he clearly will reject sentences of the form BCA,
or CBA, etc. If on the other hand, he formulates a rule, "A sentence
is formed by adding a C word before the A word of any two word
sentences," he will accept BCA, but not CBA. The study demonstrates that subjects do indeed differ in their generalizations, even

though they use the same strategy of classes and rules for their combination.

A number of related problems are suggested by this type of research. For example, it is of considerable interest to investigate the role and value of negative instances in any concept learning situation, since learning a language L may be viewed as learning the concept "grammatical sentence in L." Similarly, a crucial question one might ask is what kind of principle operates in deciding in favor of certain generalizations. Is there a tendency to formulate a general rule? Is there a tendency to formulate a rule that predicts a minimum of new sentences? How can these two be reconciled?

It is clear that these results cannot be safely generalized. However, once a convincing case can be made for a particular experimental design, it is hoped that similar results can be attained with the learning of material more closely approximating natural languages, with the only relevant variable being the model underlying the presentation, with no regard for the actual pedagogical devices or method of instruction.

References

Chomsky, N. *Syntactic structures*. The Hague: Mouton, 1957.

Edwards, A. L. *Experimental design in psychological research*. New York: Rinehart, 1960.

LINGUISTIC MODELS AND FUNCTIONAL UNITS OF LANGUAGE BEHAVIOR

Neal F. Johnson

There are developing many aspects of psychology that deal, in one way or another, with language behavior. As a beginning, it might be worthwhile to identify psycholinguistics as an area by itself by pointing out the ways in which it differs from some of the other language areas. Very often one hears the terms *verbal learning, verbal behavior,* and *psycholinguistics* used as if they were alternate labels for exactly the same thing. While there is certainly a great deal of overlap in these areas in terms of content, as well as the individuals doing the research, there are also some very important distinctions which should be kept in mind.

Verbal learning is an area of psychological research dealing with the study of the learning process in general, and it is not specifically concerned with only language. In addition it is not concerned with some of the broader aspects of language behavior that do not involve learning. As with other areas of learning, the object of interest for verbal learning is the learning process, and verbal associations are simply the vehicle used for studying this process.

The research on verbal learning is probably far more similar to the animal research on the learning process using Skinner boxes, runways, and T-mazes than it is to the areas of verbal behavior and psycholinguistics. The work with paired-associate and serial tasks is appropriately viewed as an attempt to develop an understanding of the variables that influence the formation of associations, and not as an attempt to develop an associational model for understanding the way in which we produce sequenced language behavior. The work of Underwood is a very good example of the research in this area, and certainly the implications of his research go beyond speech, per se.

The areas of verbal behavior and psycholinguistics, on the other hand, represent a concern over general language behavior. These areas of endeavor, then, have language behavior as their basic object of interest rather than just language learning. In both cases the interest is with the psychological foundations of all language behavior. For example, problems of language perception, production, encoding, decoding, concept formation, and class formation, as well as language learning, fall within this area. The interest in language learning, however, is not in learning as a basic process, but in the way the principles of learning can account for the learning of language behavior.

It is far more difficult to separate verbal behavior and psycholinguistics from one another. In practice it may be impossible to draw any real distinction between these, and for that matter there may be no real point in attempting to do so. The only meaningful distinction that seems to offer any hope would be in terms of the dependence of the investigator on both psychology and linguistics as the source of his hypotheses.

The following discussion might begin best by developing a general model or schema for psycholinguistics. The value of such a schema is not so much in its being a device for generating hypotheses as it is an integrating device into which we can cast the very diverse sets of data that are now becoming available on language behavior. If one were to look at the data Miller has presented on transformations; the data Jenkins has provided on mediation phenomena; the data Underwood has provided on the concept of a response pool; the data Osgood has provided on meaning and the acquisition of meaning; and the many other areas of language research such as verbal conditioning and learning of systems, it would be very difficult to find the way in which these are all systematically related in terms of a gradually developing account of language behavior. Yet all of this research fits into a fairly tight and integrated system providing information at a multitude of levels regarding the way in which we process language. By providing a general and over-all schema it might be easier to see the way these research endeavors are integrated and thus give each individual experiment a greater meaning in the sense that it fits into some point of a whole. As a basis for the schema I would like to propose Chomsky's (1957) transformation theory of grammar.

The plan here is to present a brief historical account of the development or evolution of transformation theories in linguistics before describing the theory. Not being a linguist, that discussion will, of necessity, be quite brief. However, such an introduction might make the implications of the theory more intelligible for other nonlinguists.[1] Following a presentation of the theory, a brief discussion will be made of some general questions regarding the psychologist's approach to language, and in light of these considerations, the model will be examined for the points at which it makes a contribution to the psychological analysis of language behavior. Finally, the way one aspect of the model can be explored for psychological correlates will be illustrated by describing a current research program at Ohio State.

PSYCHOLOGY AND LINGUISTICS

Lees (1964) and Maclay (1964) have both suggested that the contribution of the linguist to the psycholinguistic effort is to provide the psychologists with a general description or outline of the things the human must know in order to produce grammatical language behavior. They point out that the division of labor in psycholinguistics should delegate to the linguist the role of determining *what* is learned and to the psychologist that of determining *how* it is learned.

While the ultimate goal of the psychologist may be to explain

[1] The discussion of linguistics follows closely that given by Lees (1964).

how language is learned, he must first take the linguist's physical description of what is learned and ascertain its possible psychological correlates. On a practical level, the psychologist's direct goal is not to explain how a rule is acquired but, rather, how the psychological (behavioral) correlates are acquired. The first step for the psychologist is to determine these correlates. In addition to the linguist, then, the psychologist also must be concerned with what is learned, but he has an advantage in the suggestions that emanate from the linguist.

DEVELOPMENTS IN LINGUISTIC THEORY

Any attempt to draw a distinction between generative grammars and purely descriptive grammars seems most easily accomplished in terms of their goals. The goal of a descriptive grammar is to describe each sentence in its own right by identifying and labeling the linguistic units within the sentence at the several levels at which they occur (that is, the kinds of morphemes, phrases, and so forth). Essentially, a descriptive grammar is a system of classification rather than a system of rules for either producing language or judging whether a language sequence is grammatical. In a sense, then, a descriptive grammar can be viewed as a classification system that outlines the operational criteria used for determining the linguistic units of language, and it describes a corpus by attaching class labels to the units.

The goal of a generative grammar, on the other hand, is to develop a system of rules that can be used either to produce grammatically acceptable sequences of morphemes or to evaluate whether a sequence that has been produced does fit into the grammar of that particular language. A descriptive grammar would not be concerned if its system would include in the language sequences of morphemes that subjects or native speakers judge as being ungrammatical; whereas, a generative system would stand or fall on the fact that it generates only sequences that are accepted. A generative grammar, then, is concerned with developing a system of rules for determining whether a sequence conforms to the grammatical rules of that language or, better, whether the sequence could be generated using only the grammatical rules of that language.

Descriptive grammars could be translated into generative grammars fairly readily. For example, with a traditional grammar, as long as the grammarian is concerned only with identifying classes of words and he uses his grammar to analyze a corpus by attaching class labels to the words, it is a descriptive grammar. However, if the linguist should then prescribe certain sequences of classes as being allowable in the language and certain sequences as not allowable in the language, then the grammar is generative. The moment a grammar includes rules that define what is grammatical or acceptable within a language it is a generative grammar.

The linguistic units that the descriptive linguist has identified and the classes that he has established are certainly units that are used, or can be used, by both the psychologist and the generative linguist. While the contribution of descriptive linguistics for the psychologist, therefore, cannot be minimized, it also must be recognized that a generative grammar has the most points of interest for a psychological study of language.

For a psychological analysis of language behavior, as well as for a complete grammar, then, it is necessary to develop a system that will indicate which sequences of linguistic units are allowable and which sequences are not allowable in the grammar of the language. In the examination of the following models they will be viewed in terms of their adequacy as a generative model.

The earliest model that the linguists provided (i.e., traditional grammar) was simply a system of labeled word classes, and the classes were defined semantically. The system described a language corpus that had been produced by labeling each word with the class it represented. While that is a descriptive grammar as stated, it could be a generative grammar if a listing were made of all the possible class sequences and included as part of the grammar.

The model, however, has a number of inadequacies as a generative grammar. First, if sentences are interpreted as sequences of word classes, how does one account for the fact that some subword units can have an influence on the grammatical form of the sentence? Lees (1964) illustrates this point using *The psychologist was humorous* as opposed to *The psychologist was numerous*. The presence or absence of the plural *s* sound on the end of *psychologist* will determine what can or cannot occur following it (that is, *numerous* can only occur if the plural inflection is present). This particle, however, is not a word and consequently does not have any class status within the system, and therefore cannot be used.

Another difficulty with this model is the fact that the classes are semantically defined. For example, a noun is a person, place, or thing, but it is not precisely explained what is meant by a *thing*. What makes the word *love* a thing, as differentiated from *running*, which is not a thing? Furthermore, using these definitions some words can belong to more than one class. For example, *That is a blue dress* and *That is a pretty blue* both include the word *blue*, and the meaning is the same in both cases. However, in the first case *blue* functions as an adjective, and in the second case it functions as a noun.

There are a number of logical considerations, then, that preclude our using traditional grammar as a psycholinguistic model. Furthermore, if the psychologist were to use this model to explain how humans acquire grammar, it would require us to learn a set of classes and then memorize, by rote, the infinite set of possible class sequences. Then, we would still be in difficulty because of the lack of precision in the class definition.

The phrase-structure model represents an attempt to set up a generative grammar by taking the units identified by structural linguistics and formulating a set of rules for expanding or rewriting large constructions into their elements (e.g., clauses into phrases; phrases into morpheme classes). But before examining the degree to which phrase-structure grammar could serve as a psycholinguistic model, it would be worthwhile to outline some of the developments of structural linguistics.

As with the traditional model, structural linguistics deals with classes, but what is classified has been changed from words to morphemes. In making this change, the basis for determining class membership has been shifted. Instead of the old semantic definitions for classes, a system of operational criteria was developed for determining the function a morpheme plays in a sequence.

Lees (1964) stated that viewing a sentence as simply a sequence of morphemes will cause many of the same difficulties as viewing a sentence as a sequence of words. For example, he suggests the sentence *He shot the man in the red fez*. If this sentence is analyzed only as a sequence of morphemes it is not clear, and cannot be made clear, whether the intent of the prepositional phrase *in the red fez* is to identify which man was shot or to identify where the man was shot. The sequence of morphemes in both cases is exactly the same, and the meaning of each morpheme is exactly the same. The only way the alternative meaning for this sequence can be expressed is by bracketing the morphemes together into larger units and then bracketing these units together into even larger units.

The system of bracketing elements and then rebracketing these elements into larger units is called an immediate constituent (IC) analysis. The basic procedure used in an immediate constituent analysis is to take a sentence and at the first level divide it into two units. This first division probably would divide the sentence into the subject and predicate. At the next level down these two constructions (i.e., the subject and the predicate) would themselves be divided into their major constituents. On the next level the constituents from the preceding level would be divided into more constituents. This process would continue until each morpheme represented a single unit. The point to note is that the interrelation between the morphemes cannot be shown if one is to view the sentence simply as a string of morphemes. It becomes apparent only when these morphemes are grouped into units and these units into larger units, etc.

Another difficulty Lees (1964) mentioned is that there are instances where sentences can have two different meanings and these meanings cannot be clarified by bracketing. He uses the example, *They were assembled by the new machine*. He suggests in this case that whether one meant that the objects were assembled near the machine, or whether one meant that the machine did the assembling, the string of morphemes would be the same; the meaning of each morpheme would be the same; and the bracketing would be the same. He suggests that structural linguistics has overcome this difficulty by labeling the bracketed constituents. For example, in one instance *by the new machine* would be labeled a locational phrase, and in the other case it would be labeled an instrumental phrase.

If the process of immediate constituent analysis is formalized into a system of phrase-structure rules which are to be applied in a particular sequence or order, the result is a generative grammar. As mentioned above, structural linguistics has developed a rather sophisticated set of morpheme classes, but also developed have been classes of sequences of classes, and classes of these classes, etc. A phrase-structure rule is a statement of how one rewrites or expands a unit of one order into units of the next lower order. For example, "noun phrase" can be expanded to "article plus modified noun." "Modified noun" can be expanded to "adjective plus noun."

If these rules relating to the structure of phrases are applied in the correct order it should be possible to generate sentences of various kinds or types. Lees (1964) states, however, there has been no language so far discovered for which the grammar can be expressed only as a system of expansion or phrase-structure rules, and Chomsky (1957) has outlined in detail the logical problems inherent in attempting such an endeavor. In addition, viewing this from a purely psychological point of view, it also seems impossible to base a psychological analysis of language behavior on a model using only expansion rules. For example, there are an infinite number of sequences of morphemes which can occur in the language. Furthermore, some of these sequences of morphemes would have different sets and orders of phrase-structure rules applied, depending on the meaning, as illustrated by the sentences mentioned above. If psychologists were to use this model to account for the way language is learned, it would be necessary to assume that subjects learn a vocabulary pool, they learn to put these vocabulary items into classes of items, they then learn the almost infinite set of possible orders, numbers, and combinations of applying these phrase-structure rules in order to generate language. This would be an impossible task for the human organism.

In addition to this problem Lees (1964) also mentioned that there are some interesting regularities in language that a phrase-structure or expansion grammar could not explain. One illustration is that very often we can say the same thing in many different ways. Each of these ways requires a different sequence of morphemes and morpheme classes, and in each case the system of expansion rules, and the order in which they are applied, would be quite different. These regularities cannot be expressed in the grammar using only phrase-structure rules. Furthermore, there are certain general types of sentences like interrogatives and passives that have a basic similarity. Again with a grammar based only on phrase-structure rules the similarity could not be expressed.

As a final illustration of the difficulty of basing a grammar only on phrase-structure rules, Chomsky (1957) has pointed out that it would be impossible to develop a well-formed sentence that consisted of many conjunctions. For example, in English it would be possible to construct a sentence of infinite length using conjunctions between the units, but a phrase-structure grammar could not outline the system of phrase-structure rules that, when applied, would generate such an infinite sequence. For the above reasons a phrase-structure grammar can be rejected as a model for psycholinguistics.

The final generative model is Chomsky's (1957) transformation theory. This theory retains, to a certain extent, the major characteristics of the preceding models, but adds a system of transformation rules as well. At its bottom level this theory deals with classes of morphemes, although the number of classes that it assumes far exceeds the number of classes in the phrase-structure model. At its next level the theory employs a system of phrase-structure rules. However, rather than infinite sets of ordered phrase-structure rules, the transformation theory selects one of these types (or at most, a small set) and derives other types or forms of sentences by transforming these paradigm or kernel sentences into the more complex forms. Chomsky (1957, p. 107) describes the kernel or basic sentence as being ". . . simple, declarative, active, with no complex verb or noun phrases. . . ." *John hit Mary* would be an illustration of a kernel sentence.

Transformations are accomplished by using a relatively small set of transformation rules, any one of which can be applied to the same sequence any number of times. The above sentence could be changed or transformed into its passive form *Mary was hit by John* by applying to the kernel one transformation rule which describes how the passive is formed. This rule would apply irrespective of the sequence. In order to generate these two sequences, then, the transformation theory requires the ordered application of one set of expansion rules and one transformation rule. The phrase-structure model would require the ordered application of two quite different sets of phrase-structure or expansion rules.

Lees (1964) points out this theory assumes that every complex sentence has an abstract representation in terms of one or more of the simple kernel sentences. The kernel sentences are changed into the complex forms by the application of transformation rules which either modify a single kernel or combine several kernels, or both. By these refinements the Chomsky theory overcomes most of the difficulties encountered by the previous models.

PSYCHOLOGICAL CONSIDERATIONS

If, as Lees states, the linguist's role is to define what is learned, the previous considerations would suggest that it is the elements of the Chomsky theory for which psychologists must account. There are, however, at least four general psychological considerations that must be recognized in developing an integrated psycholinguistic model.

First, there are a number of ways humans can process language. When the psychologist becomes concerned with language behavior, in reality his concern seems to be with making inferences regarding the way organisms process language, using the behavior as the basis for inference. If psychologists are concerned with language processing, the different ways in which the organism can process language should be examined.

First is language production. The question is, how does the human organism spontaneously produce or generate speech? A second mode of language processing is perception. In that case concern regards the way in which the organism receives language symbols, decodes these symbols, and interprets them. It is not necessary to assume that perception and production are simply mirror images of one another. As a matter of fact, these processes may be quite different.

A third mode of language processing is language learning that involves both perception and production. In order to learn, organisms must have a language input and perceive this input. However, if we are to measure the degree to which they have learned the sample of language to which they have been exposed, the organisms must reproduce it (i.e., production).

An unpublished experiment by Compton (1963) at Ohio State illustrates the distinction between language perception and language production. He presented subjects with simple sentences typed on a piece of paper with wide spaces between the words— e.g., The   ball   is   rolling. The subjects were asked to insert words between the presented words with the restriction that they must maintain sentences of good grammatical form. The three insertions that could be made were to modify the noun, modify the verb, or negate the sentence. After they had inserted a word they were asked to insert a second word. The subject did not make a third choice, and it was assumed that whatever was left would have been his choice. Compton's data indicate that for a very large percentage of the subjects the choice was to modify the verb first, the noun second, and negate the sentence last, and the pattern held up irrespective of the sentence used.

As a second phase of his experiment Compton used sentences that subjects generated in the first phase, and he asked new subjects to delete words. The process was the same as in the first experiment except for deleting rather than inserting words. For any one sentence there was a definite pattern of deletion, but there was no constant pattern across the sentences (i.e., each sentence had a different pattern).

One possible interpretation of Compton's experiment is that when subjects are generating or producing a sentence they go by some kind of general syntactic rule for the process. However, in the process of degenerating a sentence there is a general pattern, but the pattern differs from sentence to sentence, and meaning could be the determining factor.

When examining the Chomsky transformation theory in terms of its adequacy as a general schema for a psychological analysis of behavior it might be worthwhile to keep in mind possible differences that could exist in the degree to which the model is useful for explaining language production as opposed to its usefulness in accounting for language perception.

The second general consideration involves the role of reinforcement. Skinner (1957) has tried to outline the kind of reinforcement mechanisms that could influence natural language, as well as attempting to explicate the way in which these mechanisms operate. The research being collected on the problem of verbal conditioning is certainly appropriate to this problem. More knowledge is needed on the kinds of reinforcers that are used in natural language, the way in which they operate, and the reason why they work. In addition, however, the question of what is reinforced must be studied as well.

The third general area of concern for language research is the old psychological bugaboo *purpose*. There are many examples in everyday language where the form of a word is selected on the basis of words that have not been said, but will be said in the future. In the same experiment by Compton (1963) sentences were presented to subjects that had a number disagreement between the verb and the noun. One set of his sentences can be illustrated by, *Do the girl have many clothes?* The subjects heard a sentence over a tape recorder, and they wrote out the sentence, correcting any errors they had heard. Across all sentences, 65 per cent of the subjects changed the verb in accordance with the noun given, rather than changing the noun in accordance with the verb. To do this requires the subject to modify his behavior at the onset of the sentence on the basis of a response that he will make in the future. While these data are far from conclusive, they do suggest the possibility that present behavior can be modified on the basis of future behavior. Certainly some explication of this phenomenon must be made in order to give a complete psychological account of language behavior.

The final point is the interesting relationship between semantics and syntax. While these are often discussed as being completely separate, there may be a real question as to the degree they can be separated in natural language. In such sentences as *John hit Mary* as opposed to *Mary hit John* the relationship between syntax and semantics is very simple and very obvious. In sentences such as *He shot the man in the red fez* or *They were assembled by the machine* the relationship is less obvious, and at the same time far more complicated.

In terms of developing an account of the way in which language is learned there are some interesting possibilities regarding the contribution of semantics to the process of learning classes. For example, the class of words that we label nouns generally conforms to the class of labels for objects in our environment. Common elements like this can be found for verbs and adjectives as well. As far as a psychological explanation is concerned, these common characteristics could facilitate the process of forming the classes. Some data are available on this point (Johnson, 1961), but the relation between syntax and semantics is far from clear.

A PSYCHOLINGUISTIC SCHEMA

If we attempt to use a linguistic theory as a base for a psychological analysis of language behavior, we must first examine the theory in terms of what it assumes. Such an analysis can be done most effectively by attempting to outline the functional requirements of using each level of the theory in producing language behavior and then examining the psychological data available. The four levels of Chomsky's theory are (1) a pool of vocabulary items; (2) the class structure of the vocabulary pool; (3) phrase-structure or expansion rules; and (4) transformation rules. For each level the psychologist must demonstrate both the existence of the function and how the function was acquired.

At the lowest level the theory presupposes a vocabulary pool from which the speaker selects items. The elements of the vocabulary pool are either morphemes, which represent the minimal sequence of sounds that either carry meaning or modify meaning, or words. The job of the psychologist is to demonstrate the psychological existence of the population or pool of items and to demonstrate how the items were acquired. The mere fact that we talk is probably all the evidence necessary to demonstrate the psychological existence of this pool. The explanation for the way the vocabulary pool is acquired is more difficult, but there is a growing body of data available.

One attack on the problem of acquisition is to view a morpheme as a response that consists of a complicated sequence of chest, larynx, tongue, mouth, and lip movements. The psychologist must explain the process whereby this chain of molecular responses was acquired, and how it came to represent a kind of functional unit of language behavior. The research on response generalization, shaping, and reinforcement is all appropriate to this question.

If a child utters a word in the presence of the appropriate stimulus, and only in the presence of the appropriate stimulus, we say he knows the meaning of the word. This criterion for determining whether meaning is known, however, does not give any insight as to precisely what is meant by "meaning." The problem of meaning acquisition is a second aspect of acquiring a vocabulary pool. As far as content words are concerned (e.g., nouns, adjectives, verbs) there is some research regarding what we mean by "meaning" and the way the child acquires this meaning. The work of Deese, Osgood, and the Staats is representative of the research on the problem.

The meaning of function words (e.g., prepositions, connectives) and how it is acquired is a different problem and less well understood. As opposed to content words, function words cannot be given an ostensive definition. Whatever meaning function words have must be seen as bound quite intimately to the syntax or the grammar of the language, and the ultimate explanation will probably be in terms of the way in which they modify meaning carried by the structure of the sentence.

This lowest level of the Chomsky theory, then, requires an explanation for how the sound system is learned, how specific verbal utterances are acquired, and how these operants acquire meaning. Furthermore, it will be necessary to explicate the distinction between structural meaning and referential meaning.

The next level of the theory presupposes the items in the pool have been formed into functional classes. While the traditional models employ seven or possibly eight word classes, the transformation theory presupposes an extremely large set of classes. Again, the job of the psychologist is twofold. He must demonstrate first that the morpheme classes are psychologically real, and second he must give an explanation for the way the classes of behavior are formed.

Regarding the psychological reality of word classes Jenkins (1964) has reviewed a series of studies which suggest that in word association studies a stimulus word tends to elicit a word of the same part of speech and one that readily can be substituted for the stimulus word in a sentence. If subjects are requested to construct a sentence using the stimulus words, and after doing so the stimulus word is crossed out and the subject is asked to replace it with a different word, the word used for replacement is frequently the primary associate of the word that had been crossed out. Furthermore, their data suggest that the tendency to do this is highly correlated with the frequency with which they have experienced the stimulus word in natural language. In addition, Jenkins and Palermo (1961) have illustrated how mediation mechanisms can explain the formation of these natural language morpheme classes.

Another interesting problem related to the idea of morpheme classes is that many of the classes have characteristic endings. Not only do these endings modify the meaning of the preceding morpheme, but also they can function to signal the class membership of the preceding morpheme. For example, the morpheme -ed when added to a second morpheme will not only change its meaning, but signal that the second morpheme is a verb. The psychological interest in the endings revolves around the question of how they are learned and the way in which they are used in natural language to signal class membership, if indeed they are used at all.

The next level in the transformation theory presupposes a finite set of phrase-structure or expansion rules. To date, psychologists have done little in terms of exploring possible correlates of these rules and/or the way they are implemented to produce language behavior. The work of Braine (1963) is one of the few attempts.

In terms of identifying the psychological reality of the rules both Lounsberry (1954) and Maclay (1964) have suggested that their influence on natural language may be seen by studying hesitation phenomena. Maclay and Osgood (1959) have reported a study that offers partial support for this idea.

The psychological description of a rule is far less understood than is a psychological description of response classes. That is, it is very difficult to state precisely what we mean when we say someone has learned a rule, other than the fact that we can generate a formal statement from which their behavior can be predicted. There is no ready-made psychological characterization of the "thing" that is learned when a subject learns a rule. Jenkins (1964), however, has suggested one possible alternative. It may be that we can talk about phrases, clauses, etc., in terms of being higher order classes. That is, it may be that there are certain recurring sequences of morpheme classes, and these recurring sequences represent classes themselves. The contribution of structural linguistics also suggests that there are higher order classes. For example, there are noun phrases, verb phrases, modified noun sequences. It may be that the only meaningful way of psychologically defining phrase-structure rules is in terms of higher order classes.

The last level in a transformation theory assumes a finite set of transformation rules which operate on simple strings of morphemes generated using the phrase-structure rules. Miller (1962) has reported a study that involved testing the psychological reality of transformation rules. The vehicle used for study was to explore reaction time to sentences that involved various numbers and kinds of transformation rules in their generation. Miller presented subjects with a column of sentences with a column of transformations of the sentences next to it. The subjects' task was to read a sentence in the first column and then identify its proper transformation in the second column. A control group received identical sentences in the two columns. Miller suggested the difference in time between the two groups as a rough index of the time to make the transformations or their inverse. The data he reports using this technique illustrate psychological differences between these linguistic operations.

One problem with Miller's design is that sentences increase in number of words as transformations are added, and his differences could reflect that increase. To overcome that problem, Gough (1963) suggested a design where subjects are shown a sentence and then a picture. The task is to indicate whether the picture conforms to the sentence, and the measure is the time between presentation of the picture and the reaction.

While contributing inductive support for the psychological reality of these transformation rules, the Miller experiment does not explicate the way these rules were acquired. Here again, as at the previous level, there is a need for formulating a psychological definition or reduction for the concept "knowing a rule." On the previous level it seemed possible to define phrase-structure rules in terms of complex psychological classes, but how such a reduction could be made for transformation rules is less apparent.

Functional Units of Language Behavior

One way of integrating the psychological questions that arise at the four levels of Chomsky's theory rests on the fact that in all four cases the considerations deal with the response units a subject uses or the way he manipulates these response units. Viewed in this way, the psychologist may be able to reduce the four-part linquistic model to two basic issues. The first issue involves identifying the language units the subjects use and determining the way in which the units are formed or integrated. The second issue involves identifying the operations the subjects use to manipulate the units and studying the way they are learned.

The first difficulty encountered by such a characterization of the problem is defining what is to be meant by a *functional unit of behavior*. The problem of behavioral units has been with psychology for a long time, and in line with the influence of Dewey and Hall pushing psychologists toward studying the problems of mind at whatever level they are found, there has been a tendency for behavioral units to be defined as whatever is meaningful in terms of the nature of the task. In general, that has resulted in a rather happy solution to the problem, but, in most cases, the unit has been defined or stipulated by the experimenter. The problem presented by language is somewhat different to the extent that the experimenter must determine empirically what subjects are defining as a response unit rather than stipulating the unit.

Even though the behavioral units themselves should be identified empirically, there must be some general characterization of the functional properties that a set of response elements must possess before they are to be identified as a functional unit. Generally, there seem to be two important characteristics of the behavior which, in the past, psychologists have labeled as a single response. First, the response usually can be scored dichotomously as having occurred or not occurred. That is, the behavior tends to occur in an all-or-none manner, with partial responses rather rare. Second, the introduction of a new variable tends to influence all of the behavior, not just certain elements. These two points suggest, then, that the behavior psychologists have defined as response units seems to maintain a certain internal integrity and interdependence among the response elements.

With such a characterization of the nature of behavioral units it does seem possible to reduce the four levels of the Chomsky theory to two psychological issues (i.e., unit formation and unit manipulation). The difference between the acquisition of the vocabulary pool and the acquisition of the phrase structure of a language can be viewed as a quantitative difference in the size of the unit a subject has to integrate.

Using the above characterization, the development of morpheme or word classes also evolves into a question of unit formation. In the case of a class the unit is not a behavioral sequence but, rather, a set of responses that, to a degree, are functionally equivalent.

There are certain class sequences that occur with high frequency in English (e.g., article-adjective-noun) and certain sequences that never occur (e.g., article-noun-adjective). At the same time, specific sequences of words or morphemes do not occur very often, but when they do, subjects are able to emit them with speed and ease. Furthermore, there are some sequences the subjects emit for which they have never been reinforced in the past.

It would seem that the most reasonable way of accounting for these factors would be to assume that the behavioral elements integrated in learning the phrase structure of a language are response classes rather than responses themselves. To do so, however, assumes that the classes represent functional units to the extent that an influence on one of the members also influences the other members of the class. Jenkins (1964) presents a discussion as well as some supporting data on this point.

Finally, the transformation level of Chomsky's theory can be viewed as a set of operations for manipulating the behavioral units. Miller's (1962) data offer some psychological support for the existence of these operations, but the conditions under which they are learned remain to be determined.

PHRASE STRUCTURE AND FUNCTIONAL UNITS

There are a number of illustrations in everyday language behavior which suggest that language might be encoded in units larger than the morpheme or the word. For example, there are stress and intonation patterns that span several morphemes. These patterns give the listener a subjective or intuitive feeling that the sequence of morphemes within the span represents a unit for the speaker. In addition, there are hesitations between certain words in an utterance that are longer than between other pairs of words (Maclay and Osgood, 1959). The spans between these hesitations also seem to represent functional units in language behavior. Furthermore, there seems to be an interesting correspondence between the spans governed by intonation patterns and the boundaries identified using hesitations.

The point of these intuitive considerations is that there may be a correspondence between the morpheme sequences described by phrase-structure rules and the functional units into which subjects have encoded their language. The question, then, concerns the degree to which the influence of phrase-structure rules can be detected in language by exploring for the psychological units into which it has been encoded.

One possible way to detect the language units subjects use in their behavior is to study the process of response integration as subjects learn grammatical sentences. If subjects do handle language in large units, they should integrate the units before they put the units together to integrate the sentence. That is, during the course of learning, the subjects should learn to go from one word to the next word within a unit before they learn to go from the last word of one unit to the first word of the next unit. Therefore, if subjects are scored for the probability of going from a right word to a wrong word (i.e., a transitional error) for each transition within a sentence, the probabilities should be lowest for transitions within units and greatest for between-unit transitions.

As a first approximation it would seem that subjects should treat short phrases as units. If subjects learn sentences as responses in a paired-associate task, they should learn the intraphrase transitions before the interphrase transitions, and therefore the probability of an interphrase transitional error (TE) ought to be greater than the probability of an intraphrase TE.

An experiment was designed to test the above unit hypothesis (Johnson, 1963a) in which single digits were used as stimuli, and sentences like those in Figures 1 and 2 were the responses. Each subject learned eight pairs presented on a memory drum at an eight-second rate. A subject's response protocol was scored by com-

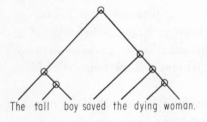

Figure 1 *Tree diagram reflecting the constituent structure of the two-phrase sentences.*

Figure 2 *Tree diagram reflecting the constituent structure of the three-phrase sentences.*

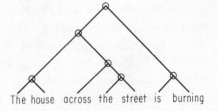

puting the probability of a transitional error (TE) at each of the six word-to-word transitions within the sentences.

The results of the experiment are presented graphically in Figures 3 and 4. The interesting result is that not only did subjects tend to have a greater probability of a TE on interphrase transitions ($p < .001$), but the TE pattern seemed to reflect the intraphrase structure as well.

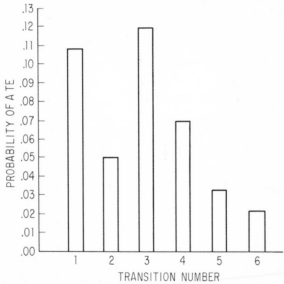

Figure 3 *Pattern of transitional error probabilities obtained when subjects learn the Fig. 1 sentences.*

When performing an immediate constituent (IC) analysis on a sentence it seems possible to rank order the transitions in terms of the level at which they represent a constituent division. For example, using the sentence in Figure 1, the first division is between the subject and predicate, then between the verb and its noun phrase, etc. The Kendall rank correlation between that rank order and the rank order of TE probabilities in several experiments using different structures has been varying between .60 and .95.

Viewing these data in a general way, they appear to give at least some inductive support to the hypothesis that there are psychological correlates of phrase-structure rules. The substantial correlations between the probability of making a TE and the "linguistic depth" of a transition (defined in terms of an immediate constituent analysis) suggest that a theory of verbal behavior that utilizes a hierarchical conception of language organization may be quite realistic.

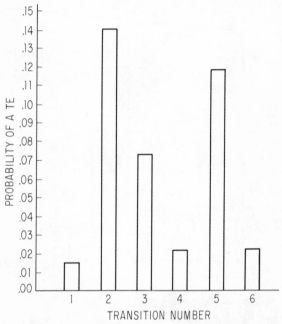

Figure 4 *Pattern of transitional error probabilities obtained when subjects learn the Fig. 2 sentences.*

There still remained a number of questions. For example, it would be possible to account for the above data in terms of a single-level analysis if the pattern of TE probabilities simply reflected pre-existing word-to-word associations. That is, *house-across* may be a harder pair to learn than *across-the*, or *is-burning* may be easier than *street-is*. To test that possibility a pair of experiments were designed to study the ease of learning the second versus the third and the fifth versus the sixth transitions of the Figure 2 sentences in both paired-associate and serial tasks. In the paired-associate task the word preceding the transition was used as the stimulus, and the word following the transition was the response. In the serial task the words occurred adjacently in the lists, and the subjects were scored for the frequency the second word of the pair was correct given the first word was also correct. When these transitions were embedded in sentences, the third and sixth transitions were clearly less difficult than the second and fifth, but no differences appeared when they were taken out of context and put into the two kinds of lists (i.e., paired-associate or serial). From that preliminary data it seemed unlikely that the results of the first experiment could be explained in terms of pre-existing word-to-word habits.

While the influence of grammatical structure may be needed to account for the previous data, that does not suggest that word-to-word habits could not have an influence on the TE pattern within response sequences. A new paired-associate experiment was designed which used as responses an ungrammatical sequence of seven words (Johnson, 1963b). The first word was a Kent-Rosanoff (K-R) stimulus word, and the second was its primary response (Russell and Jenkins, 1954). The third was another, but unrelated, K-R stimulus word; the fourth word was the K-R primary response to the third; and the fifth was the primary response to the fourth word. The sixth and seventh words consisted of another K-R pair. In sequences constructed in that manner the first, third, fourth, and sixth transitions were spanned by relatively strong pre-existing associations, while the second and fifth were not. The habit units of these sequences were the same as the phrase units of the Figure 2 sentences. The results indicate the subjects did have significantly greater TE probabilities on the low association transitions than on the high. While pre-existing associations may not account for the earlier data, the results of the above experiment indicate that pre-existing associations can have an influence on the learning of sequences when grammatical structure is absent.

A final experiment in the sequence (Johnson, 1963c) was designed to study the influence of physical structure of the response on the pattern of TE probabilities. If both grammatical structure and association can influence the way subjects "chunked" the responses, can the physical structure of the response have a similar influence? Again a paired-associate task was employed, but this time the responses were seven letters, with successive letters being low frequency pairs—e.g., SBJHFZC (Underwood and Schulz, 1960). When the responses were typed for presentation successive letters were typed adjacently, except that a blank was left between the second and third and the fifth and sixth letters for one group and between the third and fourth for another—e.g., SB JHF ZC and SBJ HFZC. With such an arrangement the units are the same as the phrase units in the first study except that the letter units have no internal structure as did the phrases. In the first study the intraphrase TE probabilities were unequal, and it was attributed to structure. If that is the case, when the units have no internal structure the intraunit TE probabilities should be equal. The results of the experiment showed the interunit transitions as having a significantly greater probability of a TE than the intraunit transitions. In addition, the intraunit transitions were all approximately equal in probability of a TE. That is, when intraunit structure is absent the intraunit TE probabilities do not differ significantly from one another.

It seems, then, that while patterns of TE probability can result from sources other than grammatical structure, those sources cannot account for the effect obtained in the first study. Consequently, it was felt that before proceeding further in the laboratory it would be worthwhile to develop at least an ad hoc account for the psychological implications of grammatical structure.

While all the data discussed above come from learning studies, the learning process itself was not being studied, but, rather, a learning task was used as a vehicle for studying the process of producing or reproducing a response. The question dealt with the degree to which the units linguists identify in a physical analysis of language also might be used in processing the responses at the time of recall or use. The learning task was used to identify the units a subject could use to process his language behavior. The role of the following model is to suggest the most probable way the units identified in the first study could be used in generating language.

Originally, it was suggested that the probability of a TE should be related to the "linguistic depth" of the node governing the transition. The prediction stemmed from the intuitive assumption that as subjects are learning a response that they organize into subunits, they should attempt to integrate the smallest units first, then the units which use the smallest units as elements, etc. When the response units are organized into a hierarchy, the element-to-element transitions within the lowest level units should be learned first and the transition between the two highest level units last. Also, subjects should hesitate to generate a unit they cannot complete, and the larger the unit (i.e., the more words) the more improbable is completion. Finally, when subjects are producing or reproducing the responses, they should tend to do so using the units in some way.

A PSYCHOLINGUISTIC MODEL

It has been argued (Jenkins, 1964; Miller, Galanter, and Pribram, 1960) that language may be best seen as generated from "top to bottom" rather than from "left to right." At least, a process of generating from "top to bottom" seems most reasonable if a hierarchical structure of units is to be used during the process of generation. As a first step in the account a simple mechanism for "top to bottom" generation might be described.

Miller (1956) outlined a process he called *recoding*, which involves learning a single encoding representation for recurring response sequences. In using the encoding representations of recoded units he suggests that subjects learn complex response sequences by retaining the sequence of encoding units and when reproducing the original sequence they simply decode or translate the recalled encoding units into the response items they represent. While he illustrates his idea with an experiment using a sequence of recoded binary digits (e.g., $00 = 1$, $01 = 2$, $10 = 3$, $11 = 4$), there is no reason why the recoded units could not themselves be recoded at a higher level.

The translating or decoding of encoding units seems a simple account for generating a response sequence from "top to bottom." For example, "sentence (Σ)" can be decoded into "subject (S) plus predicate (P)." "Subject" can be decoded into "article (T) plus modified noun (MN)," etc. In this way language generation can be viewed as a sequence of decoding steps rather than the execution of a series of S-R habits between words. That is not to say that S-R bonds or associations are not used, but only that they might occur between decoding operations rather than words.

Returning for a moment to the linguists' "tree diagrams" of a sentence, they might serve equally well as a schematic description of the encoding units and decoding operations used in producing a sequence. Figure 5 can be used as an illustration with the labeled nodes being encoding units and the lines the decoding operations. By following the lines from any encoding unit the set and order

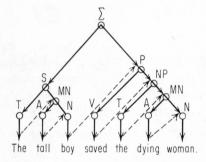

Figure 5 *Expanded tree diagram reflecting the model for sentence generation.*

of the decoding operations it entails can be seen as well as the response items (words) it governs. The broken lines in the diagram represent the steps taken when a terminal event occurs (i.e., a response is generated).

With such an operational schema the generation of a sentence can be viewed as a sequence of decoding steps which reduce high order encoding units into lower order units. As a subject decodes his way down the hierarchy each encoding unit is reduced to one, two, or more subunits. In each case he further decodes the first subunit, storing the others in his immediate memory. Such a process continues until a terminal event (i.e., a response) occurs, at which time the subject takes from his immediate memory the most recently stored encoding unit. He then proceeds to decode that unit in the same manner until a terminal event occurs, etc.

The pattern of errors obtained in the preceding experiments can be explained by assuming that subjects decode ahead of their speech. Before they begin to generate a response unit they have it at least partially decoded. However, the higher the level of the unit, the more operations necessary to decode it and, hence, the greater the probability of not even starting to generate the response items contained within the unit.

Characterizing the process of generating a sentence in that way brings up a problem concerning the metric to be used for quantifying the order of a unit or linguistic depth of a transition. The original method was to inspect the sentence diagram and crudely determine how "high" a node occurred. That runs into obvious problems, and it is difficult, if not impossible, to use the method consistently when the grammatical structure becomes complex.

A second alternative would be to use the steps in an IC analysis. The correlations reported above between the probability of a transitional error and the height of a node in a "tree diagram" seem to offer empirical justification for using the operations of an IC analysis for identifying the encoding units. However, the order of the steps taken in an IC analysis will not work as a metric for quantifying the units because there is so much room for an arbitrary decision as to when a step will be taken. For example, using the sentence illustrated in Figure 2 (*The house across the street is burning*), when is the predicate construction *is burning* to be broken into its two constituents *is* and *burning?* Is the predicate an encoding unit (i.e., construction) of the same order as the subject *The house across the street?* If so, the predicate should be divided into its constituents when the subject is divided between the noun phrase and prepositional. However, on an intuitive basis, the predicate construction appears more like a modified noun construction than the subject construction, and the data (Figure 4) look that way as well. Under those circumstances the predicate should be divided at the same time as the modified noun.

For the linguist's purpose the above decisions can be made in an arbitrary manner as long as constructions are always divided into their immediate constituents. That is, given two constituent constructions, the order in which they are then further divided into their constituents is unimportant provided they are both eventually divided into their *immediate* constituents. For that reason, then, the order in which constructions are divided in an IC analysis cannot be used for quantifying the order of encoding units, even though the operations of an IC analysis can be used for identifying the units.

If the metric is to be used for predicting the characteristics of an Ss behavior that are correlated with his processing an encoding unit, then the metric should bear some logical relation to the reasons or basis for making the behavioral predictions. As an alternate to the above suggestions a metric involving the operations implied by an encoding unit seems more reasonable. That is, the hierarchy of encoding units might be identified in an IC analysis, but the order of a particular encoding unit could be defined in terms of the number of decoding operations necessary to generate the sequence of words it includes.

One final consideration about the model concerns the appropriate behavior to be examined in testing it. Decoding operations cannot be studied directly, nor can the "existence" of encoding units be studied directly. Therefore, in testing the decoding of a unit the behavioral characteristics of its constituents are probably the most direct data that can be obtained. Generally, it would seem that most of the predictions regarding the decoding process would be about events prior to the occurrence of the first response items (i.e., what operations lead to the generation of the constituent responses). In addition, it would seem that the most immediate and apparent consequence of an operation should be on the occurrence of the first response item of the first constituent. In general, the other items within a constituent ought to be the result of other operations. Therefore, the best index as to whether a unit was decoded or a particular decoding operation occurred should be the occurrence of the first response item contained within, or implied by, the unit.

To use the above considerations in explaining the results of the first experiment necessitates predicting that the probability of a TE for any transition is some function of the number of decoding operations implied by the encoding unit that begins with the word immediately following the transition. The tau between predicted and obtained TE probabilities using "height of the node" as the basis for predicting was .75 ($p < .06$) for the Figure 2 sentences. Using the new metric as the basis for predicting, the tau is .86 $p = .028$). "Height of the node" and the new metric result in the same prediction for the Figure 1 sentences.

To summarize, it is hypothesized that when a language response is produced a subject has generated it by proceeding through a sequence of decoding operations. The decoding operations translate a high order encoding unit into two or more lower order units, which themselves may need further decoding. Based on the results of the first experiment it was suggested that the operations used in an IC analysis might be used for identifying the encoding units. Secondly, based on previous data, it was hypothesized that the associations used in producing a response seem not to exist between response items, but it was suggested that the bonds might link decoding operations instead. Finally, a metric was suggested for quantifying the level of an encoding unit within a hierarchy. The measure is the number of decoding operations necessary before the unit is completely decoded. It was hypothesized that the probability that an encoding unit would begin to be decoded should be inversely related to the number of operations needed to complete the task. The occurrence of the first response item in the first constituent was suggested as a behavioral index of whether an encoding unit was decoded.

One of the implications of the model is that subjects do not integrate the response sentences by forming word-to-word associations, but, rather, they learn a *system* for response generation which involves decoding a hierarchy of response units, and the decoding operations are the elements between which associations are formed. That conclusion, however, is not necessitated by the pattern of TE probabilities obtained in the first study reported above, and it

seems there are at least three possible ways those results could
have occurred without making any assumption about units beyond
the word level.

The first alternative is that the data could reflect pre-existing
habits between words. That, however, is contraindicated by the
other data reported above.

The second alternative is that the structure makes certain word-
position to word-position associations either difficult or easy to
form. While it cannot be assumed that there are pre-existing habits
between words, it may be that given a grammatical structure
there are differential pre-existing associations between word classes.
For example, within a sentence the class *noun* may follow the
class *adjective* more reliably than the class *verb* follows the class
noun, and hence there may be a stronger *A-N* association than
N-V. Such an explanation would not require any pre-existing
strength between particular words. Also, it would not necessarily
predict that the differential class-to-class strength should be apparent when the items are removed from the sentence context because part of the stimulus for arousing the expectancy for the next
class may be the grammatical context in which it appears. As with
the first alternative, this explanation assumes subjects learn and
generate sentences in terms of a single level of response-to-response
associations.

The third alternative is that the structure of a sentence might
be used by the subject to determine the *order* in which word-to-
word (or response-to-response) associations are formed. That would
imply the structure represents a learning strategy, rather than some
characteristic of the response itself. Also, it would not be necessary
to assume that the associations vary in difficulty. The subject may
adopt, or even learn, the structure to be used as a learning strategy,
but the structure would not determine *what* is learned, only the
order in which single-level associative bonds are formed. None of
the above data are inconsistent with either the second or third
interpretation, and certainly if either were the explanation it would
be unnecessary to assume a hierarchy of response units.

One important distinction between the model and the three
alternative explanations concerns the way a subject would use an

association. If, using a paired-associate task, an association between two adjacent words in a sentence was formed before subjects were required to learn the sentence, the various explanations would make somewhat different predictions as to how subjects would use the association. Both the second and third alternatives above would predict that the probability of a TE for the learned transitions would be reduced, irrespective of which transitions had been involved in the original learning. They would differ, however, in predictions regarding relative magnitude of change for various transitions. The model would predict that the influence of a pre-existing association should be apparent only for certain transitions.

The results of standard learning experiments indicate that the amount of improvement in performance as a result of a learning experience (e.g., a trial) is inversely proportional to the level of performance before the experience. That is, the amount of new material acquired on each trial decreases as the trials increase, resulting in a negatively accelerated learning curve. The second alternative assumes differential pre-existing habits between word classes and that the pattern of TE probabilities results from using these in forming word-to-word associations while learning the sentence. If that is the case, it would be predicted that the influence of a prior learning experience would be detectable for any transition involved in the prior learning, and the magnitude of the change would be directly proportional to the probability of a TE without the prior experience.

The third alternative, however, does not involve assumptions regarding pre-existing strength. Therefore, while it also predicts that the effect of the prior learning should be apparent on any transition involved, the amount of the influence should be independent of the probability of a TE without the experience.

The model, on the other hand, would predict that the influence of a prior learning experience should be detectable only for some transitions within the sentence. If the associations are between generating operations, then, during the original paired-associate learning, associations are being formed between the operations producing the two responses. When the subject learns the sentence the influence of the prior learning should be detectable only where the operations producing the two response items are adjacent. For example, the operational program presented schematically in Figure 5 shows the operation following the one used to decode A into *Tall* to be the one that will decode N into *boy*. In that case the two response-producing operations are adjacent, as well as the responses themselves. However, after the operation producing *boy* has occurred, the next operation does not produce *saved*, but, rather, it produces $V + NP$. Only after that is V decoded to *saved*. While *boy* and *saved* are adjacent responses within the sequence, the operations producing them are not adjacent. The execution of the intervening operations might be expected to reduce or eliminate the influence of the pre-established *boy-saved* association, and the reduction of the influence should be directly proportional to the number of intervening operations. If it is hypothesized that the pattern of TE probabilities also results from the intervening operations, then it would be predicted that the magnitude of change resulting from the prior learning should be *inversely* proportional to the original probability of a TE.

An experiment was designed to explore the above considerations (Johnson, 1964). A set of eight sentences was constructed using Thorndike-Lorge AA words. The grammatical form of the sentences followed that presented in Figure 1. Before the subjects learned the sentences they learned word pairs from the sentences in a paired-associate task. The transitions used in the paired-associate task were the first adjective-noun transition and the noun-verb transition (i.e., the second and third transitions). Every subject learned the second transition from four sentences and the third transition from four sentences. The respective transitions from the other sentences served as controls. During the original learning the subjects pronounced both the stimulus and the response. They also received familiarization trials during which they pronounced the second, third, and fourth words, in the control sentences. The subjects then learned the sentences as responses to digits in a paired-associate task.

The results indicate that during OL while the *A-N* pairs were learned more rapidly than the *N-V* pairs, the *N-V* pairs were learned to a high degree. On the last learning trial about .93 of the subjects' responses were correct for the N-V pairs. When the subjects learned the sentences, the probability of a TE for the A-N transition was reduced significantly, while the N-V transition remained unaffected by the prior learning experience.

In general, the results tend to support the model to the extent that the influence of the prior learning experience was as predicted. One interesting discrepancy, however, was the difference in learning rate between the A-N and N-V pairs during the original learning task. That result was particularly striking in light of the earlier results where the interphrase and intraphrase transitions were learned at about the same rate in both paired-associate and serial tasks. It does seem possible, however, to reconcile these results with the earlier data within the framework of the model.

If associations are between operations rather than the responses, an association can be formed between two classes of words only if their generating operations are adjacent or contiguous in many natural language instances. The strength of the association should be directly proportional to the frequency that the operations have been contiguous in normal spontaneous speech. In addition, the strength of the association should be inversely related to the frequency that the operation generating the first class also has been contiguous with operations that generate other classes. These would form competing associations and would result in interference. The earlier study compared the second against the third and the fifth against the sixth transitions in sentences like that diagrammed in Figure 2. The third transition involved going from a pronoun to a verb or a preposition to either an adjective or an article. In the sentences used in the experiment, and in natural language, it would be rare, if ever, that the operations generating these responses would occur adjacently. In addition, both pronouns and prepositions can be followed by more than one class of words. Therefore, there should be no pre-existing strength between these classes. The sixth transition involved going from a form of the verb "to be" to a verb. While these decoding operations are frequently contiguous in natural language, forms of "to be" are also frequently followed by adjectives, which should result in some competition. Therefore in the earlier study it would not be predicted that the pairs from the third and sixth transitions should be learned at rates different from the second and fifth transition pairs when they are taken from the context of the sentence.

In the present study the adjective-noun transition was compared with the noun-verb transition. In natural language the operations generating adjectives and nouns are almost always contiguous, whereas those generating nouns and verbs are not usually contiguous. On those occasions when an adjective-generating operation is not followed immediately by a noun, the adjective occurs at the end of a constituent and, hence, is not immediately followed by any response-generating operation. As a result, it might be expected that adjective-noun pairs would be learned at faster rates than noun-verb pairs. In addition, there is the related finding in word-association studies (Deese, 1962) that while all stimuli tend to arouse paradigmatic associations, adjectives tend to elicit a syntagmatic noun associate more often than nouns elicit syntagmatic verb associates.

Deese (1961) has suggested that when subjects are required to remember connected discourse they do so by retaining certain key items and they use these items at the time of recall and construct the surrounding items using their grammatical habits. That hypothesis can be incorporated in the present model by suggesting that Deese's key items function as symbolic representations of high order encoding units. If an association were established between the operation generating the first noun and the symbolic representation or key item of the P encoding unit of Figure 5, the probability of a TE for the third transition should be reduced by that proportion of the error attributed to the subject's inability to recall the correct P. That portion of the error attributed to the subject's inability to construct the correct filler items within P should not be reduced, however. The failure to obtain any reduction as a result of the prior N-V association might suggest then that either subjects do not use the verb as the P symbol or that subjects differ as to what they use.

The value of the above model for explaining the way sentences are generated remains to be seen. The supporting data are very fragmentary and do not even begin to deal with many critical issues.

One very important question that is completely avoided is the role of meaning, in terms of both the meaning of individual words and the meaning or sense of the sentence. For example, if a common word were used in a sentence but the meaning of the word did not fit within the sentence context, it might be expected that a high TE probability would result even though it would not be predicted from the structure.

In relation to that point we have repeatedly found that whenever there is a marked deviation from a predicted pattern of TE probabilities, the deviation has occurred on a transition to an adjective. In one study sentences like those in Figures 1 and 2 were used in an immediate memory experiment. The pattern of TE probabilities for the Figure 2 sentences conformed very well to the predicted pattern. However, the subjects had a great deal of trouble with the two adjectives in the Figure 1 sentences. The TE probabilities on the transitions to these items were about three times greater than for any other items, and the other transitions were about equal. It appeared as though the subjects redefined the units as the spans between difficult items rather than using the grammatical structure. Following Deese's (1961) suggestion that the sentences might be retained in terms of key items, with subjects constructing the others using grammatical habits, the key items may be nouns and verbs. The construction from grammatical habits would help the subjects fill in function words but would be of no value for the adjectives. The subjects may attempt some kind of semantic encoding rather than using the grammatical structure when they must retain difficult adjectives.

Another important question that has been neglected concerns when the subjects perform decoding operations. Do they decode as they generate responses, or do they completely decode a sequence before any attempt is made to generate the response? The fact that we can modify our verbal behavior on the basis of responses that will be made in the future suggests that decoding does occur ahead of generation, but how far ahead is unknown.

These questions and many more need an answer before a complete theory of sentence generation can be developed. The most that can be said with any certainty at this time is that there does appear to be a hierarchical structure to language behavior, and the structure seems to be used.

References

Braine, M. D. S. "On learning the grammatical order of words." *Psychol. Rev.*, **70**, 1963, 323–348.

Chomsky, N. *Syntactic structures.* The Hague: Mouton, 1957.

Compton, A. J. "Studies on the psychological correlates of linguistic theory." Unpublished paper, Ohio State Univ., 1963.

Deese, J. From the isolated verbal unit to connected discourse. In C. N. Cofer (ed.). *Verbal learning and verbal behavior.* New York: McGraw-Hill, 1961, pp. 11–31.

———. "Form class and the determinants of association." *J. verbal learn. verbal behav.*, 1962, **1**, 79–84.

Gough, P. "Understanding of sentences of different grammatical forms." Paper read at Minnesota. Group for Study of Verbal Behavior, Chicago, May 1963.

Jenkins, J. J. A mediational account of grammatical phenomena. *J. Comm.*, in press, 1964.

———, and D. S. Palermo. "Mediation processes and the acquisition of linguistic structure." Paper read at the Conference on First-Language Acquisition, Cambridge, October 1961.

Johnson, N. F. "The cue value of sentence frames for the acquisition of speech categories." Unpublished doctoral dissertation, Univ. Minn., 1961.

———. "The psychological reality of phrase-structure rules." Unpublished manuscript, Ohio State Univ., 1963a.

———. "Utilization of pre-experimental associations between elements of complex unstructured responses." Unpublished manuscript, Ohio State Univ., 1963b.

———. "The integration of subunits of structured responses." Unpublished manuscript, Ohio State Univ., 1963c.

———. "The influence of association between elements of structured verbal responses." Unpublished manuscript, Ohio State Univ., 1964.

Lees, R. B. "Models for a language user's knowledge of grammatical form." *J. Comm.*, in press, 1964.

Lounsberry, F. C. "Transitional probability, linguistic structure, and systems of habit-family hierarchies." In C. E. Osgood and T. A.

Sebeok (eds.). "Psycholinguistics: A survey of theory and research problems." *Int. J. Amer. Ling.*, 1954, **20**, No. 4 (Memoir II), pp. 93–101.

Maclay, H. "Linguistics and language behavior." *J. Comm.*, in press, 1964.

———, and C. E. Osgood. "Hesitation phenomena in spontaneous English speech." *Word*, **15**, 1959, 19–44.

Miller, G. A. "The magical number seven, plus or minus two: Some limits on our capacity for processing information." *Psychol. Rev.*, 1956, **63**, 81–97.

———. "Some psychological studies of grammar." *Amer. Psychologist*, 1962, **17**, 748–762.

———, E. Galanter, and K. H. Pribram. *Plans and the structure of behavior*. New York: Holt, Rinehart and Winston, 1960.

Russell, W. A., and J. J. Jenkins. The complete Minnesota norms for responses to 100 words from the Kent-Rosanoff Association Test. Tech. Rep. No. 11. ONR Contract, N8 ONR-66216 (1954).

Skinner, B. F. *Verbal behavior*. New York: Appleton-Century-Crofts, 1957.

Underwood, B. J., and R. W. Schulz. *Meaningfulness and verbal learning*. Chicago: Lippincott, 1960.

MEDIATION THEORY AND GRAMMATICAL BEHAVIOR[1]

James J. Jenkins

This article is divided into five parts. The first part attempts to make clear why the psychologist ought to be concerned with grammar. The second part takes up the question of what such a concern involves in terms of behavior. In essence, it tries to treat with what is entailed in a psychology of grammar. The third part is aimed at explaining mediation models and their implications for a psychological approach to grammar. The fourth part presents the evidence currently available suggesting that mediational models may be adequate to account for at least some grammatical phenomena. Finally, the fifth part treats with directions of research that seem to be fruitful in the more complete exploration of mediational and grammatical phenomena.

[1] Much of the thought in this article has been stimulated by discussions with Philip Gough, Kirk Smith, and Charles Clifton. Gough's thesis (1961) includes a thorough treatment of mediation phenomena in the most general sense. Smith's dissertation (1963) contains an extensive discussion of the nature of linguistic models and of the relation between psychology and linguistics. The preparation of this article has been supported in part by Grant G—18690 from the National Science Foundation and in part by the Graduate School, University of Minnesota.

Why Study Grammatical Behavior?

Grammar is to most of us, as G. Miller (1962) says, "a grim and forbidding subject . . . it still reminds us vividly of all those endless and incomprehensible rules that our teachers tried to drum into us in grammar school." If we are tolerant, we may admit that it is a possible topic of concern for a linguist or a language teacher, but few of us experience any glow of excitement in contemplating the structure of the passive negative query or anything but annoyance in deciding about the use of the subjunctive in a conditional construction. Grammar smacks of arbitrary prescription and artificial constraint on expression. It connotes dead tradition and dry and dusty libraries. Why should an enthusiast for the young and vigorous science of behavior bury himself in such a dreadful (and unbehavioral) subject matter?

The facts of the case, of course, are at variance with our emotions and attitudes, most of which probably stem from exposures to a variety of poorly taught language lessons. The modern linguist, as we shall see, is not at all concerned with prescription, is happy to throw off the fetters of the past, and regards himself as a student of behavior, though he is glad to maintain that he is not a psychologist. He is interested in formulating descriptions of a set of behaviors that we call linguistic. It is my contention that his formal treatment of these behaviors focuses our attention on a set of neglected problems with which the psychologist *must* cope. These are problems that we have recognized many times but still have failed to deal with effectively.

The most general problem here is the problem of serial order in behavior which Lashley so nicely set forth in his important paper on this topic (1951). The obvious fact that language has a structured and sequential nature makes it a particularly striking example of the psychologists' failure. Lashley wrote:

In spite of the ubiquity of the problem, there have been almost no attempts to develop physiological theories to meet it. In fact, except among a relatively small group of students of aphasia, who have had to face questions of agrammatism, the problem has been largely ignored.

Lashley pointed out (as must be clear now to all students of psycholinguistics) that the phonetic elements in a language string are relatively unpredictable at their own level, being determined by the word, and that the words themselves are unpredictable in a "left to right" sequence, since they are determined in turn by higher levels of organization, and so on. This led Lashley to challenge traditional psychology by asserting specifically that combinations of associations between words in sentences could not account for the grammatical structure observed in language behavior. He argued for a series of hierarchies of organization but confessed that he had not been able to systematize a set of assumptions concerning selective mechanisms which "was consistent with any large number of sentence structures." Clearly, the general form of Lashley's argument is that a psychology based on associations of elements *cannot* effectively deal with any behavior that so clearly appears to demand hierarchies, classes, and patterned structural relationships.

An attack with a similar conclusion has been launched from quite a different point of origin by Chomsky (1957) and Chomsky and Miller (1958) in their consideration of finite-state languages. Finite-state languages are those that proceed from "left to right" unit by unit, on the basis of given transitional probabilities. An associative explanation of language, it can be argued, would be much like a finite state, Markov process explanation of language. Since it can be shown that (with the word as the unit) the finite-state process is insufficient to deal with natural languages, it can be further argued that an approach through associational psychology cannot *by its very nature* be adequate to account for language phenomena.

If one gives credence to these arguments, it must be apparent that grammatical behavior itself is to be a battleground on which traditional associational psychology may well be slain. If this important behavior *cannot* be dealt with, the associationist may well be written off as far as human behavior is concerned, for it is likely that the explanation of all higher mental processes will be beyond his reach. I believe the psychologist must rise to the challenge or prepare to retire to the dim corners of his laboratory where he deals only with narrow segments of behavior which happen to fit his theoretical formulations.

Are language phenomena really so difficult to deal with? I think we must agree that there is at present no systematic psychological approach to the discussion of structure in behavior. Yet the language behaviors, so available and obvious to all of us, persist in demonstrating structure. Let us look for the moment at instances of language behaviors of children. I find these are most compelling in exposing structured behavior, on the one hand, and in exposing our inadequacies, on the other.

The speech of children is further especially interesting because it is usually understood by adults even though it does not fit the adult formal grammar and cannot be viewed as simple imitation. With only a little difficulty parents seem to apply sets of rules that enable them to understand the utterances of children. They know how to make them intelligible by correcting for the child's distortion of the phonemic system, and most important for our purposes, they know how to make them meaningful or grammatical. At a trivial level this might indicate nothing more than the fact that the child attacks the language with certain characteristic defects which in time the adult detects and learns to correct for. But the fact that parents can compensate for these "defects" not only in some particular instance but in a variety of circumstances suggests that to some extent the child's behavior is systematic and is relatable through modifications to the adult grammar.

These errors that children make, particularly the unique errors that can be understood, are potent proof of the systematic nature of the development of language in the child and, I believe, evidence of the systematic nature of language itself.

Let us consider a few instances. These are, unfortunately, anecdotal, but may readily be supplemented by the reader who troubles to observe young children even for a brief time. Systematic data will shortly be available from the excellent studies in progress by Brown and his associates (Brown and Fraser, 1963, Brown, Fraser, and Bellugi, 1964), W. Miller and Ervin (1964) and Bullowa and her collaborators (Bullowa, Jones, and Bever, 1964).

A small child says (approximately):

wan uh bear

wan uh car

wan uh daddy

These are variously translated by the parent as:

I want *the* bear

I want *a* car

I want daddy

In this case we have a systematic form, *uh*, introduced at a particular place in the sequence, which is (we might say) over-generalized with respect to its translation. It serves as an article, both definite and indefinite, and it also serves as a "zero" form given the unique case that there is only one daddy or that *daddy* is a proper name. One might hypothesize that the verb is *wan uh* except that this element is observed in the same child in a different context: "*where uh bear?*" etc.

A more complex and more interesting case which virtually all parents have observed is that of the past tense of an irregular verb. Children frequently have the correct past tense as an apparently independent element at some early age, but when they begin acquiring regularized past tense, a systematic change in the irregular verb can be seen. This change constitutes evidence that there is some "class" here, that the verb is an element of the class, and that the class is modified in a particular way under certain circumstances. For example, the child, apparently using the verb *take* in the past tense, says *taked*. This is analogically correct for a member of the broad class but is incorrect for that particular entry. When this is corrected to took by the parent, the form *tooked* may be observed, as the child apparently persists in carrying out the systematic modification. Finally after further tuition, example, and learning, this becomes *took*. At this point, we might think that the child has mastered this particular irregular verb only to find that the whole process has to be repeated with the perfect form, which emerges spontaneously as *have took* or *have tooken* long before the correct *have taken* is achieved.

I have observed still a different phenomenon in my children which similarly seems to be based on analogy and seems to call for an explanation. One child, aged six, came in and asked me to come out and *higher the swing*. This is readily understandable after a moment (given the language and the constraints on what one may do with a swing). The utterance is presumably generated through the contrast of *high* and *low* as adjectives and *higher* and *lower* as comparative adjectives. All adults know that for the verb we have *to lower* and *to raise*. But the child has generated for this grammatical position a verb form that is appropriate for the operation that covers the opposite of lowering the swing, the *highering* of the swing. *To higher a swing* clearly means to raise it. Given that the child has never heard this utterance and yet that it is understandable as to both its meaning and its probable derivation, we must conclude that it is generated by the child to meet both the situational and grammatical demands of the moment. It implies a complex framework within which an analogy may be formed and some mechanism for its formation.

We can observe similar analogical developments on other levels. For example, we get incomplete transformations when the child is learning how to ask certain kinds of questions. The child who wishes to ask where someone is going shows that the dominant word order from the kernel form is what is being acted on. He asks, *Where you are going?* and, *What your name is?* Part of the question format is acceptable, and the first rule (so to speak) of questioning has been learned, but the second part of it has yet to undergo its more subtle transformation. Here again we may be sure that the child is not imitating adults but is generating (incompletely to be sure) a question according to some systematic rules. Even when the simple questions are mastered, more complex sentence forms may still show the question-forming process in midstream. A father says to a child, *Ask your mommy what dessert we should have for dinner*. The child asks, *Mommy, what dessert we should have for dinner?*

In addition to these kinds of error we see abundant evidence of a kind of "grammatical-semantic" equivalence which is as yet undiscriminated in the emerging language of the child. All parents have seen remarkably persistent errors between the so-called opposites, *up-down, in-out, bring-take, momma-daddy* and the like.

Errors of this sort may continue for years after the semantic distinction itself is well made. It seems apparent that the fact that these elements fit into particular positions in otherwise identical sequences must play a key role in the confusion. The difficulty lies apparently in making the final discrimination between the particular elements in the minimal pair when each member of the pair plays such a similar grammatical role to the other member of the pair.

Over-all we must be impressed with the weakness of current psychological theory in dealing with the common phenomena that we see so abundantly in grammar. We must further recognize that simple associative strings are insufficient on a variety of theoretical and evidential grounds to account for language behavior. Finally, we must be aware that both the development of language skills and their manifestation in the mature speaker demand an account of behavior that can deal with structure, hierarchy, class, and combination as basic phenomena.

What Must We Explain?

While a complete explanation of grammar entails nothing less than a complete theory of the mind, a beginning may be made by attempting to treat with *classes* and *relations*. Throughout the first section and particularly in the discussion of children's errors, one is impressed with the operation of what may be broadly termed "analogy." The analogies involved are on different levels and different dimensions in the examples given. Some analogies are in form, some are analogies in the way elements in a class are modified, some are analogies in transformational operations from sentence to sentence, and some are analogies that appear to be under the joint control of grammar and semantics, but all may be considered analogies nonetheless.

We might begin then with a simple question, what is the psychological status of an analogy? The answer to that, as far as I can see, is that it has none. Analogy has not been studied deliberately by psychologists (except as material for intelligence testing) for many years. It is noteworthy that the first American psycholinguist, E. A. Esper, studied word association under this rubric in 1918 and suggested at that time (along with Thumb and Marbe) that word association would prove to be an important process in affecting change in language diachronically. Unfortunately, this whole conception has received little attention since that day. It is remarkable, however, in spite of the lack of systematic study, how often the psychologist is forced to make an appeal to the mechanism of analogy when he begins working with language processes. Even such a no-nonsense psychologist as B. F. Skinner, who explicitly disclaims any interest in grammar *per se*, invokes the mechanism of analogy in his book *Verbal Behavior* (1957) when he attempts to discuss past tense and its extension. But, sadly, we must acknowledge that from the psychological point of view analogy is undefined.

When we seek a psychological definition of analogy, we must inevitably be led to think in terms of systems of relations as Esper was led in his subsequent work to think of systems as a key to language behavior. At the heart of analogy is *equivalence* of some sort. In the simplest form of analogy, two items are presented, bearing some relation or set of relations to each other. A third item is given and a fourth item must be generated (e.g., Fuzz is to peach as _____ is to fish). Something is required. The required term is multiply determined by the first pair and by the first pair in relation to the given element of the second pair. An analogy is not unique with respect to any particular set of its determining elements. Given even such a simple relation as "*1* is to *2*," it is not clear whether the desired pair is "as 2 is to 4," or "as 2 is to 3," or "as January is to February," or "as smaller is to larger," or "as part is to whole," or "as straight is to curved," or "as thin is to thick," or "as point is to line." All of these (and many other possible responses) are unresolved until we get further information.

An analogy is made up of an educed relationship, but that relationship itself may be determined by the next stage as it indicates the area to which the relationship is to be applied. Practically all pairs of elements may be considered to be multiply related, and the question as to what relationship is to be teased out is in part a function of further stimuli supplied in the situation. It is therefore, even in the simplest case, multiply determined by complex cues.

I think we can see how this operates and at the same time get a foothold for the examination of grammar by considering briefly one of Esper's early experiments (Esper, 1925).[2] This experiment involved colored shapes with systematically related names. In miniature it can be represented by presenting a colored square and an uncolored square (see Figure 1). The colored square is called ZUBGEX and the uncolored square is called RELGEX. Now a colored circle and an uncolored circle are presented. If one is told that the colored circle is called ZUBTEF, then one is in a position to predict that the uncolored circle is called RELTEF. Given the psychological set that one may assume in all the readers of this article, that is unquestionably the prediction that must be made. Though Esper used a much more subtle setting, this is the essence of his experiment. Esper generated a 4×4 system with 4 colors and 4 nonsense shapes yielding 16 unique color-shape combinations. In his experimental group he systematically applied bisyllabic names according to the formula that can readily be educed from the examples above. In another group he applied names that were similarly partitioned but not at the syllable boundary, and in the third group he applied unique names to each color-shape combination. He withheld two of the stimulus instances, however, from all groups. These were used later in test trials after original learning on 14 of the color-shapes had been accomplished.

When the two previously withheld items were presented to the first experimental group, the subjects named them according to the system and did not even report that the entries were new. The second group did not completely master the system and had difficulty naming the new items. The group that was attempting to learn discrete names had great difficulty learning the original task and, when given the new test items, either failed to name them or borrowed a name from some other item in the matrix in a nonsystematic fashion.

[2] For a more intensive discussion of the Esper experiments see Jenkins and Palermo (1964).

The response of most psychologists to this study, if they consider it at all, is that it is not really something new. Responses are all under specific stimulus control. The subject somehow, for unknown reasons, fractures the stimulus into color and form and fractures the response into first syllable and second syllable and simply runs off first-order habits. When the color comes up, he says the first syllable and then attends to the shape and says the second syllable. In effect then, he has no new stimulus to deal with when the withheld stimuli are presented. But this in itself is not sufficient. There is, in the first place, an ordering rule here. Something is being ordered. What is it? Is it a particular syllable or is it a class of syllables? Why and how does the subject learn to fracture the stimulus? Why and how does he fracture the responses? What experiences in his history determined these behaviors?

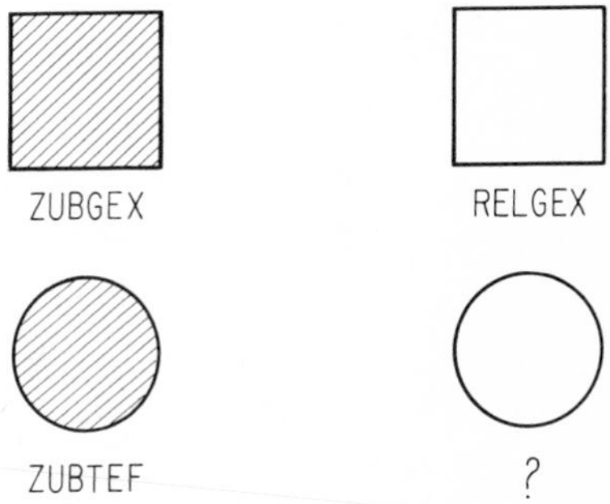

Figure 1 *A miniature Esper experiment.*

ZUBGEX   RELGEX

ZUBTEF   ?

We see the effects of language history when we move to the group that had its response system fractured at nonsyllable boundaries. This group had extraordinary trouble trying to learn to co-ordinate aspects of the stimulus with aspects of the response. In effect the subjects continued to utilize a response division they had learned to make in English, dividing morphemes at syllable boundaries. It will not do to say that this is simple transfer of the habit unless one is willing to admit morphemes and syllables as units. Even worse, one must admit the generalized syllable because we may assume that the subjects had no experience with these particular constellations of sounds prior to the experiment. Something indeed seems to have transferred, and its transfer was instrumental in making a system available to the subjects, but what was it that transferred?

Portions of this experiment have been replicated in our laboratories by Erwin Segal with different sets of dimensions and different response units with essentially the same results obtained by Esper as regards the learning of coordinate stimulus and response systems (Segal, 1962).

We are driven, then, into a hoary old set of questions at this point: what is the stimulus, what is the response, and finally, what is it that is learned? It is my opinion that this can best be dealt with by asserting that what is learned is a set of classes on both the stimulus and response sides and arrangements of classes on the response side. Following this line of analysis our problems become, how are classes generated and how does one learn their arrangements? These are *the* basic problems at each level of language function from the phoneme up to the completed utterance.

This may appear to be scarcely more than a reassertion of the trite contention that language is a system, a system in which classification and sequential organization play the key roles. But even the trite may be important. When the famous linguist Jakobson (1957) examines language, he sees two cardinal principles, *selection* and *combination,* which may also be expressed as reference and context or even as general meaning and contextual meaning. Jakobson writes (p. 159):

These two operations provide each linguistic sign with two sets of *interpretants,* to utilize the effective concept introduced by Charles S. Peirce: two referents serve to interpret the sign—one to the code, and the other to the context, whether coded or free; and in each of these ways the sign is related to another set of linguistic signs. A given sign may be replaced by other . . . signs of the same code, whereby its general meaning is revealed, while its contextual meaning is determined by its connection with other signs within the same sequence.

We must confront these two processes over and over again. Grammar enters into our work in that it provides a description of some of the kinds of classes manifest in language behavior and specifies some of the kinds of organizations and ways of changing organizations that we find in natural language. Viewed in this fashion, grammar is a target for our theories. A theory of language must *at least* be able to account for the regularities observed by the linguist in his study of language. If the linguist finds that his most efficient description is composed of classes and sequences, we must at least have a mechanism for language behavior that permits such a description to be effective.

A somewhat different approach to the question of grammatical behavior is also possible. We may view grammar as a logical apparatus, a formal calculus, which is intended to generate and discriminate grammatical sequences as opposed to ungrammatical sequences. Here one might propose to develop a theory of language that embraces the formal calculus and combines it with a theory of behavior in an attempt to test the adequacy of both via a series of construct validation experiments. It should be possible to test jointly the grammar and the theory by their capacity to predict and explain specific verbal behavior of given subjects at given times. Certainly this is the most severe test we can construct, and yet in all honesty it should be one of our important goals. Of course, we must entertain the hypotheses that the grammar may be insufficient, the theory of behavior may be inadequate, or the test may be inappropriate with respect to our variables. (i.e., it may be unreliable, poorly formulated, uncontrolled, etc.). In spite of the difficulties and uncertainties, what I wish to suggest is that we ought to attempt to test ourselves with problems of prediction and control of constrained language instances in the laboratory to see whether we can in fact employ our theory and formal apparatus to account for the behavior that ensues.

Regardless of which of the approaches we intend to employ (and of course, most of us will do some of both), it is necessary at some point to make contact with the linguists' description. Where shall we make such contact?

At least some modern grammars can be construed, as Hockett (1961) has proposed, as item and arrangement grammars. This is the equivalent of what Chomsky calls phrase-structure grammars. In such grammars there are given classes of items and given possible arrangements of items. This conception has been further modified by Chomsky with the notion that a set of transformations of

arrangements is possible. He proposes that one take a set, E, of
"initial strings" and a set, F, of rewrite rules and proceed from a
string produced by a phrase-structure grammar to generate the remainder of grammatical utterances in the language that involve the
contents of that string. There are two general sets of rules involved
in operations past the phrase-structure grammar. The first set consists of transformation rules that can be applied to the outputs of
the phrase-structure grammar to produce different forms of sentences. These rules have received considerable attention, of course.
The second set is the set of morphophonemic rules that tell how different elements in lists are rewritten when they occupy given positions in given transformations (e.g., *take* + past tense = *took*).

The psychologist who wishes to incorporate the linguists' con-
ceptions as part of his logical calculus-behavior theory combination
can enter this linguistic hierarchy at any point, as we shall see in
later examples. He may formulate a problem in learning, recall,
perception, generalization, etc., in such a manner that his independent variables correspond to a manipulation of a formal linguistic variable and examine outcome effects that correspond to
the varied inputs. Equally as readily, if he is ingenious and patient,
he may perform longitudinal studies of behavioral situations in
which the linguistic sophistication of the subjects is his independent
variable and observe corresponding changes in behavior as linguistic changes of given sorts are witnessed.

For the psychologist who wishes to view grammar itself as a target to be accounted for, however, it seems to me that the point of
contact is dictated. He must begin with the process of class formation. If he cannot carry off the notion of class formation theoretically, I cannot see how he can ever find a meeting ground with the
linguists' conception of grammar. If a class may be treated as a
stimulus and as a response, the problems of sequence learning and
varied arrangement can be handled at least approximately with
more traditional theoretical notions. Given the formation of classes,
attention can then be turned to the problems of learning the "rules
of combination" which govern acceptable sequences in the language.

I take it that the readers of this article will recognize that language must in some sense be a generative mechanism; that it must be "rule governed" as opposed to "rote learned." It is clear that speakers can utter sentences they have never learned in a word-for-word manner, and it is equally clear that listeners can understand such sentences though they may be unique in the listener's experience. Phrase structure reduces the difficulties of learning these strings to the learning of certain rules. Compared with rote learning or the finite-state generation of language, this introduces great simplicity in what it is that must be learned.

It should be remarked that one must not assume, of course, that the rules of language behavior are known in the sense that they can be verbalized or that they need to be explicitly learned as such. It is assumed, rather, that rules are demonstrated in the behavior and are descriptive of the behavior. It will be fruitful for our purposes to see how such behavior is acquired, and what sets of experiences are necessary to induce behavior that is in accordance with certain rules whether the rules are explicitly learned or not.

Mediation Models

American psychology has followed in the tradition of British associational psychology. For the most part theorists have chosen contiguity in temporal sequence as a necessary condition (in one way or another) for the formation of associations. This conception has focused attention on many interesting dimensions of learning and performace but chiefly has stressed those having to do with sequences of stimuli, sequences of stimuli and responses, sequences of responses and reinforcing stimuli, and sequences of stimuli and responses constituting "chains" of behavior. Studies of events affecting both the beginning and end of the behavior chains (stimulus generalization along "natural" dimensions, parametric studies of drive, amount, delay, and schedules of reinforcement) have further expanded our knowledge of powerful manipulators of behavior. There has been little occasion to consider complex behaviors that involve alternative responses or that involve vastly different sets of stimuli where the responses and the stimuli play functionally equiv-

alent roles. Until recently, little attention has been given by theorists to the effects of past learning on new learning, and one can
easily gather the impression that the psychologist is only "at home"
with the naïve organism, which is to be discarded as soon as it has
served its purpose and learned its one task.

However, a rapidly growing body of experiments may be found
that deliberately involve several learning stages and that demonstrate that the organism has (as everyone knew, of course) an appreciable carryover from one experience to the next. Harlow's work
(1949) on learning sets illustrates the facilitating effects of having
to solve "similar" problems in a series (even though the stimuli are
physically dissimilar). Other studies showing "latent learning," "expectation," and "latent extinction" also show marked and sometimes
dramatic effects of the interaction of several learning experiences.
(See Gough, 1961, for a detailed discussion of this issue.)

It is precisely such an interaction pattern that I believe we must
exploit if we are to achieve an explanation of the formation of
classes and ultimately of grammar. The particular vehicle with
which I have been working may be termed a general mediation
model.

The notion of mediated associations is a very old one deriving
from the thinking of the British associationists on the "association of
ideas." In an effort to achieve simplicity in their accounts of observed associative phenomena, these philosophers invented the
notion of mediate (as opposed to immediate) association. They
argued simply that two ideas which were both associated with a
third idea would come to have some association with each other.

In its modern form this essential notion has been pressed into the
mold of the stimulus-response theorist by hypothesizing implicit
responses having stimulus properties. Such specially produced
stimulation is the heart of mediation theory. These implicit responses and their stimuli are then employed, via the conventional
contiguity rules, to tie together sets of stimuli or responses which
may not have occurred together observably during the organism's
experience. While the philosophers would have said, "Idea A is associated with both idea B and idea C. Therefore B and C will be
associated," the modern theorist would detail this as follows:

Stimulus A has a high probability of eliciting response B as a result of a given set of learning experiences.

If now, stimulus A is presented, we can assume that response B will tend to occur. It may occur overtly, or if there is no possibility for it to occur overtly, it will occur covertly. In either case it will be followed by its stimulus consequences.

If in the presence of stimulus A, response C is now required, that response will become conditioned not only to stimulus A but also to the stimulus consequences of implicit response B.

Therefore, I will expect that response C will now be likely to occur in the presence of response B or following any other stimulus that elicits response B.

While this may not appear to the reader to be a particularly elegant formulation, it has rather surprising power to cope with some difficult situations and, more importantly here, offers a potential solution to the problem of the formation of classes. Consider for a moment what might be expected to happen if the following sequences were learned: A–B then C–B, followed by learning A–D and C–D, and that, in turn, followed by learning A–E and C–E, and that by A–F and C–F, etc. Surely, we must believe that our subject will begin anticipating the C– sequences correctly. If whatever is learned to A is then learned to C, we will have created "equivalent stimuli"—that is, we may now expect that if a new response is learned to A, our subject will *without specific training* transfer it to the C stimulus.[3] While this may appear trivial, it is in effect a novel but presumably appropriate response to the stimulus in this situation. Further, it is precisely what would be predicted by the clumsy theoretical formulation given above. Would not such a demonstration be sufficient to claim that a class of stimuli has been established?

Alternatively, on the response side suppose that we employed a sequence that was the reverse of the one above: learning B–A then B–C, followed by learning D–A and D–C, followed by E–A, E–C, and that in turn by F–A, F–C, etc. Clearly, here we would expect the correct use of the C response in the presence of a novel stimulus, given only that A had been paired with it. Such a prediction

[3] This situation is explicitly diagrammed in Cofer and Foley (1942).

again follows directly from the mediational hypothesis. Does this not constitute a demonstration of a response class?

It can further be seen that a sequence of learning such as A–B, C–B, A–D, C–D, consists simultaneously of a stimulus-classing and response-classing operation or, more elaborately, constitutes an intermixed stimulus-equivalence and response-equivalence model. I have elsewhere (Jenkins, 1963) referred to a sequence of experiences such as this as a four-stage equivalence paradigm. It might also be referred to simply as a miniature grammar. It is easy to see that the grammar of this series could be described as: $S \rightarrow X–Y$; $X \rightarrow A, C; Y \rightarrow B, D$.

If one maps this description back into Esper's experiment, it is easy to see that a given color-form stimulus sets the occasion for an "utterance." The utterance may be rewritten as X–Y. X may be rewritten as the four nonsense syllables Esper used for colors, and Y may be rewritten as the four nonsense syllables Esper used for shapes. Esper's system, then, affords a simple grammar which (as the subjects demonstrated) may be learned on the basis of an incomplete sample of the utterances and applied with accuracy to the new instances when they arise on the test trials. It is at the same time an instance of our mediation model.

In addition to the Esper experiments and the "thought experiments" above, there is impressive evidence that such learning experiences do indeed mediate stimulus generalization and response transfer. The first clear experimental demonstration was given by Shipley (1935) and analyzed by Hull (1939) in the fashion already suggested here. It furnishes a useful illustration of the processes sketched above.

Shipley gave his subjects the following experiences over a period of several days. First, they were presented with either a light or a tone stimulus (in random order) followed by a tap on the cheek which induced a reflex wink. When these pairings were well established, the light was presented alone followed by a shock to the finger which induced finger withdrawal. This pairing was continued for many trials. Finally the tone alone was presented as a test to see if it would induce finger withdrawal. In a significant number of cases, it did. Shipley concluded that the conditioning had transferred from one stimulus to another as a result of the functional equivalence they had previously acquired.

The situation may be viewed as one in which the transfer of the second response was mediated by the implicit occurrence of the first response. The situation may be diagrammed in the following manner:

```
A................................B
(light)     (tap) ─────────────→ (wink)
C................................B
(tone)      (tap) ─────────────→ (wink)
A..........(implicit B)..........D
(light)     (shock) ───────────→ (finger withdrawal)
C..........(implicit B)..........D
(tone)                          (finger withdrawal)
```

This explanation requires the occurrence of some sort of implicit response with relatively stable stimulus characteristics as a result of the first two stages of training. If this may be assumed, in the third stage the stimuli from the implicit response become conditioned to the finger withdrawal response. When the tone is introduced in the fourth stage, the implicit response and its subsequent stimuli afford an explanation of the observed finger withdrawal.

That this paradigm is effective has now been demonstrated in many different situations, although there are still difficulties in stating the sufficient conditions for its operation (see Jenkins, 1963). Birge (1941) showed that verbal responses learned as common names for disparate stimuli could mediate appropriate motor responses toward those stimuli and, conversely, that when stimuli shared an appropriate motor response, they were likely to be named with the same name. Birge worked with young children and found the paradigm to be effective only when the mediators were made explicit (i.e., the children were required to name as they performed the motor response). Wickens and Briggs (1951) gave a much more impressive demonstration of the paradigm when they paired a light and a tone with a common verbal response

("Now") and showed transfer of a conditioned response (finger withdrawal) from one stimulus to the other as a consequence of the earlier learning.

Eckstrand and Morgan (1953) showed that if a set of verbal labels (color names) were learned as responses to color stimuli and, separately, as responses to nonsense forms, motor responses learned to the color stimuli transferred readily to the nonsense forms, whereas this learning was difficult for subjects who had learned unrelated names to the nonsense forms. Morgan, Eckstrand, Rockway, and Newton (1954) went on to demonstrate that transfer of motor responses from one set of nonsense forms to another set of forms was similarly facilitated if the appropriate forms had been previously used as stimuli for a common verbal response (here, abstract nouns). They further found that the order in which the first stages were learned was an important consideration in determining the degree of transfer, much as the Hullian analysis would predict.

In experiments in our laboratory, James Greeno and I have found that the general model can be seen in experiments with natural associates. We used real words as stimuli which were known to elicit certain associates in a free-association test. The learning lists were so arranged that three stimuli, all of which elicited a common word on the word association test, were paired with a common nonsense syllable response (e.g., the stimuli *germ, crumb,* and *atom* all elicit the response *small* in the Underwood-Richardson norms [1956]). After the subject has learned to respond to these three stimuli with a particular nonsense syllable, he can rapidly learn a new pair made up of any other stimulus that elicits the response *small* and the appropriate nonsense syllable. Martin, Oliver, Hom, and Heaslet (1963) have also shown that the four-stage paradigm may be demonstrated in verbal learning under somewhat different conditions.

In other experiments Kirk Smith, James Tweedy, and I have explored the generalization of a motor response from pictures to words and vice versa. If one assumes that the subject responds to a printed word by saying the word subvocally, and that he responds to a picture by naming it, again subvocally, then it follows that we must predict that a motor response learned to a picture will transfer to the printed word which names the object pictured. This is confirmed by the experiments. The transfer from pictures to words is higher than the transfer in the other direction, which we view as attributable to the unique characteristics of any particular picture as opposed to the absence of distinguishing characteristics in a printed word.

All of these examples illustrate that there is real substance in the paradigm given above. As more studies appear, we will be able to specify more clearly the circumstances under which stimulus and response equivalence are achieved and the conditions that afford an occasion for their manifestation. We know that a mere specification of the paradigms themselves and their coordination with ostensible stimuli and responses is not in itself any guarantee that the critical behavior showing the equivalence will ensue. In an extensive series of experiments in our laboratories we have found more ways *not* to get the equivalence effects than we have found ways to achieve them (Jenkins, 1963). It is becoming clear that the nature of the stimuli and the responses, the number of association stages employed, the strengths of the associations, the sequences of the stages, the nature of the subjects' tasks, the type of appraisal stage employed, and the time intervals involved, all play some role in the process. In addition it is reasonable to suppose that a variety of subject variables (age, linguistic sophistication, learning experiences, etc.) affect both what is learned and what may be demonstrated in the test stage.

It may appear odd to the reader that one should choose such a fragile and incompletely understood device to make the center of such a powerful set of behaviors as those involved in language. Nevertheless, I believe that the principles involved in these simple paradigms will prove to be adequate to the task in the long run. As we come to understand the controlling variables and as we begin to bring these paradigms under multiple stimulus control (as was true in the Esper experiment and as must be true in the case of natural language), demonstrations of their effectiveness will become commonplace, and their extensive application will be revealed.

Relations Between Grammar and Behavior

Evidence from a variety of sources presses the psychologist to
consider the relations between the formal analytic system of grammar and the behavior of human beings. The kind of argument
given in the first part of this article could easily have been made
40 years ago. However, argumentation of the form, "Psychologists
ought to . . . ," is probably never very effective. Peculiarities of
data, curious lawfulness, and hints of emerging relationships, on
the other hand, may lure even the most narrow investigator into
hitherto unexplored areas. Certainly, those of us working on language processes at Minnesota did not set out to study grammatical
phenomena *per se.* We were, rather, slowly forced into the consideration by the nature of the data we collected during the course
of our extensive work on word associations.

Psychologists have observed for many years that word associations to common words bear a curious relation to one another grammatically. In adult subjects stimuli and responses tend, surprisingly,
to be of the same grammatical class. While this may be easily
rationalized by postulating a variety of logical relationships between stimuli and responses, it is puzzling nonetheless. An association theorist would suppose naïvely that stimulus words would have
a strong tendency to elicit as associates those words which most
frequently followed the stimulus in the language as it is heard and
spoken. In fact, however, this is rarely the case in the responses
of adult speakers. Nouns tend to elicit other nouns, verbs other
verbs, participles other participles, adjectives other adjectives, etc.
(see, for example, Deese, 1962). When we sought cases for which
the stimulus-response matching breaks down, we found, for example, stimuli such as adverbs. This is an especially interesting
case because in English the linguistic class is itself in doubt, the
treatment of adverbs linguistically being a difficult problem as yet
unresolved. Other instances included rare words, particularly adjectives, for which two general types of responses were found: first,
clang responses, suggesting that the subjects did not know the word

as a word and simply responded to its formal characteristics much as subjects do to nonsense syllables; and, second, continuation responses (e.g., the response *missile* to the adjective *ballistic*), suggesting that we had broken into a single unit of high strength and, there and chiefly only there, found the kind of association one would predict from a simple association chaining theory.

Saporta and I suggested as early as 1954 (see Jenkins, 1954) that it would be fruitful to analyze associates into *paradigmatic* (same form class) and *syntagmatic* (sequential form class) responses. We felt that the very strongest associates could be represented in both groupings—that is, they shared the same class and occurred in many of the same contexts, but in addition they were frequently used in nearly contiguous series—e.g., *tables* and *chairs, black* and *white, light* or *dark*. We overlooked, as Howes (1957) later pointed out, that one rarely finds responses of the "function classes" to the contentive words which should occur in the sequence, and our use of syntagmatic was loose in the extreme.

In later work (with Gough, Hakes, and Segal) it was possible to demonstrate that grammatical relations were indeed useful. Response hierarchies were highly manipulable in terms of the particular form of the stimulus. If the stimulus *man* were changed to *men,* content of the response hierarchy was virtually unchanged, but most of the noun responses were pluralized. Similarly as verbs were changed in form, the hierarchies were modified systematically. When subjects were asked to use stimulus words in sentences and then directed to strike out the key word and substitute another, they substituted the most frequent paradigmatic associate. When we studied the remaining content of such sentences we found some evidence for the use of the so-called syntagmatic associates scattered throughout the sentences. Over-all, the set of studies became for us a convincing demonstration of grammatical control of stimulus-response relations in a "free" responding situation.

If one examines these findings in the light of acquired equivalence through use (ignoring the logical and functional relations present) and considers the explication via mediational models, it is apparent that a partial explanation is available. If we suppose that a child repeatedly encounters two different words in the same contexts, A-B-C-X-D and A-B-C-Y-D, for example, the first order relations should emerge: C should elicit X and Y, and both X and Y should elicit D. If these sequences are repeated often enough and if other contexts are available in which X and Y play similar roles, they should, via the mediational models, come to be members of the same class (which the linguist would also tell us by his analysis of the sequences) and should have the capacity to elicit one another. If this is in general true, one would predict that children would tend to give sequence-like associates and, as they became linguistically more facile, would tend to shift to paradigmatic associates. Further, one would predict that paradigmatic responding would be earlier for more frequent words than for less frequent, etc.

Evidence on children's associations bears out this whole line of thinking. The data collected by Woodrow and Lowell (1916) for fourth and fifth grade children early in the century shows remarkably high incidence of sequential and completion responses in comparison to adults of about the same period (Kent and Rosanoff, 1910). In place of the *Deep-Shallow* associate of the adults, for example, the children responded *Deep-Hole;* in place of *Dark-Light* the children's norms show *Dark-Room,* etc.

Ervin (1961) and Brown and Berko (1960) have provided modern studies directly aimed at the examination of grammatical hypotheses in the context of children's associations with enlightening results. Both studies show that increasing experience with language and competence in its use are correlated with an increased tendency to respond paradigmatically on word-association tests. They also found differential rates of paradigmatic responding for various parts of speech that seem reasonable in terms of the probable use of these parts of speech by children.

McNeill (1963) performed a laboratory test of this hypothesis concerning the origin of associates by requiring subjects to learn short sentences with embedded nonsense words. The nonsense materials were in particular patterns such that two different nonsense "nouns" randomly appeared following a particular nonsense "adjective." He tested for both sequential and paradigmatic associations at different degrees of learning and found that paradigmatic responding appeared in significant amounts only after sequential recall had reached a high (and asymptotic) level. This appears to strengthen the case for serious consideration of the grammatical status of associates and at the same time argues for a particular source of origin.

If to these considerations we add the fact that parts of speech do *tend* to have certain consistencies, as Brown (1957) has pointed out, and that these may well reinforce and contribute to their "psychological reality," it becomes reasonable to regard them as important classes that must be explicitly included in any work on verbal processes when we are interested in discrete words as units.

An interesting aside here is furnished by the research of Werner and Kaplan (1950) who presented their subjects with a "meaning assignment" problem. Here children were given sentences containing nonsense words and asked to give the nonsense words meaning. Younger children tended to give contextual associations as meanings—that is, they reported something else from the sequence as the meaning—but older children gave potential substitutions for the term in the sentence context. The investigators saw this as reflecting the interdependence of meaning and structure, much as we would be led to interpret it here.

Another series of experiments has similarly forced us into further considerations of a grammatical nature. This series began with a concept formation study by Johnson (1961) which attempted to show that a sentence position that called for a particular part of speech, a noun or an adjective, could serve as a stimulus for the selection of a response marked with a given formal characteristic, in this case a final syllable. Subjects were presented with sentences of the form, article-adjective-noun-verb, with one of the two middle positions represented by a blank. They were required to learn a specific nonsense word for each of eight sentences, four with the noun missing and four with the adjective missing. Each of the noun forms ended in the same syllable (e.g., *pod*) and each of the adjective forms ended with a common syllable (e.g., *lef*). Examples: *The green dupod rolled. The bilef boat sank.* Test conditions then presented the old sentences with a choice of two new forms (one a *pod* and one a *lef*), or new sentences with a choice of two old forms (one a *pod* and one a *lef*), or both new sentences and new forms of each kind.

To our great surprise Johnson found that while subjects showed generalization to old sentences with new response words and generalization to new sentences with old response words, when presented with new sentences and new words, their performance was essentially at the chance level. In other words, it was possible to achieve stimulus generalization *or* response generalization but *not both* simultaneously. Clearly our formulation appeared to be in trouble with nothing more complex than a simple concept learning experiment.

Further work revealed that subjects could readily sort the sentences into two groups on the basis of missing structure (though they usually described the sorting in some other manner), and they could readily sort the response forms on the basis of differential endings (though they usually failed to report that the entire last syllable was common for each class) but apparently could not put the covariation of these two classes together when members of both classes were new.

Johnson found complete stimulus *and* response generalization, however, when, during the presentation of the training words, a picture accompanied the *pod* words and a color square accompanied the *lef* words. With this mere hint of meaning, the generalization was complete. Control procedures that employed the reference alone failed to produce stimulus and response generalization. The results of this experiment led us strongly to the considerations of multiple determination of responses, which have been alluded to throughout the paper.

Subsequent to the Johnson research, John Warner has undertaken a series of studies attacking the problem in a different fashion. He reasoned that a single context in English rarely (and perhaps never) defines the part of speech of a word form unambiguously. Consequently, he prepared materials of a more complex nature in which nonsense nouns, adjectives, and verbs were illustrated in a variety of sentence forms and in a variety of positions.

With these materials he demonstrated stimulus generalization, response generalization, and stimulus and response generalization within an experimental setting in which subjects had no opportunity to learn the material completely but only heard and studied it. While the results of the experiments are not directly comparable, it was clear that in a more complex situation with more parts of speech to learn and less opportunity to learn them precisely, subjects were demonstrating much more "class learning" than in the Johnson experiment.

Warner has gone on to study in a variety of fascinating experiments the effects of semantic and syntactic manipulations on nonsense words used in varying contexts. He has found recently systematic hierarchies in the substitution patterns found for nonsense nouns, adjectives, and verbs when they are not used in the "correct" class or when subjects are forced to use them in completion tests on which the "correct" blanks are not available.

Duane Martin has also taken this as a point of departure and has performed a series of experiments in a programmed learning format manipulating the same kinds of variables. Clearly, one early outcome of the studies of both of these investigators is that diversity of position of a supposed member of a class is an important variable in the assignment of that member to the class in the subsequent behavior of the subject. This, of course, suggests that the determination of class membership is more complex than our simple model would imply and affords a partial explanation for the delay in the emergence of paradigmatic responding in children. It also seems to suggest that complex and varied stimuli may play an important role in leading the subject to attend to the relevant aspect of the stimulus, just as bringing in cues from a different domain did in the Johnson experiment.

While further examples could be cited here, perhaps this is sufficient to illustrate the point that the psychologist who works with verbal materials at all is today having a difficult time trying to stay away from grammatical considerations. Even supposedly simple rote-learning tasks are not immune as Glanzer (1962) showed when he found grammatical variables intruding to determine rate of paired-associate learning for words of different parts of speech and affecting response integration when words of different parts of speech had to be integrated into sets of nonsense terms.

Directions of Research

While it is doubtful that any reader of this article needs an external stimulus as to the direction of his research (or would accept such direction if it were needed), it is tempting to suggest problems to others and in the usual tradition of the field to do so.

As pointed out earlier, I believe that there are two major and complementary thrusts to the research effort at this point. One is to begin with the grammatical variables and demonstrate behavioral correlates, and the other is to start from some theoretical position and attempt to build up toward an elaborated model that will account for the grammatical phenomena themselves. While both are being pursued at the present, I suspect that the first will proceed faster than the second and will in fact provide guidelines in identifying the major phenomena that must be the target of the second.

The first line of research is well illustrated by the work of Miller and his students (see for example, Miller, 1962, and Mehler, 1963) and by such work as Johnson has already reported here. It is currently exemplified in our laboratories by a series of studies of the rated similarity of sentences when the sentences are various transformations of the same basic kernel sentence. This work, which was begun by Ida Kurcz, a postdoctoral fellow in our laboratories, is now being extended by Charles Clifton and Penelope Odom to studies of the generalization of a motor response from one member to another of such "sentence families." The results obtained thus far suggest that the response of subjects to sentences that have undergone different transformations is fairly heavily weighted semantically. Various transformations have vastly different effects in terms of how much they alter the subjects' responses. In general, all questions are seen as being pretty much the same, and passive transforms are not seen as being much different from their active forms, but the negative transformation makes rather great differences in response.

The second line of research is rather less well represented in the literature. Braine's work (1963) is clearly the best example and offers the excellent illustration of model building that attempts to secure its footings by careful experimentation and tries to extend itself up slowly by offering limited accounts of restricted sets of phenomena. There is, of course, much in common between Braine's proposed "contextual generalization" and "focal points of association" and the general approach through mediational models suggested here.

In general, studies in the Esper tradition seem to me to be most fruitful here. Studies that manipulate *systems* of responses seem to afford insights into the mechanisms that may underlie grammar and afford convenient tests of the generality of the system when missing cells are evaluated.

In our laboratory Smith (1963) has pursued this systematic approach in a series of structured recall experiments. Subjects are presented with sets of letter pairs that may be systematically related in a variety of ways. These structures may be thought of as more or less complicated grammars, and the generalization of the grammatical system may be evaluated in the "errors" made in the process of attempting to recall the pairs heard. Smith has already shown that a simple grammar of the Esper type is quite productive in filling in the missing cells of the system and that such "systematic errors" increase steadily as the subjects are given more training trials on the incomplete system, while nonsystematic errors decrease.

It appears to me that our next steps may well be to expand experiments of this type, adding such variables as a simple referential field, a variety of orders of "utterances," systems of cues such as intonation pattern and emphasis, to bring ourselves to an understanding of the acquisition and operation of these more complex systems which more and more directly approximate real language.

Throughout all of this work I would suggest that we may well be guided by the considerations of the simple mediational models and that part of our research will be directed to the more thorough exploration of the simple system represented in the four-stage equivalence model. My faith is that this represents a minimal cornerstone in linguistic process and that it will be productive for us to determine those conditions which maximize its effectiveness.

References

Birge, J. S. "The role of verbal responses in transfer." Unpublished doctoral dissertation, Yale Univ., 1941.

Braine, M. D. S. "On learning the grammatical order of words." *Psychol. Rev.*, 1963, **70**, 323–348.

Brown, R. W. "Linguistic determinism and the part of speech." *J. Abnorm. Soc. Psychol.*, 1957, **55**, 1–5.

———, and Jean Berko. "Word association and the acquisition of grammar." *Child Devel.*, 1960, **31**, 1–14.

Brown, R. W., and C. Fraser. "The acquisition of syntax." In C. N. Cofer and Barbara S. Musgrave (eds.). *Verbal behavior and learning.* New York: McGraw-Hill, 1963, 158–197.

———, ——— and U. Bellugi. "Explorations in grammar evaluation." In U. Bellugi and R. W. Brown (eds.). "The acquisition of language." *Monogr. Soc. Res. Child Devel.*, 1964, Serial No. 92, 29, No. 1, 79–92.

Bullowa, M., L. G. Jones, and T. G. Bever. "The development from vocal to verbal behavior in children." In U. Bellugi and R. W. Brown (eds.). "The acquisition of language." *Monogr. Soc. Res. Child Devel.*, 1964, Serial No. 92, 29, No. 1, 101–107.

Chomsky, N. *Syntactic structures.* The Hague: Mouton, 1957.

———, and G. A. Miller. "Finite state languages." *Inform. Control,* 1958, **1**, 91–112.

Cofer, C. N., and J. P. Foley, Jr. "Mediated generalization and the interpretation of verbal behavior: I. Prolegomena." *Psychol. Rev.*, 1942, **49**, 513–540.

Deese, J. "Form class and the determinants of association." *J. Verbal Learn. Verbal Behav.*, 1962, **1**, 79–84.

Eckstrand, G., and R. Morgan. "A study of verbal mediation as a factor in transfer of training." *WADC Tech. Rpt.*, 53–34, 1953, AD 13030.

Ervin, Susan M. "Changes with age in the verbal determinants of word association." *Amer. J. Psychol.*, 1961, **74**, 361–372.

Esper, E. A. "A technique for the experimental investigation of associative interference in artificial linguistic material." *Language Monogr.*, 1925, No. 1.

Glanzer, M. "Grammatical category: A rote learning and word association analysis." *J. Verbal Learn. Verbal Behav.*, 1962, **1**, 31–41.

Gough, P. B. "The study of mediation in animals." Unpublished doctoral dissertation. Univ. Minnesota, 1961.

Harlow, H. F. "The formation of learning sets." *Psychol. Rev.*, 1949, **56**, 51–65.

Hockett, C. F. "Grammar for the hearer." In R. Jakobson (ed.). *Structure of language and its mathematical aspects* (Proc. 12th symp. in appl. math.), Providence, R. I. Amer. Math. Soc., 1961, pp. 220–236.

Howes, D. H. "On the relation between the probability of a word as an association and in general linguistic usage." *J. Abnorm. Soc. Psychol.*, 1957, **54**, 75–85.

Hull, C. L. "The problem of stimulus equivalence in behavior theory." *Psychol. Rev.*, 1939, **46**, 9–30.

Jakobson, R. "The cardinal dichotomy in language." In R. N. Anshen (ed.). *Language: an enquiry into its meaning and function.* New York: Harper and Brothers, 1957, 155–178.

Jenkins, J. J. "A study of mediated association. Report No. 2. Studies in verbal behavior." N. S. F. Grant, Univ. of Minnesota, 1959.

———. "Mediated associations: paradigms and situations." In C. N. Cofer and B. S. Musgrave (eds.). *Verbal behavior and learning.* New York: McGraw-Hill, 1963, pp. 210–245.

———. "Transitional organization: association techniques." In C. E. Osgood and T. A. Sebeok (eds.). "Psycholinguistics." *Suppl. J. Abnorm. Soc. Psychol.*, 1954, **52**, 112–118.

———, and D. S. Palermo. "Mediation processes and the acquisition of linguistic structure." In U. Bellugi and R. W. Brown (eds.). "The acquisition of language." *Monogr. Soc. Res. Child Devel.*, 1964, Serial No. 92, 29, No. 1, 141–169.

Johnson, N. F. "The cue value of sentence frames for the acquisition of speech categories." Unpublished doctoral dissertation, Univ. Minnesota, 1961.

Kent, Grace H., and A. J. Rosanoff. "A study of association in insanity." *Amer. J. Insanity*, 1910, **67**, 37–96, 317–390.

Lashley, K. S. "The problem of serial order in behavior." In L. A. Jeffress (ed.). *Cerebral mechanisms in behavior: the Hixon symposium.* New York: Wiley, 1951, pp. 112–136.

Martin, J. G., M. Oliver, G. Hom, and G. Heaslet. "Repetition and task in verbal mediating-response acquisition." *J. Exp. Psychol.*, 1963, **66**, 12–16.

McNeill, D. "The origin of associations within the same grammatical class." *J. Verbal Learn. Verbal Behav.*, 1963, **2**, 250–262.

Mehler, J. "Some effects of grammatical transformations on the recall of English sentences." *J. Verbal Learn. Verbal Behav.*, 1963, **2**, 346–351.

Miller, G. A. "Some psychological studies of grammar." *Amer. Psychologist*, 1962, 17, 748–762.

———, E. Galanter, and K. H. Pribram. *Plans and the structure of behavior*. New York: Holt, 1960.

Miller, W., and S. M. Ervin. "The development of grammar in child language." In U. Bellugi and R. W. Brown (eds.). "The acquisition of language." *Monogr. Soc. Res. Child Devel.*, 1964, Serial No. 92, 29, No. 1, 9–34.

Morgan, R., G. Eckstrand, M. Rockway, and J. Newton. "Verbally mediated transfer as a function of order of tasks." *WADC Tech. Rpt.*, 54–41, 1954, AD 33353.

Segal, E. M. "Stimulus perception as a function of response set." Unpublished Ph.D dissertation, Univ. Minnesota, 1962.

Shipley, W. C. "Indirect conditioning." *J. Gen. Psychol.*, 1935, 12, 337–357.

Skinner, B. F. *Verbal behavior*. New York: Appleton-Century-Crofts, 1957.

Smith, K. "Recall of paired verbal units under various conditions of organization." Unpublished Ph.D. dissertation, Univ. Minnesota, 1963.

Underwood, B. J., and J. Richardson. "Some verbal materials for the study of concept formation." *Psychol. Bull.*, 1956, 53, 84–95.

Werner, H., and E. Kaplan. "Development of word meaning through verbal context: an experimental study." *J. Psychol.*, 1950, 29, 251–257.

Wickens, D. D., and G. E. Briggs. "Mediated stimulus generalization in sensory preconditioning." *J. Exp. Psychol.*, 1951, 42, 197–200.

Woodrow, H., and F. Lowell. "Children's association frequency tables." *Psychol. Monogr.*, 1916, 22 (5, Whole No. 97).

III

PSYCHOLINGUISTICS
AND
VERBAL LEARNING

THE LANGUAGE
REPERTOIRE AND
SOME PROBLEMS IN
VERBAL LEARNING

Benton J. Underwood

As a reference point, let me think of the *experimental* psycholinguist as one who is asking questions about the acquisition and use of verbal and conceptual habits which encompass larger units of the language than those customarily dealt with in the usual verbal learning study. More particularly, the habits with which the psycholinguist deals may be referred to in general as grammatical habits. Since grammar receives its full meaning only by referring to relationships among words, it may be said that the units of analysis used by the psycholinguist are larger than those commonly dealt with in verbal learning studies.

Much of the work in the modern counterpart of classical verbal learning is secondarily a study of the operation of simple linguistic habits. To understand how meaningfulness influences rote learning of lists of simple verbal units, we must of necessity inquire about the subject's linguistic habits. Meaningful similarity is defined in terms of established habits, and to understand how similarity influences rote learning we must understand these habits. So, perhaps the major difference between the experimental problems facing the psycholinguist and those facing the experimenter in verbal learning lies in the complexity as inferred from differences in the size of the units of analysis—e.g., a sentence versus a word. If this is a major difference, it is almost inevitable that the fields draw closer together as research continues. Application of experimental analysis leaves no alternative, for an inevitable outcome of such analysis is the need to break down complex phenomena into more elementary units; to understand the complex it is necessary to understand the constituents. Very likely some of these more elementary units may be found to be those which have been extensively studied in the verbal learning laboratory. On the other hand, as will be seen in later discussions, some work in verbal learning is pointing to the possibility that conceptual-like habits are of considerable importance in so-called rote learning. Such a trend would clearly move the thinking in the direction of problems faced by the psycholinguist. Thus, there is every reason to believe that sooner or later the outcome of the efforts of the experimental psycholinguists and of the workers in verbal learning will cleanly mesh.

In the remainder of this article I will examine some problems currently tantalizing workers in the verbal learning laboratory. These particular problems have been chosen because they seem to involve the linguistic repertoire of the subjects and may, therefore, be of some interest to the psycholinguist.

Covert Habit Systems

Much work in verbal learning is essentially a study of covert processes which are said to insert themselves between a stimulus term and the elicitation of the response term. More particularly, these covert processes are usually identified as pre-established habit systems. The formal aspects of this situation are rather curious and are, perhaps, worth examination.

In the paired-associate task we present a stimulus term and a response term, with the interest centered in the mechanisms by which the subject is sooner or later enabled to produce correctly the response term upon presentation of the stimulus term. When the subject can give the response term, we say learning has occurred. The use of the term learning for this situation might not be judged appropriate for several reasons. Learning may be considered a construct. In this sense it means a change in the organism inferred from the correlation between trials and the number of correct response terms elicited. Some who personally dislike theory refuse to use the term learning in this sense. On the other hand, it is quite reasonable to define learning operationally, thereby merely applying the term to the correlation between practice and performance without any implication that it represents an intervening construct; in this sense it is simply a shorthand expression for the operations. We might also wish to avoid the use of the term on the grounds that we are not usually measuring new learning. Rather, it might be argued, we are only measuring the output of habits, already learned, as they combine to elicit the response term. Thus, a true distinction between performance and learning might be made. Nevertheless, as a general rule, we continue to call this change in performance with successive trials learning, and it does not seem to me that we find ourselves in great difficulty because we do so.

In the more formal theoretical systems, as exemplified by Hull, we may find hypothetical constructs or intervening variables inserted between the nominal stimulus term and the response elicitation. As has often been said, there is no necessary implication that the processes implied by these constructs be real or palpable. Formally, concepts like reactive inhibition are hypothetical constructs and are supposed to stand or fall on the basis of the predictions they mediate, not on the basis of whether or not they can be measured directly. The verbal learning situation presents an odd contrast to the Hull-type theory. When a stimulus term is presented a subject in a verbal learning situation and a response term is evoked, all sorts of things are presumed to happen in between, just as one might imagine things happening via a Hull-type theory. But, in the verbal learning situation, these happenings have nearly as firm a sense of reality as do the manifest stimulus term and the response elicited by it. This sense of reality (or palpability, insofar as habits can be said to be palpable) is produced since, by various operations, the in-between events—the in-between habits—may be studied and measured independently. Thus, the only critical assumption is that the particular stimulus situation used will elicit the habit systems known to exist. The term now used for this is *associative arousal*. If the habits are "aroused" by the stimulus situation, and if they combine in the manner in which they are known to combine when studied independently, then the response must occur. In any particular experiment these covert events are just as hypothetical as a formal construct, but unlike the processes implied by a formal construct, they can be studied directly. Indeed, when a prediction goes awry, a prediction based upon the operation of presumably known habit systems, the investigator may go back and study these habit systems in more detail. Much work in verbal learning is concerned with habit composition or habit chaining, but these intervening events are often as real to the experimenter as is the objectively measured response.

For those who do not like to stray too far from the data, the above situation has considerable attraction. It allows the investigator to include pre-experimental habits in his accounting for the performance of the moment, but the accounting mechanisms may themselves be studied independently. I do not believe that any comparable situation exists in any other area of behavioral psychology, and its exploitation proceeds at a very rapid pace. Yet, having thumped our chests over the beauty of the situation with which we often work, we must at the same time be the first to admit that we are not dealing with learning at a fundamental level. We are dealing with habit composition or transfer of habits that have already been formed, thereby escaping (perhaps happily) the problem of specifying how the habits became formed in the first place. Nevertheless, there is a wide range of phenomena that may be studied which appear to depend upon the transfer of habits and which are being systematically investigated. It is to some of these phenomena that attention will be directed.

Loosely speaking, many covert processes represent what have been called association aids. The subject makes use of habits he has already learned to acquire or perform the particular associations required by the laboratory situation. There is nothing new here.

Generations of research workers in verbal learning have known that subjects *do* use such devices, and one will find periodic reports in the literature that classify the various aids, the most recent being that of Bugelski (1962). But discipline can be brought into this area only by devising situations in which the operation of particular association aids can be specified by the experimenter.

Studies under the heading of *mediation* represent just such attempts to devise paradigms wherein specified habit utilization will produce given outcomes. Since mediation is discussed by Jenkins elsewhere in this volume, only passing reference to mediation need be made. The fact that expectations are not always confirmed in mediation studies only forces more careful scrutiny of the transfer properties of habits on which expectations were based, and also forces us to look for other habits which have not been adequately assessed but which may disturb predictions based only on the habit systems for which we do have normative data (e.g., word-association norms). I want to discuss some of these other habits. As will be seen, in some cases, at least, a minimum amount of direct evidence is available concerning these habits while for others the evidence is quite indirect and hence the remarks are speculative.

SELECTION HABITS AND DOMINANCE OF HABITS

We now recognize that the stimulus term we present may "have things done to it" by the subject. Among other things, there may be stimulus selection (e.g., Underwood, Ham, and Ekstrand, 1962). If the nominal stimulus consists of more than a single elementary unit, the subject may select a portion of the nominal stimulus as the functional stimulus. For example, if a stimulus compound consists of a difficult trigram and a three-letter word, the association is established between the word and the response term; it is as if the subject ignores the trigram. We do not know much about the variables of the material nor of the characteristics of the subjects that lead to stimulus selection; at the moment we only know that it occurs in a dramatic manner given the situation where the elements of the stimulus compound are widely different in nature.

A second fact that is known is that selection habits vary in dominance. This is to say that given two or more selection habits which may be elicited by a given stimulus, one may be more dominant than the other. Indeed, the strength of some of these habits may be so great that unadaptive behavior results, given an appropriately devised situation. If patches of easily discriminable colors are used as stimulus units in a paired-associate list, learning occurs as rapidly as if the stimulus terms were common words. However, if we use names of colors as stimulus terms but print those names in ink colors which are inappropriate—e.g., the word red printed in green ink—and if from trial to trial only the ink color is the consistent cue, learning is severely retarded (Saufley, unpublished). Thus, in spite of the fact that the subject is told to ignore the word and attend only to the ink color, he seems quite incapable of doing this easily. Responding to the printed word is so dominant a habit that it interferes heavily with other habits.

Studies of stimulus-selection habits is a new area of research. It is apparent that these studies are dealing with the covert processes or habits which insert themselves between the presentation of a given stimulus term and the occurrence of the response. But, by appropriately devised situations, they are quite amenable to study. It is a little frightening to speculate on the number of possible selection habits about which we know nothing, for assuredly we are making errors of inference about learning mechanisms when, as at the present time, we know so little about selection habits.

TRANSFORMATION OF VERBAL UNITS

There is still another way in which a verbal unit may have things done to it. Recent studies (Underwood and Keppel, 1963) have shown that verbal units may be transformed so that the unit of memory differs from the unit presented to the subject. We have called this coding, meaning that the subject encodes the unit for storage purposes and then, at the time of recall, decodes back to the unit presented him that is required for correct responding. If the trigram RAI is presented along with others in a free-learning situation (in which the subject need only learn the units without regard to order), he may encode the unit as AIR and decode at recall back to RAI. Thus, the memory for this unit consists of the unit AIR plus a decoding rule (e.g., "put R at beginning"). It seems quite evident that if a list of such units is given, the subject may or may not encode, depending upon the complexity of the decoding. In unpublished experiments we have shown that this expectation is borne out. If all trigrams in a list can be encoded to form words, and if a single decoding rule holds for all units, the subject does indeed code, and learning is very rapid. If there are two decoding rules for the same number of units as above, most subjects will attempt to learn by coding, but performance is poorer than with one decoding rule. With four different decoding rules very few subjects will use this particular form of coding—that is, they will not transform the trigram to a word for storage purposes.

We have also shown that what may be called "sound coding" will occur. This is to say that the functional stimulus for an association is a sound rather than, say, the three letters in sequence as presented the subject. For example, if a stimulus term in a first-learned paired-associate list is PHO and the response term 7, and if the corresponding pair in a second list is FOE-7, positive transfer occurs in learning the second list. We infer from this that the covert or implicit response to the stimuli in both lists is essentially the same. Again, until we know more about such encoding-decoding processes, we may expect predictions of in-between events to be in error. The habit systems evoked by an encoded or transformed unit must be different from those we would say are evoked if we assume an isomorphic relationship between the unit as presented and the unit of memory. Nevertheless, there appears to be nothing in these problems that prohibits straightforward analysis of the intervening processes. We simply need to know more about the specific habit systems in order to fill in the gap.

SECOND-ORDER HABITS

Even the above brief exposition may make it appear that the experimenter is a hopeless victim of habit systems which the subject brings to the verbal learning situation. If so, we are willing victims, for the acknowledgment of such habits and the realization that they may be studied objectively have greatly expanded the scope of classical verbal learning. This expansion will be further enhanced by what I will call second-order habits. Although the remarks to be made about second-order habits will be quite speculative, I venture to make them on the grounds that they provide the most promising bridge between classical rote learning and the study of more complex linguistic processes.

As I look with my verbal learning eye at certain problems in sentence comprehension or sentence learning, I cannot help but assert that a major role of grammatical habits is that of ordering. Studies that vary the degree of approximation of a sequence of words to formal linguistic ordering are varying the degree to which grammatical ordering habits that the subject brings to the situation are appropriate. The more closely a series of words approaches grammatical ordering, the less the interference from grammatical habits. Or, to put it positively, the more closely a series of words approaches grammatical ordering, the greater the facilitating effect of grammatical habits in reproducing the order of the words. A sentence is a serial learning task, but unlike the usual serial task, second-order habits place restrictions on the positions that can be occupied by the discrete units.

By a second-order habit I mean one that determines the category or class of response at any moment but does not determine the specific instance of the class or category. If I comprehend one of the major problems which tantalizes the psycholinguist, it is with regard to the development of grammatical habits, and these are second-order habits. These habits are conceptual in nature; they supersede any particular instance. The critical problem, it appears to me, is that of specifying the communalities that exist among the instances which in turn leads to the development of the concept. What is there about the wide variety of nouns that leads to the development of the habit of placing them appropriately in a sentence? What is the critical stimulus, or stimulus complex, that allowed Berko's (1958) child subjects to provide the appropriate syntax to a nonsense syllable used in a sentence?

I do not know the answers to these questions. In fact, there are really two independent questions involved. The first is that mentioned earlier—namely, what communalities provide the basis for the concept learning? The second question concerns the nature of the stimulus needed to elicit the second-order habits. We know from simple word-association procedures that a single-word stimulus need not, indeed, usually does not, elicit these second-order habits. The stimulus "dog" may elicit "cat," which is not appropriate, grammatically. However, if we insert one more word, the single letter *a*, before the word *dog*, so that the stimulus is "A dog," we would very likely elicit a verb, indicating the operation of a second-order habit. This particular illustration suggests that function words, which are sharply limited in number, may be involved in the development of some grammatical habits. However this may be, I wish to turn to some rather speculative remarks about second-order habits involved in the verbal learning laboratory.

I will insist that it is reasonable to suppose that a nonsense syllable has a grammar that is just as real as the grammar of a sentence. Let me first indicate that beyond doubt it can be shown that concept utilization occurs in rote learning (Underwood, 1964). If a subject is given a list of 16 words consisting of 4 common animal names, 4 birds, 4 countries, and 4 musical instruments, and is given these in a random order for a single presentation with recall requested immediately, concept memory is essentially perfect although memory for the particular instances is not. Thus, it is clear that the subject has not reacted to these 16 words as independent, unrelated words. His implicit responses must also include category responses. This concept utilization—this second-order habit—immediately precludes his recording at recall any words but animals, birds, countries, and instruments. In the same sense that grammatical habits make certain classes of words appropriate at certain positions in a sentence, the conceptual habits elicited in this situation have restricted the classes of responses appropriate at recall.

Now, let us turn to the nonsense syllable, or, more generally, a three-letter trigram which does not form a word. A difficult consonant syllable, such as RZL, is a three-unit serial list. The problem for the subject is not that of acquiring the separate units (the three letters), but is that of the appropriate ordering of the three units. In effect, he has no grammar to cope with this situation, and the grammar he does have interferes. His natural grammar for a three-letter unit may be assumed to be a CVC order (consonant-vowel-consonant) because this is the order of three-letter units with which he most frequently deals. A count shows that two-thirds of all three-letter words in the 20,000 most frequently used words have the CVC structure. The next most frequent structure is VCC, but only 9 per cent of the three-letter words have this structure.

Generally speaking, CVC trigrams are much easier to learn than CCC trigrams. This would be expected, since the CVC structure corresponds to the natural grammar of words and restricts the particular positions within the three-letter sequences for certain classes of letters. Unfortunately, this situation is badly contaminated by other differences, such as pronunciability, so that no clear case can be made that grammar is the differential characteristic. Yet, differences in pronunciability may reflect the grammar; pronunciability may serve as a serial-placement mechanism because it mirrors the grammar.

The notion that trigram learning is differentially influenced by consonant-vowel grammar must face difficulties from at least two sources. At the most critical level is the fact that I know of no data that unequivocally support it, although I know of no data available that are entirely appropriate for making the test. However, peculiar results keep cropping up which suggest that we may be overlooking something when we pay attention only to specific associations and ignore the possible role of second-order habits. For example, a recent study by Lindley (1963) showed no relationship between pronunciability and learning when all trigrams in the list had the CVC structure. The odd thing about this result is that pronunciability has been shown in many studies to be an extremely acute predictor of learning when the lists of trigrams had mixed consonant-vowel structure (Underwood and Schulz, 1960). Could it be that pronunciability is reflecting only the grammar and becomes irrelevant when all items in the list have the same grammar?

A second major obstacle to accepting the operation of grammar in learning trigrams concerns the means by which the grammar is developed. In spite of the fact that among three-letter words the CVC structure is overwhelmingly more frequent than any other structure, and in spite of the fact that we know the organism is very sensitive to differences in frequencies of environmental events, these alone will not allow one to insist that a second-order habit has developed. Again, we must face the communality problem. Just as it is troublesome to specify the communalities that lead to the development of second-order habits governing placement of words in sentences, so too it is difficult to specify the communalities leading to second-order habits governing the placement of letters. Specifically, what are the common properties of vowels that differ from the common properties of consonants? I do not know. But again, I think we will in the long run find it necessary to include second-order habits in our thinking about the learning of even the simplest of verbal units. These second-order habits, like many simple direct associations, become a part of the covert processes that occur as the subject learns to give the response term when the stimulus term is presented.

SEMANTIC GENERALIZATION

One of the clearest situations in which we attempt to account for observed performance in terms of intervening processes which in themselves have been studied is the situation yielding semantic generalization. This could be the study of generalization *per se,* the study of transfer as a function of similarity, or the study of the role of intralist similarity. But in all cases the performance is "explained" by referring to associative habits evaluated independently. Thus, two words may be said to generalize because by simple word-association procedures they are known to elicit each other or to elicit a common response. Or, conceptual similarity is said to produce a detrimental effect in learning a paired-associate list because again, by separate procedures, it is known that certain of the words elicit a common concept name. Because many of these matters have been discussed previously by others, I will not spend time on them. However, there is one problem I think has been overlooked by those who have drawn up conceptual schemes that are presumed to represent the covert habit sequences in semantic generalization. Two different situations will be examined to demonstrate the puzzle.

Assume an experiment in which paired associates are used and in which conceptual similarity is manipulated. The similarity will hold among all stimulus terms (e.g., all words are animal names) in one case, with the response terms neutral, and with the similarity holding among all response terms in a second case, with the stimulus terms neutral. There will, of course, be two other corresponding lists with low conceptual similarity. Such an experiment (unpublished) will show that conceptual similarity among response terms will retard learning as much as, or more than, will the similarity among the stimulus terms.

The conceptualization of how stimulus similarity produces the negative effect in learning seems quite straightforward by any of several schemes. For example, if some or all of the animal names produce an implicit response "animal," it can only be a nondifferentiating implicit response and associative interference should result in acquiring the specific association. However, when the similarity holds among the response terms the category name must somehow "get ahead" of the specific response if the same mechanism of associative interference as used for stimulus-term similarity is to be maintained. That is, the stimulus term (neutral, in this case) must elicit "animal" prior to the subjects attempt to give the specific animal name. Initially, however, the appearance of the specific animal name was required to produce the category response "animal." The sequence was: neutral stimulus term, specific animal name, and the implicit response of "animal." How, then, do we get the sequence to be: neutral stimulus term, implicit response of "animal," and then the attempt to give the specific animal name paired with this particular stimulus? If this can be accomplished, the explanation of in-between events producing interference becomes quite comparable to that for stimulus similarity.

One possible way of getting the implicit category response appropriately ordered so as to produce the associative interference would be as follows. Assume that on initial trials each response term does elicit the implicit response "animal." As a consequence, this response becomes more frequent than any of the specific response terms and should, therefore, have generalized strength as a response to all stimuli. Therefore, when the stimulus term occurs, the first response is the implicit "animal" response. Again, since this is a nondifferentiating response, associative interference would occur.

Another set of data (also unpublished) does not support this interpretation, and the experiment producing these data constitutes the second situation which demonstrates the extent of the puzzle. The situation is changed only slightly. Rather than having all stimulus terms or all response terms instances of the same category, subgroups of terms are used so that more than one concept is represented. For example, let there be four animal names and four names of birds, again paired with neutral response terms. Interference in learning is again produced (as compared with no conceptual similarity). However, the subject apparently learns rather quickly that a given response term "goes with" one of the words within a concept. This is inferred from the fact that he rarely makes an error that is inappropriate for the concept—e.g., if the response term is paired with an animal name, it will rarely be given to a bird name. The interference occurs in associating the particular response term with a particular stimulus term within the concept.

Now, however, when the same words are response terms (with the stimulus terms neutral), there is no evidence of the limiting effect noted with the stimulus similarity. A given stimulus term elicits response terms for all concepts with equal frequency. It would seem that if the concept name was "moving ahead" of the specific response terms by the frequency principle noted above, it should be elicited by the stimulus terms paired with instances of the concept. If so, the errors should be appropriate to the concept just as in the case of similarity among stimuli. As noted, the errors are essentially random. Of course, it is possible that the assumption is in error—that is, the assumption that the concept name, initially elicited by the response term, gets associated to the stimulus terms appropriate to the concept. We may have, in effect, two free-floating category names, either or both of which may be elicited by any stimulus. In any event, the rather neat systems used to conceptualize covert habit systems involved when stimulus similarity is manipulated cannot be applied easily to the situation in which response similarity produces a negative effect on paired-associate learning.

LEARNING IN THE RAW?

The above illustrations of the manner in which interpretations of verbal learning phenomena seem to depend heavily on rather complex intervening habit systems may make it appear that not much room is left for simple, direct, associative learning. The habit systems that the subject brings to the situation had to be learned. How were they learned? How does "raw," simple associative learning occur in the first place? Actually, the appropriate place to attempt to get answers to such questions is with the very young child. With the usual college-student subject, some approximation may be made through the use of incidental learning procedures. And yet interpretation of these studies also requires some minimum amount of speculation concerning the manner in which the subject implicitly responds to the verbal units. I will illustrate with a particular study (Spear, Ekstrand, and Underwood, 1964).

We attempted to set up a situation for simple associative learning in which the likelihood of intervening habit systems being elicited was at a minimum. Pairs of low-frequency words were presented as a verbal discrimination task. One member of each pair was arbitrarily designated as correct, and the subject's task was to learn the correct member of each pair (being told "right" or "wrong" after each choice). Following this learning the subject was, without being forewarned, given a paired-associate task in which the two words appearing together in verbal discrimination were paired. The question we asked was whether or not an association had developed between the two words merely as a consequence of their contiguous occurrence in the verbal discrimination list.

The results show that upon the first presentation of the paired-associate list the subjects gave a third of the response terms to the correct stimuli. Thus, it did appear that an association had developed between the members of some of the pairs. We could not see how mediation or any other elicited covert habit could account for this. There were two things wrong, however. First, not all items were associated. Second, other investigators (Battig, Williams, and Williams, 1962) had failed to find such associations developing when nonsense syllables were used. An examination of our data showed that the more difficult items in the paired-associate list (as gauged by a control group) were also the ones least likely to become associated in the verbal discrimination procedure. Thus, it appeared that associations did develop with the more meaningful units, but less so or not at all with low-meaningful units. In short, simple contiguity does not inevitably lead to an association. Since we felt some obligation to suggest why this should be true, we found ourselves once more suggesting differences in the nature of the implicit responses made to high-meaningful units as compared with low-meaningful units. More specifically, we speculated that with high-meaningful units the implicit response that occurs is much more stable than the implicit response made to low-meaningful units, and that contiguity is most effective if the same implicit response is made from trial to trial. So, once again we were speculating about intervening events in a situation that seemed initially to preclude the necessity of such speculation.

Language Habits and Forgetting Theory

In all of the above illustrations we have been concerned with the role of language habits in learning. We turn next to the role of the linguistic repertoire in understanding forgetting. Perhaps it is more appropriate to say that in theory we have applied notions about the linguistic repertoire to the refinement of an interference theory of forgetting. As will be seen, this has not been very successful, for reasons that to date we have not been able to discover. Two steps will be taken in the exposition. First, a rather rapid summary of developments will be given which led to the current theory accounting for forgetting produced by interference generated within the laboratory. This need be no more than a summary of the basic notions, since Postman (1961) has recently summarized and cited references for the developments. Second, the extension of the theory to account for interference from pre-established habits will be given, together with such tests as have been made of the extension to date.

Interference theory has long held a firm grip on explanatory accounts of forgetting. The reason for this appears quite simple. For decades, studies of retroactive inhibition had shown that very severe losses in retention could be produced by introducing an interfering task in the laboratory. The variables that could be manipulated within the retroaction paradigm, variables such as similarity and degree of learning, all produced results that refined the notions of the operation of interference and added to the belief that a general interference theory of forgetting is difficult to deny. Then, in more recent years, the powerful role that proactive interference plays was discovered. Thus, by introducing interfering tasks prior to the learning of the task to be recalled, large amounts of forgetting could be produced. Interference theory appeared to be built on exceptionally solid ground, and the more modern work was directed at exposing in more detail some of the precise mechanisms producing the interference. Here are the key developments:

1. Associations, when followed by the learning of contradictory or opposed associations, appear to undergo extinction. Thus, if as one pair in a first list the subject learns *DAX-icy*, and then in the second list is required to learn *DAX-giant*, the association between *DAX* and *icy* appears to be extinguished. Such extinction has been shown to occur for such direct associations, for backward associations, and for associations between the general experimental context and a verbal unit. Indeed, this extinction or unlearning appears to be great enough so that all retroactive inhibition measured in the laboratory immediately after interpolated learning may be due to it.

2. If associations are extinguished, with the passage of time there should be some sort of spontaneous recovery. Inferential

evidence suggests that this does occur with verbal associations, and by analogy with the work in conditioning there was every reason to accept it as a reasonable mechanism. By making an assumption of spontaneous recovery, several sets of facts could be accounted for. We could account for the fact that proactive inhibition increases with the length of the retention interval; if previously extinguished associations recover with time, as time passes the greater should be their interference potential. It would account for the fact that retroactive inhibition may actually decrease with time between interpolated learning and recall. In this case, the extinguished associations are the correct ones at recall, and the longer the time allowed for recovery, the better the recall.

3. The use of the extinction-recovery assumptions, plus an assumption that re-extinction of recovered associations results in more permanent extinction than a single extinction, allowed us to account for the fact that distributed practice will reduce the amount of proactive inhibition. This effect can be enormous if the distribution interval (hence, recovery interval) is long. For example, Keppel (1964) had subjects learn four lists in which the stimulus terms were identical in each list but the response terms different. On the fourth list, for certain subgroups he introduced a 24-hour distribution interval between each two learning trials, while for other groups (massed practice) 4 seconds elapsed between all trials. With the distribution interval of 24 hours, 34 per cent retention was observed after 29 days, while for massed practice forgetting was essentially complete after 8 days.

Generally speaking, then, the use of the extinction-recovery assumptions proved to be extremely satisfactory in accounting for many of the facts found when interference is manipulated between lists in the laboratory, for both retroaction and proaction paradigms. Other developments only tended to make the theory more firmly entrenched. Following the pioneering work of Peterson and Peterson (1959) in retention of single verbal units over very short time intervals, a burst of experiments using their basic techniques appeared. Certain of the analyses made it highly plausible that proactive inhibition was a major factor in this forgetting (Melton, 1963). The laws of proactive inhibition also appeared to hold quite well when Slamecka (e.g., 1961) used sentences as his learning material rather than the traditional paired-associate list. So the facts of proaction and retroaction had generality across materials, and the extinction-recovery theory used to account for variations in interference was, if not right, at least extraordinarily useful in making predictions and in accounting for results already obtained.

I suppose that the meshing of theory and fact so beautifully should have aroused our suspicion. Nevertheless, to say that we entered the next phase with a sanguine attitude is something of a euphemism. But, the next step was absolutely necessary, and the fact that we took it with great confidence as to the outcome only makes this outcome more shattering. Let us examine this required next step.

If a naïve subject is given a *single* list of verbal units (either a paired-associate or serial list), and retention is measured after 24 hours following learning to one perfect recitation, we may expect about 80 per cent of the items to be recalled. To be consistent in the application of interference theory we must assume that the loss is due to interference from linguistic habits. Furthermore, most of the interference would have to be identified with proactive sources. If indeed this forgetting was being produced via proactive inhibition from contrary language habits, then the amount of forgetting of the list should be capable of being "shoved around" by varying the nature of the associations required in the list. So, Professor Postman and I worked out the mechanisms to show not only how linguistic habits could produce forgetting but how differential forgetting must be expected as a function of the nature of the associations learned in the single list in the laboratory (1960).

In this theory we simply extended the mechanisms used to account for proactive inhibition in forgetting when two or more lists are learned in the laboratory. Two sources of interference were identified. One of these sources we spoke of as the unit-sequence hypothesis to refer to the fact that words, as a result of extensive use in common linguistic contexts, will have associative connections. If the laboratory task requires acquisition of habits that are contrary to these pre-established associations, extinction of these "old" associations will occur. Then, with the passage of time, these extinguished associations will recover to produce proactive interference at recall. A differential prediction is that words with high frequency of linguistic usage will be forgotten more rapidly than words with low frequency of usage. This prediction must follow because high-frequency words have more and stronger pre-experimental associations than do low-frequency words.

The theory also had to account for the forgetting of verbal units that are not words. To such materials we applied the letter-sequence hypothesis. When a very difficult trigram is learned, associations between these letters and other letters must be extinguished. That is, if two letters must be associated and if these two letters rarely occur together in words, other letter associations to each must be extinguished in the process of learning. With the passage of time the extinguished associations will recover to produce interference at recall. A prediction of differential forgetting was clear. A list of nonwords in which the associations between letters within a unit have high initial association should be forgotten more slowly than a list with low initial association between letters, since in the former case there are fewer associations that could interfere at recall. The letter-sequence hypothesis specifies a gradient of interference to be expected at recall; roughly speaking, maximum interference would be expected with a difficult consonant syllable, minimum interference with a nonsense syllable of high association value.

The two gradients, one generated by the unit-sequence hypothesis, the other by the letter-sequence hypothesis, were assumed to meet somewhere at about the point where very low-frequency words become nonsense syllables. At this point interference should be at a minimum and, therefore, retention at a maximum. Whatever else one may wish to say about the theory, two aspects are clear. First, it seemed a very accurate translation of the theory developed in the study of the effects of the formal proactive and retroactive paradigms; the mechanisms developed to account for interference in the proactive paradigm were faithfully applied to the operation of the interference expected from habits established outside the laboratory. Second, the theory was quite explicit in its predictions; it said precisely what must happen in retention as word frequency was varied and what must happen as the degree of initial integration of nonword letter sequences was varied.

Initial tests of the theory have now been made. Professor Postman has examined the expectations from the unit-sequence hypothesis, while in our laboratory we have examined the predictions from the letter-sequence hypothesis. Without detailing the results from Postman's studies, I think it is fair to report that only suggestive evidence in support of operation of the unit-sequence gradient is found in his studies (e.g., 1962). In somewhat more detail I will give the procedures and results of our tests of the letter-sequence hypothesis.

Two lists of paired associates were constructed, each list consisting of single-letter stimuli and single-letter response terms. For one list, the initial associative connection between the letters of each pair was essentially zero by our norms, and for the other the initial associative connection was moderate. The theory must predict that the former list—the list with the low initial associative connection—will be forgotten more rapidly than the second list. The reasoning is as follows. Consider a pair, M-K. The K, as a response to M, does not occur in the letter-association norms, and K rarely if ever follows M in words. But other letters *do* have strong associative connections to M, letters such as N or O. Therefore, it was presumed that these associations have to be extinguished during learning and that they will recover with the passage of time and produce interference at recall. The amount of this interference should be greater than for the list with moderate initial associative strength between the letters of the pairs, for in this latter case there are fewer associations to extinguish, hence fewer to recover to cause interference at recall. There were nine pairs in each list, and the differences in initial associative connection between the two lists was supported by the fact that the list with low initial associative connection took significantly longer to learn than the list with moderate initial associative connection.

The degree of learning was also varied at six levels, and retention was taken either after one day or after seven days. At all degrees of learning and for both retention intervals the null hypothesis could not be rejected; the amount of forgetting shown by the two lists was essentially equivalent. Not even a trend was apparent to which we could cling. Subsequently another experiment was performed with a much greater difference in initial associative connection between the letters of the two lists. Enormous differences in rate of learning appeared but absolutely no difference in rate of forgetting. These experiments left us no conclusion other than that something was wrong with the letter-sequence hypothesis, for we believe that our test of the hypothesis was adequate. Predictions of differential interference were simply not supported. If the forgetting that was observed is to be attributed to interference, it appears that we must account for the constancy of the interference across different kinds of material.

This is the rather perplexing situation that exists at the moment with regard to accounting for the role of linguistic habits in forgetting. It does not seem quite possible that these habits are irrelevant to the forgetting we observe, either in the single-list situation in the laboratory or in everyday life. They certainly influence learning. Why, then, do they not influence forgetting in a manner comparable to habits built in at the laboratory. These are the puzzles we face at the moment in generalizing the interference theory of forgetting.

References

Battig, W. F., J. M. Williams and J. G. Williams. "Transfer from verbal-discrimination to paired-associate learning." *J. Exp. Psychol.*, 1962, **63**, 258–268.

Berko, J. "The child's learning of English morphology." *Word*, 1958, **14**, 150–177.

Bugelski, B. R. "Presentation time, total time, and mediation in paired-associate learning." *J. Exp. Psychol.*, 1962, **63**, 409–412.

Keppel, G. "Facilitation in short- and long-term retention of paired associates following distributed practice in learning." *J. Verb. Learn. Verb. Behav.*, 1964, **3**, 91–111.

Lindley, R. H. "Association value, familiarity, and pronunciability ratings as predictors of serial verbal learning." *J. Exp. Psychol.*, 1963, **65**, 347–351.

Melton, A. W. "Implications of short-term memory for a general theory of memory." *J. Verb. Learn. Verb. Behav.*, 1963, **2**, 1–21.

Miller, G. A. "Some psychological studies of grammar." *Amer. Psychologist.* 1962, **17**, 748–762.

Peterson, L. R., and M. J. Peterson. "Short-term retention of individual verbal items." *J. Exp. Psychol.*, 1959, **58**, 193–198.

Postman, L. "The present status of interference theory." In C. N. Cofer (ed.). *Verbal learning and verbal behavior.* New York: McGraw-Hill, 1961.

———. "The effects of language habits on the acquisition and retention of verbal associations." *J. Exp. Psychol.*, 1962, **64**, 7–19.

Slamecka, N. J. "Proactive inhibition of connected discourse." *J. Exp. Psychol.*, 1961, **62**, 295–301.

Spear, N. E., B. R. Ekstrand, and B. J. Underwood. "Association by contiguity." *J. Exp. Psychol.*, 1964, **67**, 151–161.

Underwood, B. J. "The representativeness of rote verbal learning." In A. W. Melton (ed.). *Categories of human learning.* New York: Academic Press, 1964.

———, M. Ham, and B. Ekstrand. "Cue selection in paired-associate learning." *J. Exp. Psychol.*, 1962, **64**, 405–409.

———, and G. Keppel. "Coding processes in verbal learning." *J. Verb. Learn. Verb. Behav.*, 1963, **1**, 250–257.

———, and L. Postman. "Extraexperimental sources of interference in forgetting." *Psychol. Rev.*, 1960, **67**, 73–95.

———, and R. W. Schulz, *Meaningfulness and verbal learning.* Philadelphia: Lippincott, 1960.

THE INFLUENCE OF
GRAMMATICAL AND
ASSOCIATIVE HABITS
ON VERBAL LEARNING[1]

Sheldon Rosenberg

The area of research activity to which I have addressed myself in the studies to be reported here is verbal learning. On the independent variable side, I have been concerned chiefly with the question of the effects of grammatical structure, or, more specifically, with the question of the possible influence of the serial word-order habits that might be aroused by natural language materials.

In a more general linguistic sense, of course, the term grammatical structure would have to include in its definition both syntactic (word order) and morphological (word composition) structures (Hill, 1958). If one were to employ an auditory mode of presentation for natural language materials, however, instead of the usual printed representation, additional factors would have to be considered.

Interestingly enough—although there is every indication that the

[1] Thanks are due the following individuals who contributed in one way or another to the preparation of materials, data collection, and data analysis in the present series of studies: Mrs. Genny Kamback, Miss Mary McGavern, Mr. David Martin, Mr. Walter Porter, and Miss Iris Willoughby. Part of the research included here was also presented at the meetings of the Psychonomic Society, August 1963.

situation is changing rapidly—this is not a problem that has generated much research in the past in the area of verbal learning. Recent developments in the field of psycholinguistics and in linguistics proper are perhaps most responsible for the sudden upsurge of interest. One thing appears to be clear: these developments have raised many issues for verbal learning that cannot be fully resolved through the use of lists of words, syllables, or letter combinations, or through the use of a single-item response term in paired-associate learning.

A major contribution has been made to our understanding of language processes by Chomsky (1957) and the descriptive linguists who preceded him. Miller, Galanter, and Pribram (1960) have leaned heavily upon Chomsky's theory of syntactic structure in their attempt to account for the way in which language is acquired and sentences generated. They have also offered some very strong arguments against the adequacy of left-to-right associative-chain and Markov-process models of language acquisition and sentence production. They were not clear, however, as to what extent these models might be applicable in verbal learning. Miller (1962), in a review of research and theory on the psychology of grammar, has suggested that such factors as (1) reduction of the number of competing alternatives, (2) recoding into memory units larger than the word, (3) the meaningfulness conveyed by constituent structure, and (4) memory for grammatical structure *per se*, may all act to facilitate the learning of sentences. An important implication of Miller's ideas is that the learning of grammatically structured sequences is not simply a matter of rote *reproduction*, but may involve elements of *construction* as well.

Perhaps the most important implication for psychology of Chomsky's approach is in the area of the acquisition of grammar. According to this view, what the child learns when he acquires the language of his culture is a system, a set of basic or kernel sentence patterns—possibly not many more than ten (Roberts, 1962b)—and a set of rules that permit him to transform these basic patterns into a variety of syntactic structures. If this is the case, it would seem reasonable to expect that in the course of language development and experience, these basic sentence patterns (as well as their lower level constituents) and their transformations would be encountered and used over and over again. Syntactically equivalent word classes should begin to form quite early, supported, possibly, by morphological cues and external reference. At the same time, sequential dependencies should be established between adjacent form classes and phrase structures. Ways in which such developmental changes might be accomplished by the young child have been suggested by Braine (1963), Brown and Fraser (1963), and Jenkins in the present volume.

It is in these sequential dependencies between adjacent form classes that I am most interested. Although some psychologists would prefer a term such as "conceptual schema" or "syntactic structure" to label the sequential dependencies that are found in grammatical structures, I have found the term *grammatical habit* to afford more continuity with previous research in the field of verbal learning. It is possible, however, that the sequential dependencies associated with grammatical habits might be more accurately described as cognitive *rules of serial order* rather than as S-R contingencies. In any event, it seems to me that we would at least have to represent them as being conceptually mediated.

It is also necessary to recognize that strengthened during the course of language development and experience are not only grammatical habits but *associative habits* as well. I am referring here to the kinds of verbal habits that have been revealed by cultural norms of free association and found to affect learning and behavior in a variety of situations (e.g., Deese, 1961; Jenkins and Russell, 1952; Russell and Storms, 1955). For present purposes, I have found it useful to distinguish between sequential and nonsequential associative habits. If one examines, for example, the hierarchy of responses to common adjectives that appears in associative norms, one finds words that are in the same grammatical form class as the stimulus word and words that appear in a form class (in this case nouns) that is observed to follow the adjective class with great frequency in our language. The former I have termed nonsequential and the latter sequential. Unless otherwise specified, when the term *associative habit* is used here, it is limited to sequential associates.

To summarize the foregoing, in an adjective-noun form class combination, for example, the grammatical habit shows up in the fact that the noun form class *per se* is highly predictable; however, *particular members* of the noun class will vary in their likelihood of occurrence as a function of associative habit (e.g., as estimated from associative-norm frequency). As an illustration, words in the sequence *dark night* not only represent an instance of a highly familiar series of form classes in our language, but are associatively related as well. With respect to verbal learning, the question that arises is whether any increment of strength is added to the ease of recall of such sequences as a function of grammatical habit *per se*. Certainly, the strength of the grammatical habit, even in the case where the associative relationship is minimal (e.g., *dark coat*), should at least make syntactic errors highly unlikely.

It is in the context of the foregoing ideas that I set out to compare the extent to which grammatical and associative habits might mediate verbal learning at the level of two-word form class combinations. Familiar sentence structures (Roberts, 1962*a*) contain such combinations as adjective-noun, noun-verb, verb-adverb, and verb-noun. Only in adjective-noun combinations, however, were the needed associative norms (Russell and Jenkins, 1954) found to be at least partially adequate, so I have limited myself to these two form classes. To avoid complicating matters, I have also limited myself in these initial studies to the content classes. Ultimately, however, as Glanzer (1962) has demonstrated, we will have to consider grammatical habits that involve function words as well. The choice of linguistic levels was also one of convenience and does not necessarily reflect the view that lower level laws will most likely be found to account for relationships observed at the level of the sentence.

Before attempting to describe these studies, it will be fruitful to look at some of the work of others.

Review of the Literature

The literature on associative processes in verbal learning is very extensive, and some studies of grammatical structure have appeared in recent years, but I have been unsuccessful in my attempts to locate studies in which grammatical and associative habits were compared directly. I will limit my review, therefore, to some of the more interesting studies in which an attempt was made to manipulate grammatical structure or in which grammatically structured materials were used to study other aspects of verbal learning. A more thorough review of theory and a review of current research not discussed here can be found in Miller's (1962) paper on the psychology of grammar.

Lambert and Paivio (1956) explored the relationship between noun-adjective order and learning in a study in which two groups of subjects received seven sets of four words each. Each set consisted of a noun and three appropriate adjectives. In one group, the noun in each set appeared first, followed by the adjectives, and in the other, the adjectives in each set were presented first, followed by the noun. Learning was by serial anticipation. When nouns preceded their appropriate adjectives, serial learning was facilitated. It was hypothesized that this finding might have been the result of an increased tendency for related items to cluster when the noun occurred first. Another possibility, however, is that for the particular words these investigators selected, associative habits were stronger in the noun-adjective direction than in the adjective-noun direction. If this was the case, these results could not be attributed to form class order *per se*. Another factor that complicates matters is that from the standpoint of grammatical habit, the adjective-noun order should at least be as easy to learn as the noun-adjective order. Adjective-noun combinations occur contiguously in connected discourse, whereas in the noun-adjective order, members of the two form classes are separated by at least a verb.

Data from a study by Gonzalez and Cofer (1959), on clustering in free recall of nouns modified by adjectives, indicated no differences in clustering or recall of nouns attributable to form class order. The possibility also exists, therefore, of an interaction between word order and type of learning task.

In other studies reported by Gonzalez and Cofer (1959), various combinations of form classes (e.g., adjective-noun, verb-adverb) were used to study clustering in free recall. The clearest results appeared in the case of adjective-noun combinations, where it was found, among other things, that the likelihood of occurrence of clustering in members of one form class influenced total recall and clustering tendencies in the other. In addition, these investigators reported that inappropriate adjective modifiers paired with nouns reduced clustering and total recall in the noun category. Unfortunately, Gonzalez and Cofer did not, in general, report results for total number of pairs recalled, which, for present purposes, would have been very useful. In a subsequent study, Cofer (1960) has related some of these findings to associative factors.

Newman and Saltz (1960) embedded adjective-noun combinations in simple sentences to determine the relationship between similarity (synonymity) of adjectives and ease of recognition-memory for the nouns. As was anticipated, recognition was found to be poorer when the nouns were paired with similar adjectives. Unfortunately, no attempt was made to test for retention of the adjectives or of the adjective-noun pairs as such.

Taken together, the studies by Gonzalez and Cofer and by Newman and Saltz emphasize the importance of intralist phenomena at levels higher than the isolated word.

Epstein (1961, 1962, 1963) has reported the results of a series of studies in which he attempted to investigate the influence of what he called "syntactical structure" on learning, apart from the effects of meaningfulness, familiarity, or sequential dependency. In actuality, he used both morphological and syntactic cues in structuring his material. In the first of these studies, Epstein (1961) constructed sequences that varied in terms of meaningfulness (nonsense vs. real words), presence or absence of grammatical cues (function words and bound morphemes), and word order (random vs. sequential). Subjects were exposed to each sentence as a whole, and learning was tested by the method of immediate recall. The most interesting finding of this study was that grammatically structured sequences were easier to learn than nongrammatically structured sequences, even when they consisted of nonsense words. This result was confirmed in a subsequent replication (Epstein, 1962). However, in the replication, an experiment was also conducted in which the materials were learned by the serial anticipation method, one word at a time, at a two-second rate. Under these conditions, the differences between structured and unstructured sequences disappeared.

Epstein interpreted this last finding as evidence against the possible contribution of sequential dependencies to the facilitating effect of grammatical structure observed in the initial studies. As Osgood (1963) has suggested, however, sequential habits may have been reduced markedly by the slow rate of memory drum presentation as compared with the normal reading rate for sequences presented as a whole. In addition, differences in the shapes of the serial position curves for the sentence and single-word presentations suggested that subjects may have reacted to the words when presented on the memory drum as being unrelated to each other.

To return to Epstein's original findings, from the standpoint of frequency, the nonsense words would certainly tend to fall at the lower end of the distribution of familiarity, but since nothing was done apparently to control for association value of the nonsense words in grammatical context, and since the presence of morphological and syntactic cues could have permitted subjects to recode the nonsense words into highly familiar form class dependencies, it is difficult to see in what sense these results could be interpreted as being independent of meaningfulness and sequential dependency. With sentences as long as the ones he used, and with the task of the subject being to reproduce each sequence in the original serial order, sequential dependencies (grammatical habits) at the levels of form class or phrase combinations could conceivably have facilitated performance. If this was the case, one would anticipate left-to-right serial learning to be facilitated by grammatical structure. Such a finding was reported by Epstein (1963) himself in a recent study in which structured material was observed to be easier to learn in a forward direction than unstructured material, and unstructured material easier to learn in a backward direction than structured material. However, Epstein speaks here of the operation of "temporal schemata" rather than sequential dependencies.

It is my impression that Epstein's view has been influenced by a conception of sequential dependency that is limited to associative habits. The questions raised here, however, have emphasized the need to consider grammatical habits as well.

The kind of dependency that might exist between items in simple form class sequences has been suggested by Crothers (1962) for the case of adjective-noun combinations. He employed a paired-associate learning task with single nonsense syllables as stimuli and adjective-noun pairs as responses, with results that suggested that the response components were not learned independently of each other. Occurrence of the noun component appeared to be related to the likelihood of occurrence of the adjective component.

Studies of Grammatical and Associative Habit

It seemed reasonable to expect—and indeed the results of a pilot study appeared to suggest this—that the influence of the kinds of variables of interest here, especially in the case where very common words are used, might best be demonstrated in simple, relatively unstructured learning situations. The incidental learning task was found to be well suited for this purpose, and I have used it in Studies I and II and in part of Study III.

STUDY I: INCIDENTAL FREE RECALL OF ADJECTIVE-NOUN FORM CLASS COMBINATIONS

The purpose of Study I was to determine whether a randomly selected list of meaningful adjective-noun word pairs was easier to recall than a list of unrelated adjective-adjective or noun-noun pairs. It was hypothesized that since meaningful adjective-noun pairs not only were likely to be associatively related, but represented very common form class dependencies as well, they would tend to be easier to recall than the unrelated and grammatically less common adjective-adjective and noun-noun pairs.

The materials for this study consisted of four lists of eight pairs of common (Thorndike and Lorge, 1944) monosyllabic words in which no attempt was made to control or manipulate associative relationships within pairs. The first list (AN) was made up of meaningful adjective-noun pairs (e.g., *thin line, deep hole, clean room*); the second list (NA), the same pairs as the first only in reverse order; and the third (AA), a series of unrelated adjective-

adjective pairs (e.g., *wild green, clean hard, rich cold*). List AA contained the eight adjectives used in the first two lists plus eight new ones. Half of the adjectives from lists AN and NA appeared as the first words of AA pairs and half as the second words. The remaining four words in each position were the new adjectives. The fourth list (NN) contained unrelated noun-noun pairs (e.g., *truth coat, bear door, word room*), constructed in the same manner as was list AA, using the nouns of lists AN and NA and eight new ones.

In no instances were initial letters of a given pair of words identical. An attempt was made also to reduce intralist similarity, but there is a limit to the extent to which this is possible when very common words are used. In any event, there appeared to be no reason to believe that any of the lists were differentially weighted with respect to intralist factors.

A simple, group-administered orienting task was developed which insured differential response to the various word pairs without instructions to learn. Booklets were constructed which contained pages measuring $2\frac{1}{4}$ inches high and $4\frac{1}{4}$ inches wide. Just above the middle of each page a single pair of words was printed in lower case pica type. A single blank space separated the two words. Three-eighths of an inch below the pair of words, the following rating scale appeared, printed in pica capitals:

VF   F   MF   SL   O

Subjects were told that VF meant "very frequent"; F, "frequent"; MF, "moderate frequency"; SL, "slight frequency"; and O, "never or almost never." The subjects' task, specifically, was to look at the pair of words and to decide for themselves how frequently in their own experience they would estimate having heard, seen, and spoken the words together. They then indicated their choice by circling one of the scale values designated above. Each booklet contained eight pages, arranged randomly, one pair of words to a page.

Fifty-six undergraduate students were assigned at random to four groups of 14 each, and tested simultaneously in a large classroom. Each page of the booklet was exposed for ten seconds, with a verbal warning delivered after eight seconds. The signal to turn the page was the word "Turn," delivered by the experimenter. Timing was accomplished with the aid of a metronome. At the completion of the eighth page, all booklets were collected rapidly and a sheet of blank, lined paper distributed to each subject. A five-minute free recall test was then administered with the following instructions:

> Now in order to get some additional information on the level of difficulty of these pairs of words, I want to see how many you can remember. On the sheet of paper you have been given, please write down, in any order, as many of the pairs of words in your list as you can remember. Put one pair on each line. Do not hesitate to guess if you are not sure. Try to put each individual pair down in the order in which the two words of the pair appeared. If you remember only one of the words in a pair, put it down in its proper place, with a dash for the missing item.

The interval between the end of the orienting task and the beginning of free recall was two minutes. This interval was occupied with collection of the booklets, distribution of recall sheets and presentation of free recall instructions. Timing was done with a stop watch.

Recall was scored initially for total number of pairs recalled in the correct first-word, second-word order (TP), total number of first words recalled correctly in the first-word position (W1), and total number of second words recalled in the second-word position (W2). Means and standard deviations for these measures have been presented in Table 1. For all measures concerned, it can be seen that Groups AN and NA recalled more items than Groups AA or NN. Analysis of variance revealed an F of 14.74 ($df = 3,52$) for TP; 7.60 ($df = 3,52$) for W1; and 12.95 ($df = 3,52$) for W2. All values of F were significant beyond the .001 level. Tukey's significant Gap Test (Edwards, 1954) was then applied to the individual means arranged in order of magnitude, with p taken as .05. In this analysis, Groups AN and NA were found to form a cluster at the upper end of the range of means, and Groups AA and NN at the lower end on all three measures. In other words, adjective-noun word pairs were easier to recall than adjective-adjective or noun-noun pairs regardless of form class order.

A dependency can be seen to exist between words in AN and NA pairs from the fact that adjectives in both W1 and W2 positions were easier to recall when associated with a noun rather than another adjective, and nouns easier to recall when associated with adjectives rather than other nouns.

Table 1   *Means and Standard Deviations for Measures of Study I*

Group	Pairs		First Words		Second Words	
	MEAN	SD	MEAN	SD	MEAN	SD
AN	5.00	1.66	5.14	1.56	5.64	1.22
NA	4.57	1.74	4.64	1.74	4.71	1.82
AA	1.79	1.53	3.14	1.29	2.64	1.22
NN	2.14	1.46	2.79	1.58	2.86	1.70

Three additional analyses produced results of considerable interest. Protocols were scored for total number of words recalled out of place (WOP)—i.e., a W1 recalled in the W2 position or a W2 recalled in the W1 position. In all groups except AN, subjects recalled words out of place. However, means were low and distributions too skewed to permit use of a parametric test. Instead, a chi square median test was applied to these data. The number of subjects with one or more WOP (the median fell between zero and 1) in Group AN was zero; Group NA, five; Group AA, 12; and Group NN, 11. The resulting value of chi square of 26.86 ($df = 3$) was found to be significant well beyond the .001 level. In the light of this finding, it is possible that differences between groups in this study may have been due to failures to recall the order of words within pairs. If this was the case, a measure of retention that was independent of the order of words within pairs might show no differences between groups. One possible measure considered was: total number of words recalled without regard for order within pairs. The means and standard deviations for this measure for

Groups AN, NA, AA, and NN were, respectively, 10.79 and 2.49, 11.07 and 2.81, 7.64 and 1.95, and 7.64 and 2.65. It is apparent that Groups AN and NA recalled more words than Groups AA and NN. The value of F was found to be 8.12 ($df = 3{,}52$), p less than .001. The Gap Test showed Groups AN and NA to cluster at the high end of the distribution of means and Groups AA and NN at the low end.

In view of this finding, it would seem reasonable to conclude that if grammatical habits are influencing behavior in the present situation, the effect may be upon the kinds of errors subjects make rather than upon recall.

Since ratings of words have been found to predict ease of learning (Underwood and Schulz, 1960), a scale from five to one was assigned to the frequency ratings produced by subjects in the orienting task, with a rating of five for VF and one for 0. The means and standard deviations for Groups AN, NA, AA, and NN, respectively, were, 3.61 and .73, 3.44 and .82, 3.06 and .99, and 2.44 and .86. The value of F for an analysis of variance of these means was found to be 5.19 ($df = 3{,}52$), p less than .01. Upon inspection of Table 1, it will be seen that the order of frequency ratings was almost identical with the order of recall scores.

The possibility that the differences between groups associated with form class combination were not the result of syntactic errors suggested that associative relationships between words may have contributed more to the variance than grammatical habits. Study II was designed to test this hypothesis.

STUDY II: INCIDENTAL RECALL OF ADJECTIVE-NOUN PAIRS AS A FUNCTION OF ASSOCIATIVE STRENGTH

For this study, I selected eight common adjectives—dark, cold, hard, blue, loud, black, heavy, slow—from the list of stimulus words in the Kent-Rosanoff word association test, and for each of them, two common, appropriate nouns from responses in the Minnesota norms (Russell and Jenkins, 1954). One set of nouns contained associates that had appeared among the first three highest ranking responses to the adjectives in question, and the other, nouns that were given only *once* in a sample of 1,008 responses. A third set of appropriate nouns contained words of very low Thorndike-Lorge frequency—items that would most likely never be given as responses to these adjectives in free association. Thus, three lists of AN pairs were constructed, one where the pairs were of high associative strength (HA), one where they were of low associative strength (LA), and one that contained low frequency nouns (LF). These materials, therefore, represented a rough continuum of associative strength. Examples of HA items were *dark night, cold snow;* of LA items, *dark coat, cold school;* and of LF items, *dark chintz, cold knoll.* For comparative purposes, a fourth list was constructed of unrelated NN pairs from the nouns in lists HA and LA. None of the words in any of the pairs began with the same initial letter, and associative relationships within each class of words in a list were reduced as much as possible (i.e., as before, none of the lists appeared to be differentially weighted with respect to intralist factors). With the exception of list LF, the lists were comparable with respect to word frequency.

In all other respects, the procedure, instructions, and orienting task were identical with those used in Study I. Sixty-four undergraduate students served as subjects, and were assigned at random to four groups of 16 each.

The trend of means displayed in Table 2 clearly suggests, for all measures concerned, that the relationship between incidental recall and associative strength of pairs is a positive one. Group NN subjects differed very little in their performance from subjects in

---

Table 2   *Means and Standard Deviations for Measures of Study II*

Group	Pairs		First Words		Second Words	
	MEAN	SD	MEAN	SD	MEAN	SD
HA	6.38	1.09	6.44	1.15	6.44	.96
LA	5.06	1.73	5.63	1.41	5.69	1.49
LF	2.94	1.12	3.88	1.31	3.94	1.57
NN	3.13	1.46	3.75	1.00	3.88	1.50

Group LF. The value of F for TP was found to be 22.86 ($df = 3,60$), p less than .001; for W1, 18.58 ($df = 3,60$), p less than .001; and for W2, 13.35 ($df = 3,60$), p less than .001. By the Gap Test ($p = .05$), Group HA recalled significantly more pairs than Group LA, and Group LA significantly more pairs than Group NN. The difference between the means of Groups LF and NN was not found to be significant. Similar results were discovered for W1 and W2, with the exception that gaps between HA and LA did not turn out to be significant. In this respect, it should be remembered that W1 and W2 include words recalled where the other word in a pair was absent. The effect of associative strength, then, appeared most clearly in the recall of pairs.

The analysis of WOP revealed differences that one would have anticipated. No subjects in Group HA recalled WOP, two did so in Group LA, and none in Group LF. However, 13 subjects in Group NN recalled WOP. The value of chi square for the median test was 47.25 ($df = 3$), p less than .001.

The means and standard deviations for total number of words recalled without regard for order within pairs were 12.88 and 2.09 (HA), 11.81 and 1.94 (LA), 7.81 and 2.71 (LF), and 9.63 and 2.47 (NN). The value of F of 15.19 ($df = 3,60$) for this measure was found to be significant beyond the .001 level of confidence. With the means arranged in order of magnitude, significant gaps were found between LA and NN and between NN and LF. In other words, on this measure, HA and LA did not differ from each other. In general, then, it appeared that associative habits exerted their greatest effects upon incidental recall of word pairs.

At this point, it seemed reasonable to conclude that at the level of linguistic structure employed, associative habits contributed more to recall than grammatical habits. However, since no attempt had been made thus far to control for associative strength between words in AA or NN pairs, the conclusion could only be a tentative one. At the same time, it seemed advisable to raise the question of whether "instructions to learn" would interact in any way with form class combination. Study III was an attempt to deal with these questions.

STUDY III: INTENTIONAL AND INCIDENTAL RECALL OF
ADJECTIVE-NOUN FORM CLASS COMBINATIONS OF LOW
ASSOCIATIVE STRENGTH

Three lists of 12 pairs each were put together, an AN, an AA, and an NN series. In each list, the first words were stimuli selected from the Kent-Rosanoff test, and the second words, responses to these same stimuli that appeared only *once* in the Minnesota norms. The first words in the AN and AA lists were identical. All lists were comparable with respect to Thorndike-Lorge frequency. Common, familiar words were used throughout. To emphasize the grammatical relationships, response words were selected without reference to appropriateness. However, with the present population of materials, it was impossible to construct pairs where words were not related in some way. Initial letters were different for the words in each pair. Examples of AN pairs were *dark noise, black wagon,* and *smooth water;* of AA pairs, *dark lonely, black good,* and *smooth narrow;* and of NN pairs, *river grass, table book,* and *fruit child.*

Seventy-eight subjects were assigned at random to six groups of 13 each, three of which learned under incidental instructions, and three under intentional instructions. In all other respects, the method was essentially the same as the one used in Studies I and II. Subjects in intentional learning groups were instructed to try to learn as many of the pairs as possible, without regard for order in the list. Two different orders of the pairs were used in each list. All subjects performed the orienting task.

The results summarized in Table 3 indicate that in almost all instances, recall scores of intentional learners exceeded those of incidental learners. Performance of the AN group surpassed that of Groups AA and NN under both intentional and incidental conditions. For TP, the value of F for instructions (9.03, $df = 1,72$) and form class combination (13.21, $df = 2,72$) were both highly significant (p's less than .01). The value of F for interaction (.86), however, did not even approach significance. In view of this finding, intentional and incidental groups were combined to determine the trend of differences between means for form class combination. The groups ordered themselves, from highest to lowest, in the following manner: AN, NN, AA. However, a significant gap was not found between AN and NN, nor between NN and AA. It would appear, then, that the highly significant F for TP was the result of the large difference between Groups AN and AA.

The superiority of AN over AA pairs is difficult to understand. Perhaps it was the result of some peculiarity in the particular words selected (this, of course, would be limited to the second words, since the first words were identical in both lists), inadequacies in

Table 3 *Means and Standard Deviations for Intentional and Incidental Learners in Study III*

Group	Pairs		First Words		Second Words	
	MEAN	SD	MEAN	SD	MEAN	SD
AN						
Intentional	7.62	2.29	8.00	1.87	8.38	1.56
Incidental	6.08	2.50	7.08	1.55	7.31	1.93
AA						
Intentional	4.92	2.43	5.38	2.14	5.62	2.02
Incidental	2.62	1.71	4.15	1.52	3.92	2.10
NN						
Intentional	6.31	2.01	6.54	1.76	6.38	1.98
Incidental	5.62	2.29	6.62	1.98	5.85	2.11

the measure of associative strength, or some characteristic of free associative responses to common adjectives. The group of adjectives used as the first words in both lists were chosen, in general, from among those that usually elicit opposites as their most frequent response. Of course, one might be tempted to attribute these results to the operation of grammatical habit, but if this was the case, the difference between the AN and NN groups should have also been significant.

As far as the variable of form class combination was concerned, the main effects for W1 ($F = 15.55$, $df = 2,72$, p less than .001) and W2 ($F = 16.11$, $df = 2,72$, p less than .001) were identical with those reported for TP. The interactions with task instructions for W1 and W2 were nonsignificant, and the trend of differences between means arranged in numerical order were identical with what was reported for TP. The variable of task instructions, however, produced significant differences in favor of intentional learners only for W2 ($F = 6.17$, $df = 1,72$, p less than .025). The value of F for W1 was 2.83 ($df = 1,72$, p greater than .05).

Under conditions of intentional learning, the number of subjects who recalled WOP in Groups AN, AA, and NN was, respectively, zero, 10, and 7 (chi square = 16.80, $df = 2$, p less than .01). The corresponding cell frequencies under incidental conditions were virtually identical (chi square = 15.60, $df = 2$, p less than .01). The control of associative strength within pairs, then, appeared to have no effect upon the tendency to recall WOP. What we have here is additional evidence for the effects of grammatical habit upon syntactic errors.

The means and standard deviations for total number of words recalled without regard for order within pairs have been summarized in Table 4. Intentional recall was found to be superior to

Group	Intentional		Incidental	
	MEAN	SD	MEAN	SD
AN	16.31	3.35	14.77	2.95
AA	13.23	4.34	10.85	2.80
NN	15.08	2.87	14.08	3.38

Table 4   *Means and Standard Deviations for Words Recalled Without Regard for Order in Study III*

incidental recall ($F = 4.76$, $df = 1,72$, p less than .05), and the results for form class combination were similar to those reported for TP ($F = 7.70$, $df = 2,72$, p less than .01). The interaction between instructions and form class combination was not significant.

The results of the Gap Test applied to Groups AN, NN, and AA were identical with those reported for TP, W1, and W2.

In view of these last two findings, the difference between Groups AN and AA in the recall of pairs could not be easily attributed to the fact that no syntactic errors were made by subjects in the AN group. It is also important to note that within the limitations of this study, form class combination did not interact with task instructions.

STUDY IV: FREE RECALL OF WORDS OF LOW THORNDIKE-LORGE
FREQUENCY AS A FUNCTION OF FORM CLASS COMBINATION

As a final test of the possible influence of grammatical habits, an attempt was made to construct lists where the words in pairs were unfamiliar and unlikely to be associatively related to each other. For this purpose, a number of two-syllable adjectives and nouns of very low Thorndike-Lorge frequency (in the range from 1 to 9 in the general count) were selected and paired at random to produce an AN, AA, and NN list, with eight pairs per list. The first words in the AA list were identical with those used in list AN, and the second words of the NN series identical with the nouns of the AN set. Initial letters of words in all pairs were different. Examples of pairs in each list were:

AN—murky cohort, direful skewer, adroit hailstone
AA—murky regal, direful guileless, adroit obtuse
NN—tourney cohort, granule skewer, naphtha hailstone

Each pair of words was printed in lower case pica type on a different page of a booklet measuring $3\frac{1}{2}$ inches high and $4\frac{1}{4}$ inches wide. Two different orders of pairs in a list were constructed to reduce serial effects. Each booklet contained the eight pairs for that particular form class combination.

Because of the greater difficulty usually encountered in learning uncommon verbal materials, it was deemed advisable to employ an intentional learning task and to expose materials for a series of four trials. Subjects were instructed that their task was to try to learn as many of the pairs as possible in any order. With the aid of a metronome, each pair of words was exposed for four seconds. Fifteen seconds after exposure of a given list, a two-minute free recall task was administered. The intertrial interval was 30 seconds. Each subject's scores were the mean number of pairs, first words, and second words recalled over four trials. Syntactic errors were computed in a similar manner. Sixteen subjects served under each condition in a group testing situation.

Table 5 presents the summary statistics for this study, which show, in general, smaller differences between groups than had appeared in most of the previous studies. For all measures concerned, the NN group showed the highest mean recall, AN next, and AA last. The only value of F to reach significance at the

Table 5 *Means and Standard Deviations for Measures of Study IV*

Group	Pairs		First Words		Second Words	
	MEAN	SD	MEAN	SD	MEAN	SD
AN	3.86	1.20	4.59	1.13	4.94	1.07
AA	3.45	1.47	4.41	1.45	4.08	1.40
NN	4.53	1.33	5.11	1.26	5.16	.92

.05 level, however, was for W2 ($F = 3.94$, $df = 2{,}45$). The finding with respect to W2 is difficult to interpret, and represents perhaps a chance occurrence or an artifact of the words in question. In any event, there was no evidence to suggest any facilitation of recall associated with AN pairs. The results for WOP, however, were more striking. The number of subjects in Groups AN, AA, and NN with WOP were, respectively, 3, 13, and 9. The value of chi square for this analysis was found to be 12.60 ($df = 2$), and the value of p less than .01.

It appears, then, that when word frequency and associative strength are minimized, there are still fewer sequential errors made in recalling AN pairs. The results for total number of words recalled without regard for order were identical with those reported for TP.

Discussion

The most interesting finding to come out of the present series of studies was that the greater ease of recall of common, meaningful AN pairs was, in large measure, a function of associative habit. To be sure, grammatical habit contributed to the kinds of errors subjects made, but it was not this effect apparently, which produced the differences observed in the recall of form class pairs.

Perhaps the first question that should be raised concerning these results is whether they will generalize to other two-word form class combinations. Unfortunately, adequate associative norms are not available for common form class combinations other than those used in the present study. In order to extend the research reported here to the case where a noun is modified by more than one adjective, adjective responses to nouns selected from the Kent-Rosanoff test have been obtained under conditions of controlled association (Rosenberg and Carter, unpublished).

A question of possibly greater importance is whether the effects of grammatical and associative habits will interact with the level of linguistic structure (e.g., phrase, sentence) of the materials to be learned. It is possible, for example, that since the strings to be learned are usually longer at the level of the sentence than they are in the case of two-word form class combinations, grammatical habit might be found to contribute significantly to recall when the measure of learning is total number of complete sentences. I am involved at present in research in which an attempt is being made to compare the influence of grammatical and associative habits at the level of the sentence. In one kind of design, form class combinations similar to those used in the present series of studies are being placed in various positions in sentence structures, and in another, an attempt is being made to manipulate associative habits involving *all* of the words in a given sentence structure.

With respect to the latter approach, the results of an initial study (unpublished) suggest strongly that both associative and grammatical habits contribute significantly to the ease of learning simple sentences. Grammatical habit was manipulated by varying the order of words within sentences, and an attempt was made to manipulate associative relationships between words through the use of free association norms (Russell and Jenkins, 1954). High-associative-frequency sentences such as *Strong lions roar fiercely*, were constructed by selecting noun stimuli that had elicited, with appreciable frequency, two adjectives and a verb. A plural "s" was added to each noun and the adverb ending *ly* to one of the adjectives. Similarly, sentences of low associative frequency (e.g., *Pretty lions creep tenderly*) were constructed using the same nouns plus adjectives and verbs that had occurred very infrequently in the norms.

One of the limitations of this procedure, it should be pointed out, was that it permitted the construction of only a small number of sentences. What are needed here obviously are associative norms at the level of sentence structures. Approaches are being explored in our laboratory at present that might make it possible to generate such norms in the context of simple sentence structures of the sort outlined by Roberts (1962*a*).

A problem that cuts across all of the research reviewed thus far is the question of the possible role of form class *per se* in verbal learning. Unfortunately, if little is known about the ways in which grammatical habits influence verbal learning, even less is known about possible differences in the ease of learning words as a function of form class membership. In the first of two paired-associate learning studies, Glanzer (1962) found that content words (nouns, adjectives, verbs, adverbs) were easier to learn than function words (pronouns, prepositions, conjunctions). Glanzer hypothesized that this finding might have been due to the fact that function words possess some of the characteristics of bound forms and, as such, do not operate in isolation as content words frequently do.

To test this notion, content and function words were embedded in contexts of nonsense syllables in a paired-associate learning task where the response term consisted of a nonsense syllable-word nonsense syllable triplet. Under these circumstances, function words as a class were easier to learn than content words as a class.

While Glanzer did not report comparisons of individual means for the various form classes, it is possible to describe the learning-ease hierarchy from an inspection of his graphs. Of particular interest here are the differences between the various content classes. In the first paired-associate study, the hierarchy (from easiest to most difficult) for the English-nonsense condition was noun, adjective, adverb, verb; and for the nonsense-English condition, noun, adjective, verb, adverb. In the paired-associate triplet study, the hierarchy was adverb, noun, adjective, verb. Some of the differences between the various content classes were very slight while others appeared to be appreciable. In any event, the hierarchy appeared to vary as a function of conditions of learning and context.

What appeared to be needed at this point was a study in which content form class and meaningful grammatical context were manipulated. Miss Norma Jean Baker and I (Rosenberg and Baker, 1964) have recently reported on the results of such a study. The procedure for manipulating context was in terms of the level of linguistic structure at which the verbal materials were presented to be learned. Linguistic analysis (e.g., Gleason 1961) has revealed language structure to be hierarchically organized, and within this hierarchy, the sentence, phrase, and morpheme levels have been viewed as being fundamental to an understanding of grammatical structure. The word, which is usually found to be more useful psychologically (Osgood, 1963) than the morpheme, might be seen to operate at a level between the morpheme and the phrase (Francis, 1958).

College students were exposed to a series of words containing adjectives, nouns, verbs, and adverbs, which were equated for word frequency (Thorndike and Lorge, 1944). One group was shown the words in the form of a list of adjective-noun-verb-adverb sentences; a second group saw them as a list of noun and verb phrases; and a third group saw them as a list of isolated words.

The findings of particular interest were as follows. (1) The main effects of content form class and linguistic level were both significant, as was their interaction. (2) At the sentence and phrase levels, adjectives and nouns were easier to learn than verbs and adverbs, but the pattern changed at the level of the isolated word. (3) There was no difference between adjectives and nouns nor between verbs and adverbs at the sentence and phrase levels.

(4) The learning-ease hierarchy at the level of isolated words was noun, adverb, adjective, verb. Recall of nouns was significantly greater than recall of any of the other form classes. Verbs and adverbs were no more difficult to learn than adjectives, but adverbs were recalled significantly more frequently than verbs. (5) With the exception of a partial reversal of trend for adverbs, recall increased from the level of the word to the level of the sentence. The differences associated with linguistic level were significant for adjectives, verbs, and adverbs, but not for nouns.

The findings at the sentence and phrase levels were interpreted (in the light of other research in the literature) to indicate possible recoding into units larger than the isolated word, and the possibility of the existence of stronger associative relationships between the adjectives and the nouns than between the verbs and the adverbs.

The pattern of differences that emerged at the level of isolated words was not altogether consistent with what one would have predicted from research on the grammatical structure of free associates to the various content form classes (Deese, 1962) and from research on the effect of intralist associative relationships in free recall (Deese, 1961). One of the factors that might have contributed to our results, we suggested, was the use of a heterogeneous list of words with respect to form class. It will be necessary to repeat this aspect of the study using a different group of subjects for each of the form classes.

While the many differences between the conditions of Glanzer's (1962) study and the present one make direct comparisons very difficult, it can be shown that the learning-ease hierarchy that Miss Baker and I noted at the phrase and sentence levels is similar to the hierarchy observed by Glanzer when his form classes were presented in isolation. The differential effects that context had in our study were due, perhaps, to the use of natural language context rather than nonsense context.

Clearly, a good deal of additional research is needed, in order to be able to specify the reasons for the relationships between grammatical form class and verbal learning that have been observed thus far.

References

Braine, M. D. S. "On learning the grammatical order of words." *Psychol. Rev.*, 1963, **70**, 323–348.

Brown, R., and C. Fraser. "The acquisition of syntax." In C. N. Cofer, and Barbara S. Musgrave, (eds.). *Verbal behavior and learning.* New York: McGraw-Hill, 1963.

Chomsky, N. *Syntactic structures.* The Hague: Mouton, 1957.

Cofer, C. N. "An experimental analysis of the role of context in verbal behavior." *Trans. N. Y. Acad. Sci.*, 1960, Ser. II, **22**, 341–347.

Crothers, E. J. "Paired-associate learning with compound responses." *J. Verbal Learn. Verbal Behav.*, 1962, **1**, 66–70.

Deese, J. "From the isolated verbal unit to connected discourse." In C. N. Cofer, and Barbara S. Musgrave, (eds.). *Verbal learning and verbal behavior.* New York: McGraw-Hill, 1961.

———. "Form class and the determinants of association." *J. Verbal Learn. Verbal Behav.*, 1962, **1**, 79–84.

Edwards, A. L. *Statistical methods for the behavioral sciences.* New York: Rinehart, 1954.

Epstein, W. "The influence of syntactical structure on learning." *Amer. J. Psychol.*, 1961, **74**, 80–85.

———. "A further study of the influence of syntactical structure on learning." *Amer. J. Psychol.*, 1962, **75**, 121–126.

———. "Temporal schemata in syntactically structured material." *J. Gen. Psychol.*, 1963, **68**, 157–164.

Francis, W. N. *The Structure of American English.* New York: Ronald, 1958.

Glanzer, M. "Grammatical category: A rote learning and word association analysis." *J. Verbal Learn. Verbal Behav.*, 1962, **1**, 31–41.

Gleason, H. A. *An introduction to descriptive linguistics,* rev. ed. New York: Holt, Rinehart and Winston, 1961.

Gonzalez, R. C., and C. N. Cofer, "Exploratory studies of verbal context by means of clustering in free recall." *J. Genet. Psychol.*, 1959, **95**, 293–320.

Hill, A. A. *Introduction to linguistic structures.* New York: Harcourt, 1958.

Jenkins, J. J., and W. A. Russell. "Associative clustering during recall." *J. Abnorm. Soc. Psychol.*, 1952, **47**, 818–821.

Lambert, W. E., and A. Paivio. "The influence of noun-adjective order on learning." *Canad. J. Psychol.*, 1956, **10**, 9–12.

Miller, G. A. "Some psychological studies of grammar." *Amer. Psychologist*, 1962, 17, 748–762.

———, E. Galanter, and K. H. Pribram. *Plans and the structure of behavior.* New York: Henry Holt, 1960.

Newman, S. E., and E. Saltz. "Effects of contextual cues on learning from connected discourse." *Amer. J. Psychol.,* 1960, **73**, 587–592.

Osgood, C. E. "Psycholinguistics." In S. Koch. (ed.). *Psychology: a study of a science,* Vol. 6. New York: McGraw-Hill, 1963.

Roberts, P. *English sentences.* New York: Harcourt, 1962*a*.

———. *Teacher's manual for English sentences.* New York: Harcourt, 1962*b*.

Rosenberg, S., and Norma J. Baker. "Grammatical form class as a variable in verbal learning at three levels of linguistic structure." Paper presented at meeting of Southeastern Psychological Association, Gatlinburg, Tenn.: April 1964.

Russell, W. A., and J. J. Jenkins. "The complete Minnesota norms for responses to 100 words from the Kent-Rosanoff word association test." Tech. Rep. No. 11, Contract N8-ONR-66216, Office of Naval Research and Univ. Minnesota, 1954.

———, and L. Storms. "Implicit verbal chaining in paired-associate learning." *J. Exp. Psychol.,* 1955, **49**, 267–293.

Thorndike, E. L., and I. Lorge. *The teacher's word book of 30,000 words.* New York: Teachers Coll., Columbia Univ., 1944.

Underwood, B. J., and R. W. Schulz. *Meaningfulness and verbal learning.* Philadelphia: Lippincott, 1960.

IV

THE MODIFICATION OF VERBAL BEHAVIOR

THEORETICAL AND EPISTEMOLOGICAL ISSUES IN VERBAL CONDITIONING[1]

Charles D. Spielberger

Psychologists have been concerned with whether or not learning can occur without awareness, at least since Thorndike's (1932, 1934) early work related to this problem. During the past decade, however, interest in "unconscious" learning has increased markedly. This renewed interest in an old problem has been stimulated largely by claims that the findings of recent investigations of verbal operant conditioning (verbal conditioning) provide evidence of learning without awareness. In this article, I propose to examine this evidence along with some of the theoretical and epistemological assumptions that have guided research on verbal conditioning.

In verbal conditioning experiments, subjects are typically required only to emit verbal responses (e.g., to say words). Those responses belonging to a selected response class are followed by a reinforcing stimulus, such as the experimenter's saying "Good" or "Mmm-hmm." If the rate of emission of the reinforced response class increases as a function of reinforcement, this is interpreted as

[1] The experimental work reported in this paper was supported in part by grants from the National Institutes of Mental Health (MH 7446) and Child Health and Human Development (HD 947), United States Public Health Service.

evidence that conditioning has taken place. The findings of verbal conditioning experiments have clearly established that the frequency of emission of a variety of verbal responses can be altered by simple manipulations of the physical environment of a speaker (see reviews by Greenspoon, 1962; Krasner, 1958; Salzinger, 1959).

What relevance has verbal conditioning for students of psycholinguistics? One obvious answer is that verbal conditioning is concerned with the "learning" (modification) of language behavior. Another resides in the implications of verbal conditioning phenomena for learning theory since, as Osgood has noted, "Learning theory and learning phenomena contribute most heavily to the 'psych' in psycholinguistics" (1963, p. 249). Moreover, psycholinguists of a Whorfian orientation may be particularly interested in the competing language systems that psychologists of differing theoretical persuasion have used to describe their verbal conditioning findings. In descriptions of verbal conditioning experiments, it is apparent that "observers are not led by the same physical evidence to the same picture of the universe unless their linguistic backgrounds are similar or can in some way be calibrated" (Whorf, 1961, p. 465). Thus, in divergent theoretical accounts of verbal conditioning phenomena, support may be adduced for Whorf's linguistic relativity hypothesis.

INTERPRETATIONS OF AWARENESS IN VERBAL CONDITIONING

Claims that verbal conditioning experiments provide evidence of learning without awareness (e.g., Cohen, Kalish, Thurston, and Cohen, 1954; Greenspoon, 1955; Taffel, 1955), and of the automatic and unconscious effects of reinforcement (Dollard and Miller, 1950), are based on observations that subjects who do not report awareness of a correct response-reinforcement contingency, nevertheless, show significant conditioning effects. Within the past several years, however, these claims have been challenged on methodological grounds. It has been pointed out, for example, that in early verbal conditioning studies: (a) the interviewing procedures used in the assessment of awareness were superficial and insensitive (Eriksen, 1960; Krieckhaus and Eriksen, 1960; Levin, 1961; Spielberger, 1962); (b) the subjects' awareness of partially correct or correlated hypotheses was not adequately evaluated (Adams, 1957; Dulany, 1961; Tatz, 1960); and (c) the subjects' motivation to receive reinforcement was not taken into account (DeNike and Spielberger, 1963; Dulany, 1963; Spielberger, Levin, and Shepard, 1962). Furthermore, evidence accumulated in recent experiments incorporating needed methodological refinements has indicated that performance gains in verbal conditioning are limited essentially to subjects who report awareness of correct or partially correct response-reinforcement contingencies.

Interpretations of observed relationships between reports of awareness and performance gains in verbal conditioning have differed according to the particular learning theory to which an investigator subscribes. Those who favor stimulus-response theories[2] tend to regard subjects' verbalizations of awareness as merely complex, noncausal correlates of performance. Accordingly, they argue that the relationships obtained between performance and awareness in verbal conditioning experiments may be explained in terms of (a) the subject's *a posteriori* rationalization of his performance; (b) the suggestion of hypothesis by the cues of the interview to subjects whose rate of emission of the reinforced response class increased; or (c) the simultaneous conditioning of awareness along with the conditioning of the reinforced response class. Postman and Sassenrath (1961) have suggested the further possibility that initial increments in performance in learning experiments may result from the automatic effects of reinforcement but that performance gains subsequent to the verbalization of awareness are augmented by awareness. They state, "Since verbalization often occurs after a period of systematic improvement, *verbalization of a principle may be considered at the same time the result of past improvement and a condition of further improvement.*" It should

---

[2] Reference in the present context to stimulus-response and cognitive learning theories reflects Hilgard's (1956) usage of these terms to refer to the two major "families of theories." The major issues on which stimulus-response and cognitive learning theories differ are in their emphases upon peripheral versus central intermediaries, on the acquisition of "habits" versus the acquisition of "cognitive structures," and on the importance of problem solving and insight versus trial and error learning (Hilgard, 1956, pp. 8–11).

be noted, however, that although Postman and Sassenrath cite findings of verbal conditioning investigations as relevant to their interpretation, their conclusions are based primarily upon Thorndikian experiments in which gradual increments in performance typically precede the point of verbalization.

When verbal conditioning effects are interpreted within the framework of cognitive learning theories, verbalizations of awareness tend to be regarded as operational indices of cognitive states. According to such views, subjects in verbal conditioning experiments who show conditioning effects do so because they develop correct or partially correct hypotheses concerning the contingency of the reinforcing stimulus upon their verbal responses. Cognitive interpretations of verbal conditioning assume that subjects who discover correct or correlated response-reinforcement contingencies modify their responses in accordance with their hypotheses in order to elicit the reinforcing stimulus, provided, of course, that they wish to receive it.

I have previously suggested (Spielberger, 1962) that, given the empirical evidence currently available, verbal conditioning phenomena can be *described* more or less adequately in terms of either stimulus-response or cognitive theories and that the heuristic value of these alternative theoretical explanations will be determined ultimately by their differential success in predicting empirical relationships not previously observed. In the meantime, the existence of vigorous, competing theories might be viewed as highly desirable. In general, theory stimulates and guides research, competing theories lead to more sensitive experiments, and good experiments contribute to the accumulation of a composite set of facts that facilitate the convergence of theoretical schools and the establishment of an organized body of scientific knowledge (Campbell, 1963).

In debating the implications of verbal conditioning research with colleagues over the past several years, however, it has become increasingly apparent that the collection of new data alone will not serve optimally to advance our theoretical understanding of verbal conditioning phenomena. Until important differences in the epistemological assumptions generally associated with the particular stimulus-response and cognitive theoretical orientations that have guided verbal conditioning research are recognized, these epistemological differences will continue to be reflected in the operations by which awareness is defined in verbal conditioning experiments and will, thereby, lead to the collection of noncomparable data about which fruitless theoretical controversy is generated.

In this article, I will examine the influence of some of the implicit epistemological assumptions associated with stimulus-response and cognitive theoretical orientations as these affect the design and interpretation of verbal conditioning research. Toward this end, the methods and findings of several representative verbal conditioning experiments carried out within the general frameworks of stimulus-response and cognitive learning theories will be examined in some detail. Before proceeding to these experiments, however, the principle verbal conditioning techniques will be described, present-day interest in verbal conditioning will be documented, and the particular stimulus-response and cognitive theoretical frameworks that have guided research in this area will be briefly reviewed.

PRINCIPAL VERBAL CONDITIONING PROCEDURES

Subjects in verbal conditioning experiments typically are given minimal instructions; they are not asked to learn, nor are they generally even told that learning is involved in the study. The experimenter operates on a selected class of the subjects' verbal behavior by carefully manipulating verbal and/or nonverbal environmental cues that are assumed to have reinforcing properties. A nonreinforced period of responding prior to the onset of reinforcement usually serves to establish the subjects' operant rate for the selected response class. Also, in most verbal conditioning experiments, the conditioning performance of subjects who receive systematic reinforcement is compared with that of a nonreinforced control group. If, in response to reinforcement, the rate of emission of a selected response class is increased significantly over the operant rate of responding, and if subjects who receive systematic reinforcement give significantly more responses of the selectively reinforced response class than do nonreinforced controls, then it is concluded that the subject's verbal behavior has been conditioned.

Verbal conditioning effects have been obtained with reinforced response classes ranging from "references to mother" to the autokinetic effect. Reinforcing stimuli that have proved effective in producing conditioning effects include lights, buzzers, bell tones, and verbal statements such as "Good," "Right," and "Mmm-hmm." Although a variety of response classes have been conditioned through the use of a number of different reinforcing stimuli, most verbal conditioning experiments have employed variants of conditioning procedures first introduced by Greenspoon (1951, 1955) and Taffel (1955).

The Greenspoon Word-Naming Procedure. This procedure requires the subject "to say all the words you can think of" and to continue saying words until he is told to stop. Subjects are instructed not to count and to avoid sentences or phrases. Each time a subject says a word belonging to the selected response class, the experimenter reinforces the word. "Plural nouns" and "humans" have been the response classes most popularly employed in investigations utilizing the Greenspoon procedure. In principle, any response class that can be classified as a verbal operant may be reinforced in any experimental situation that permits the objective identification of the response class and the precise determination of its rate of occurrence. Experimental settings in which variants of the word-naming procedure have been employed include the reinforcement of selected response classes in informal conversation, in interviews, and in the context of storytelling tasks.

The Taffel Sentence Construction Procedure. In this procedure, subjects are typically presented with a series of 3 × 5-inch, white index cards. At the top or bottom of the card, the six personal pronouns *I, you, he, she, we,* and *they* are typed. The order in which the pronouns occur is usually varied from card to card. In the middle of each card there is a past tense verb. The subject's task is to make up a sentence beginning with one of the pronouns and utilizing the verb. Whenever a subject initiates a sentence with a specific pronoun (e.g., "you") or class of pronouns (e.g., the first-person pronouns, "I" and "we") that has been selected for reinforcement, the experimenter says "Good" or administers some other reinforcing stimulus. A simple variant of this task is to provide the subject with a single pronoun and a choice of verbs, varying in meaning. For example, the subject may be given a choice of neutral and hostile verbs and reinforced if he chooses the hostile verb. Such variations of the sentence-construction task have been employed in investigations of the influence of personality variables on verbal conditioning.

In verbal conditioning experiments employing either the Greenspoon or Taffel procedures, the subjects' awareness of response-reinforcement contingencies has generally been determined on the basis of oral replies to interview questions or written responses to questionnaires. It is usually assumed that a subject is aware in verbal conditioning experiments if he is able to verbalize the "correct" relationship between his own verbal responses and the reinforcement—i.e., the principle on the basis of which the experimenter administers reinforcement. In some studies, the definition of awareness has been broadened to include specification by the subject of any response-reinforcement contingency that, if acted upon, would yield reinforcement on essentially every trial or for every verbal response. In a few studies, awareness of partially correct or correlated hypotheses is also assessed.

The interview for determining awareness in verbal conditioning experiments is generally not conducted until after the conclusion of the conditioning period. The evaluation of awareness, in many studies, is further complicated by the interpolation of an extinction period between the conditioning trials and the awareness interview. In several recent investigations of verbal conditioning, awareness has been evaluated through inquiring of subjects at predetermined intervals during the conditioning period about the basis of their responding. It should be noted, however, that in a sizable proportion of verbal conditioning studies the question of awareness is not even raised.

CURRENT INTEREST IN VERBAL CONDITIONING

Investigations of verbal behavior that have employed operant conditioning procedures have been reported with increasing frequency over the past decade. A bibliography of verbal conditioning studies compiled by Kanfer[3] lists a total of 284 references, including 217 articles published in psychological journals. The number of articles on verbal conditioning published during each two-year period subsequent to 1947, as determined from Kanfer's bibliography, is indicated in Figure 1. Inasmuch as verbal conditioning procedures tend to reflect Skinner's approach to verbal behavior, the period 1947–1948 was selected as the origin for Figure 1, since it is indicated in the preface to *Verbal Behavior* (Skinner, 1957) that preliminary formulations of the book were first circulated in 1947.

The marked interest in verbal conditioning reflected in Figure 1 is undoubtedly related to the objectivity of verbal conditioning procedures and the ease with which these can be adapted for the investigation of a variety of psychological problems. Verbal conditioning has proved to be particularly appealing to clinical psychologists because of implications for psychotherapy (Krasner, 1962) implicit in the claims that complex verbal behavior can be automatically modified through the systematic presentation of external physical stimuli and that changes in verbal behavior can be predicted from these physical events without recourse to the internal processes of the speaker. The wide acceptance of such claims was evident in a recent survey made by the writer and his colleagues of verbal conditioning studies published during the past three years. We found that subjects' awareness was not even evaluated in over 40 per cent of the studies examined. The bases for this obvious lack of concern with the possibility that cognitive processes mediate verbal conditioning effects will become more

[3] Personal communication, March 1963. Only five of the articles cited in Kanfer's bibliography (see progress report on USPHS Grant MH 06921–01) were published prior to 1949, and these, strictly speaking, do not employ the verbal conditioning paradigm. Kanfer's bibliography also listed 67 unpublished references, of which 16 were doctoral dissertations.

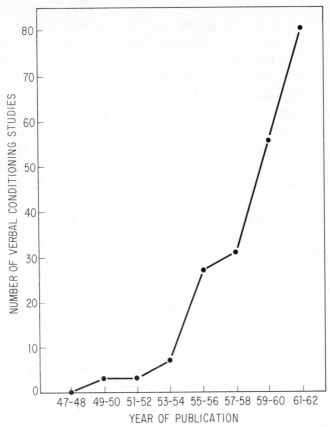

Figure 1 *Articles relating to verbal conditioning published between 1947 and 1962.* Based on unpublished data from F. H. Kanfer.

evident after examing the theoretical framework that has guided most of the research.

Theoretical Heritage of Verbal Conditioning

SKINNER'S DESCRIPTIVE BEHAVIORISM

Most investigations of verbal conditioning, including nearly all of the early studies of this phenomenon have been carried out within the conceptual framework provided by Skinner's (1957) descriptive behaviorism. Simply put, this approach to verbal behavior has as its goal the functional analysis of relationships between observable physical and environmental events and a speaker's verbal responses. Private stimuli to which a speaker alone is able to respond—i.e., his thoughts and ideas—are not given systematic scientific status as variables controlling verbal behavior because they cannot be objectively observed and described. In rejecting "ideas" and related concepts, such as "meaning" and "information," Skinner has repeatedly claimed that precise predictions of verbal behavior need only the specification of relevant external factors.

Although a detailed analysis of descriptive behaviorism is beyond the scope of this article, a comprehensive review of Skinner's *Verbal Behavior* (1957) by the noted linguist Noam Chomsky is available and should be consulted by psychologists and linguists seriously interested in verbal conditioning phenomena. In commenting on the claims and goals of descriptive behaviorism, Chomsky (1959, p. 27) notes:

What is so surprising is the particular limitations he (Skinner) has imposed on the way in which the observables of behavior are to be studied, and, above all, the particularly simple nature of the "function" which, he claims, describes the causation of behavior. One would naturally expect that prediction of the behavior of a complex organism (or machine) would require, in addition to information about external stimulation, knowledge of the internal structure of the organism, the ways in which it processes input information and organizes its own behavior. These characteristics of the organism are in general a complicated product of inborn structure, the genetically determined course of maturation, and past experience. Insofar as independent neurophysiological evidence is not available, it is obvious that inferences concerning the structure of the organism are based on observation of behavior and outside events. Nevertheless, one's estimate of the relative importance of external factors and internal structure in the determination of behavior will have an important effect on the direction of research on linguistic (or any other) behavior, and on the kinds of analogies from animal studies that will be considered relevant or suggestive.

The pertinence and cogency of Chomsky's analysis of descriptive behaviorism is readily apparent in verbal conditioning research.

Lack of interest in internal processes is strikingly evident in the proportion of verbal conditioning experiments in which the awareness issue is simply ignored and in the operations by which awareness is evaluated in most of the remaining studies. Furthermore, verbal conditioning procedures are highly analogous to experimental operations that have proved very successful in the modification of animal behavior. The degree to which analogies from the animal laboratory have been accepted by those who have investigated verbal behavior with operant conditioning techniques is revealed in the introduction to a recent review of the verbal conditioning literature in which it is stated that ". . . it should be possible to work with verbal behavior in much the same way that experimenters have worked with the behavior of rats, pigeons, etc. It should also be possible to investigate the same kinds of variables that have been investigated with the nonverbal behavior of humans and infra-humans" (Greenspoon, 1962, p. 511). Given these convictions, it logically follows that subjects' hypotheses about the experiments in which they participate are likely to be considered beyond the limits of scientific inquiry as would be those of rats and pigeons. Thus, the implicit assumption by descriptive behaviorists that mediating cognitive processes have no scientific utility implies an epistemology that has important methodological consequences, particularly with respect to the operations by which awareness is evaluated (defined) in verbal conditioning experiments.

The most direct and obvious manifestation in verbal conditioning of the epistemological assumption that subjects' awareness has no scientific value would be simply not to inquire about subjects' hypotheses. As we have already noted, this has actually been the case in a substantial proportion of published experiments on verbal conditioning. In verbal conditioning experiments in which subjects' awareness is investigated, a clear manifestation of the implicit epistemological assumptions associated with descriptive behaviorism is revealed in the interviewing procedures employed for assessing awareness. The use of brief and superficial interviews to evaluate the hypotheses of subjects who have been given minimal instructions for an ambiguous experimental task might be expected on a priori grounds to increase the probability that some subjects with correct and/or correlated hypotheses would go undetected. This would appear to be especially likely when awareness interviews were not conducted until after the conclusion of a lengthy extinction period. Moreover, we have observed that even a few instances of accidental nonreinforcement during conditioning may suffice to disconfirm subjects' hypotheses in verbal conditioning experiments (Spielberger and DeNike, 1963).

A more subtle methodological influence in verbal conditioning experiments of the epistemological assumptions associated with descriptive behaviorism is the insistence that verbalizations of awareness are nothing more than complex verbal responses which, moreover, must be treated only as dependent (noncausal) variables. As Krasner has put it,[4] "How can you *really* know whether a subject was aware at a given time . . . rather than being concerned with such insoluble problems, awareness is approached as a dependent variable in the verbal conditioning situation that in *itself* can be either influenced *directly* by reinforcement or *indirectly* as a function of . . . variables which also influence conditioning." Kanfer and his colleagues (e.g., Kanfer and McBrearty, 1961; Kanfer and Marston, 1961, 1962) have also treated subjects' verbal reports exclusively as dependent variables, noting, however, that such reports may be affected by different antecedent conditions from those which influence the acquisition rate of a reinforced response class.

The exclusive interpretation of reports of awareness as dependent response measures in verbal conditioning implies rejection, on epistemological grounds, of the possibility that verbal reports can be valid indices of cognitive states that mediate subjects' performance on conditioning tasks. Since the theoretical interpretation that awareness mediates performance is not considered "legitimate," verbal conditioning data typically are not examined as a function of awareness as the empirical independent variable, and data for subjects who verbalize a correct response-reinforcement contin-

---

[4] L. Krasner. "Verbal conditioning and awareness." Unpublished paper presented in a symposium, Interpersonal Variables and Verbal Conditioning, at the annual meeting of the American Psychological Association, St. Louis, 1962.

gency are often simply disregarded. If the relationship between awareness and conditioning is examined at all, it is generally reported in terms of a correlation between two responses. Thus, an investigator's rejection of mediating cognitive processes on epistemological grounds is concretely reflected in the manner in which he analyzes the data obtained in verbal conditioning experiments.

In sum, the epistemological assumptions implicitly associated with descriptive behaviorism lead to the rejection of awareness as a concept and/or the rejection of indices of awareness as empirical independent variables in analyses of verbal conditioning data. Ignoring subjects' reports of awareness or treating them exclusively as dependent response measures precludes comparison of the conditioning performance of aware and unaware subjects. When such comparisons have been made in verbal conditioning experiments in which sensitive procedures for assessing awareness are employed, the conditioning curves of aware and unaware subjects are found to be markedly dissimilar, and there is little evidence of learning without awareness.

APPROACHES TO VERBAL CONDITIONING GUIDED BY
COGNITIVE LEARNING THEORY

The verbal conditioning paradigm represents a literal exportation of operant conditioning procedures from the Skinner box of the animal laboratory to the domain of verbal behavior. It is perhaps not too surprising, therefore, that a relatively small proportion of verbal conditioning experiments has been guided by cognitive learning theories. Indeed, most investigators who have become concerned with the role of cognitive factors in verbal conditioning at first accepted the considerable evidence of learning without awareness reported with remarkable consistency in early studies,[5] and adapted verbal conditioning procedures for the investigation

[5] Such evidence was reported in 29 of the 31 verbal conditioning studies reviewed by Krasner (1958). Krasner also noted, however, that the role of awareness needed clarification and that ". . . perhaps the measures used to test 'awareness,' the open-ended questionnaires, are inadequate or not sensitive enough to pick up awareness when it really does exist, or even different degrees of 'awareness' " (1958, p. 164).

of other problems. For example, I was introduced to verbal conditioning by a colleague who wished to investigate the influence of individual differences in a personality variable (hostility) on the learning of a personality-related verbal response class (hostile verbs). In carrying out pilot work for this study in which conditioning without awareness was expected, it was found instead that when conditioning effects were obtained, these were generally accompanied by verbalizations of awareness. Consequently, we became interested in factors that influenced awareness, and in the relationship between verbal reports of awareness and performance on verbal conditioning tasks (e.g., Levin, 1961; Spielberger, Levin, and Shepard, 1962; Spielberger, 1962). Our observations and findings have essentially paralleled those of Dulany, who described his early experiences with verbal conditioning as follows:

> A few years ago, my associates and I set about to obtain a stable finding of verbal conditioning without awareness so that we could investigate its parameters. We have yet to find it. Using all the common tasks, we compared experimentals with controls, questioning carefully after acquisition, and setting report of a correct or correlated hypothesis as the criterion of awareness. . . . But, in every study, subjects who reported a correct or possibly correlated hypothesis made themselves conspicuous with dramatic 'conditioning' curves. It was, of course, the subjects' reports that had become the lure, reports that we had no mandate to believe, but which could not sensibly be dismissed when so clearly related to other behavior (1962, p. 103).

Most investigations of verbal conditioning that have been guided by cognitive frames of reference have attempted to clarify the mediating role of conscious processes. The epistemological and theoretical assumptions associated with cognitive approaches to verbal conditioning have usually included the following: (a) cognitive processes such as thoughts, ideas, and hypotheses exist; (b) although cognitive processes are not directly observable, they may be inferred, albeit imperfectly, from subjects' verbal responses to interview questions (within the descriptive behaviorist frame of reference, subjects' verbal reports may be viewed as operational definitions of cognitive processes); (c) cognitive processes are lawfully related to antecedent conditions (e.g., the manipulation of instructions) as well as to consequent changes in verbal behavior. The specification of the precise nature of such relationships, however, requires that motivational factors be taken into account; (d) cognitive processes mediate performance gains in verbal conditioning by permitting the selection of those responses that lead to reinforcement, provided that a subject wishes to receive the particular reinforcing stimulus utilized in the experiment. It should be noted, in accordance with the last two assumptions, that subjects' awareness of correct or correlated response-reinforcement contingencies is not considered sufficient to produce performance gains. Aware subjects must also be motivated to receive the reinforcement, or, to put it differently, the reinforcing stimulus must have *incentive* value for a subject in order for it to induce him to increase his output of a reinforced response class.

A major difference[6] between cognitive and stimulus-response approaches to verbal conditioning may be observed in the implicit definition of the "learned response" in verbal conditioning experiments. The investigator whose research is guided by the conceptual framework of descriptive behaviorism concludes that learning has taken place from observed change in the rate of emission of the reinforced verbal response class. Learning is thus defined in terms of observed gains in subjects' performance on the conditioning task, and no distinction is made between learning and performance. In contrast, learning is inferred in cognitive interpretations of verbal conditioning from subjects' verbalized hypotheses. "What is learned" by the subject is the hypothesis that the reinforcing stimulus is contingent upon his giving certain verbal responses (Spielberger and Levin, 1962). A "correct" or a "correlated" hypothesis is learned by the subject, depending upon whether the response class he calls correct is the same or correlated with the response

---

[6] This difference, which stems in part from the epistemological assumptions associated with stimulus-response and cognitive theories, bears out Campbell's (1954) contention that different learning theories imply different operational definitions of the learned response. Strictly speaking, however, stimulus-response interpretations of verbal conditioning that introduce the concept of learning depart from Skinner's descriptive behaviorism. Skinner (1950) has argued that learning theories are not necessary; the term "learning" is not even indexed in *Verbal Behavior* (Skinner, 1957).

class the experimenter calls correct (Dulany, 1961, pp. 259–260). Whether or not a subject acts on his hypothesis, however, depends on his motivation to receive the reinforcement. Thus, cognitive interpretations of verbal conditioning view the subject's performance as a complex product of his hypotheses and his motives.

An obvious potential disadvantage encountered in cognitive interpretations of verbal conditioning is the questionable validity of verbal reports as indices of cognitive states (and motivational states as well). For precisely this reason, psychologists have traditionally avoided questioning subjects and relying upon their reports as indices of conscious experience. At best, reports of private events have only imperfect, probabilistic validity (Eriksen, 1960), and this depends upon many factors—e.g., the nature of the event reported on, the subject's willingness and ability to report accurately, the methods employed for obtaining the report. However, it seems no more logically justifiable to reject reports of private events *on epistemological grounds* than it would be to insist that such reports correspond perfectly to the reporting subjects' conscious mental processes. The logic of science (positivism) on the basis of which descriptive behaviorists reject mediating states as beyond the limits of scientific inquiry prescribes that theoretical constructs must be (a) defined in terms of objectively specifiable operations that yield data on which there is reliable interobserver agreement and (b) useful in that they enter into empirical laws that relate them to other operationally defined constructs. In verbal conditioning, it has been demonstrated that awareness, defined in terms of verbal reports obtained in response to specific interview questions, meets the criterion of operational specificity, and that more empirical variance can be accounted for in verbal conditioning experiments when subjects' verbal reports, elicited with sensitive interviewing procedures, are taken into account than when these are ignored.

Dulany (1962) has advanced a sophisticated theoretical analysis of verbal conditioning in which subjects' verbal reports are employed as indices of cognitive concepts, and the validity of these reports takes the status of a testable hypothesis. In essence, Dulany sets forth a set of interconnecting theoretical propositions that specify hypothetical relationships between cognitive concepts, their antecedents, and subjects' verbal behavior. The theoretical constructs in Dulany's network include *reinforcement hypothesis, behavioral hypothesis, behavioral intention, verbal habits, subjective incentive value of reinforcement,* and *drive*. To the extent that hypothesized relationships between verbal reports and other terms in the network are confirmed empirically, then, like any other hypothesis, the validity of the verbal report is inductively supported. We shall make use of Dulany's constructs and the logic of theoretical networks as we examine epistemological factors that have influenced the verbal conditioning experiments reviewed in the next section.

Theory and Method in Verbal Conditioning Experiments

In each of the experiments described below, the verbal conditioning task was a variant of the word-naming technique. These experiments, admittedly, were selected for presentation in the present context in order to demonstrate methodological implications of epistemological assumptions implicitly associated with the stimulus-response and cognitive theoretical orientations that have guided verbal conditioning research. However, since the studies are presented in the chronological order in which they were published, the clarifications provided by the cumulative research findings also tend to reflect our emerging understanding of verbal conditioning phenomena.

GREENSPOON'S PIONEERING EXPERIMENT

Greenspoon (1955) investigated the effect of the introduction and omission of two reinforcing stimuli, "Mmm-hmm" and "Huh-uh," on the acquisition and extinction of two verbal response classes, "plural nouns" and "any word not a plural noun." His subjects were instructed to say words individually and not to give sentences, phrases, or numbers. There were four experimental groups, representing each of the four possible combinations of reinforcing stimulus and response classes. There was also a single nonreinforced control group. For the experimental groups, the experimenter introduced the contingent stimulus immediately following the first response belonging to the response class selected for reinforcement, and subsequently all responses belonging to this selected class were reinforced for a period of 25 minutes. Then, there followed a 25-minute extinction period during which the reinforcing stimulus was omitted. The control group received no reinforcement at any time during the experiment.

Any subject in Greenspoon's experiment who noticed the relationship between the reinforcing stimulus and the response that it followed was eliminated from the study. For the remaining subjects, Greenspoon reported that "Mmm-hmm" had a consistent effect upon both response classes and that this effect was greater for plural nouns than for nonplural words. Therefore, *only* the effects of "Mmm-hmm" on plural nouns will be considered here. Furthermore, since we hold that an understanding of acquisition in verbal conditioning must precede any meaningful explanation of extinction, our concern in this and subsequent experiments will be limited to the acquisition trials.

The percent plural noun responses given by Greenspoon's reinforced (R) and nonreinforced (NR) groups is indicated in Figure 2, in which the 25-minute reinforcement period has been broken down into five 5-minute time periods. These results were described by Dollard and Miller[7] in their influential book, *Personality and Psychotherapy* (1950, p. 43), as follows:

Greenspoon found that during the "training" period the experimental group, to whom he said "Mmm-hmm" after each plural noun, greatly increased the percentage of plural nouns spoken, while the control group, to whom nothing was said after plural nouns, showed no such increase. Furthermore this happened with subjects who on subsequent

[7] The findings described by Dollard and Miller in 1950 were reported by Greenspoon in his doctoral dissertation (1951), but were not generally available until the article based on his dissertation was published in 1955. The immediate and relatively uncritical acceptance of verbal conditioning findings as evidence of learning without awareness by Dollard and Miller, and apparently by the editors of psychological journals (see Figure 1), provides an interesting commentary on the *Zeitgeist* that prevailed in psychology a decade ago, which continues to influence the design and interpretation of verbal conditioning experiments.

questioning showed that they had no idea what the purpose of the "Mmm-hmm" was and were completely unaware of the fact that they were increasing their percentage of plural nouns. This clearly demonstrates that the effects of a reinforcement can be entirely unconscious and automatic. . . . A great deal of human learning seems to be of this direct, unconscious kind. Apparently, many attitudes, prejudices, emotions, motor skills, and mannerisms are acquired in this way.

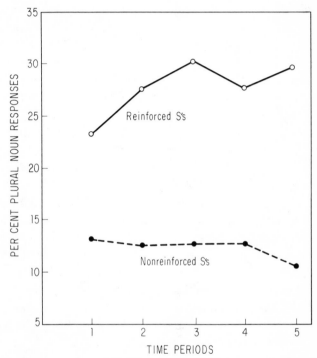

Figure 2 *Percentage of plural nouns given by reinforced and nonreinforced subjects during a 25-minute time period.* Adapted from Greenspoon (1955).

With respect to the common interpretation that Greenspoon's findings provide evidence of learning without awareness, two questions may be raised concerning possible shortcomings in his experimental procedures. Were there differences between Greenspoon's

R and NR groups in operant rate for plural nouns—i.e., readiness
to give plural noun responses prior to the introduction of the reinforcing stimulus? Were Greenspoon's interviewing procedures
adequate for evaluating subjects' awareness of correct and/or correlated hypotheses? Although both questions appear to be primarily
methodological in import, the latter is inextricably tied to the theoretical and epistemological assumptions concerning awareness as a
construct that determined the operations Greenspoon employed for
evaluating awareness. We shall consider each of these questions in
turn.

In summarizing his findings, Greenspoon (1955, p. 416) states,
"The results indicated that Mmm-hmm increased the frequency of
plural responses." The conditioning data he reported, however, revealed that the mean number of plural nouns emitted by his
R and NR groups actually declined. Furthermore, the differences
between groups over time periods were relatively constant. For
the five successive 5-minute time periods these differences were
10.03, 10.87, 11.43, 8.54, and 12.46 plural nouns, respectively (computed from Greenspoon, 1955, Table II, p. 412). Although Greenspoon's R group consistently gave more plural nouns than his NR
group, the reinforcing stimulus appeared to have little influence
after the initial time period. If Greenspoon's groups differed in
readiness to give plural nouns prior to the introduction of the reinforcing stimulus—i.e., if his R group had initially a higher operant
rate for plural nouns—then his "conditioning effect" could be attributed to uncontrolled differences between groups in operant rate
which persisted over time periods, rather than to the effects of
the reinforcing stimulus.

What evidence is there that Greenspoon's R and NR groups
were initially comparable or matched with respect to operant rate?
Greenspoon employed the ordinal position of each subject's first
plural noun response as his index of subjects' readiness to give
plural responses. Since his R and NR groups did not differ in
mean ordinal position, he concluded that they were selected from
the same population with respect to operant rate for plural responses. Ordinal position of first plural response, however, has been
found to correlate only —.34 with number of plurals given in a

nonreinforced period of responding (Spielberger and DeNike, 1962). The magnitude of this relationship suggests (a) that ordinal position of first plural response is not a very precise indicator of readiness to give such responses and (b) that groups matched for ordinal position may still differ in operant rate. A statistically significant "groups by time periods" interaction would have supported Greenspoon's contention that the reinforcing stimulus produced the observed differences between his R and NR groups, even if these groups were not initially matched for operant rate. In his generalized analysis of variance, however, Greenspoon reported only a significant main effect of groups. This finding could be attributed as readily to uncontrolled differences in operant rate which persisted over time periods as to the effects of the reinforcing stimulus.

Although a greater readiness to give plural responses in Greenspoon's R group than in his NR group may have contributed to the differences he obtained, this would not seem to account entirely for his findings. Inspection of the conditioning curves in Figure 2 reveals that the reinforced and nonreinforced groups tend to diverge over time periods. Furthermore, while the reinforced group did *not* give significantly more plurals than the nonreinforced group during the initial 5-minute time period, it did so in each succeeding time period. We have previously noted, however, that Greenspoon employed only four general questions to assess awareness in his postconditioning interview and that this interview was not conducted until after the conclusion of a lengthy extinction period. It has been demonstrated that a greater proportion of the subjects in verbal conditioning experiments are found to be aware when a detailed interview is conducted immediately after conditioning trials (e.g., Levin, 1961; Spielberger, 1962). Therefore, it was possible that awareness of correct and/or correlated response-reinforcement contingencies went undetected for at least a few of the subjects in Greenspoon's R group and that the performance of such subjects, guided by their hypotheses, may have determined the tendency for the R and NR groups to diverge over time periods. Evidence bearing on these possibilities will be considered in the experiments described later.

AWARENESS AND THE REINFORCED RESPONSE CLASS IN
VERBAL CONDITIONING

Since Greenspoon's pioneering study, the successful utilization of operant conditioning procedures to modify the rate of emission of a variety of verbal responses has been demonstrated with remarkable consistency. More specifically, with respect to the conditioning of plural nouns, positive results were obtained in all seven of the studies employing this response class included by Krasner (1958) in his review of the verbal conditioning literature. The first *published* verbal conditioning study in which the rate of emission of plural nouns was *not* influenced by verbal reinforcement was reported by Matarazzo, Saslow, and Pareis (1960). Although these investigators employed essentially the same conditioning procedures as Greenspoon (except that "Good" was the reinforcing stimulus rather than "Mmm-hmm"), they were unable to increase subjects' output of plural nouns in four separate experimental attempts. These findings are particularly notable because of the care with which the experiments were carried out, the concern of the investigators with subtle methodological factors, and their generally sympathetic attitude toward the implicit theoretical assumptions of descriptive behaviorism.

In commenting on their negative results relative to the preponderance of positive findings in the literature, Matarazzo *et al.* (1960, p. 192) noted that "colleagues from other parts of the country have reported in informal conversations similar lacks of success in conditioning plural nouns. Such experiences plus our own negative results would suggest that either the type of verbal reinforcement used or some other presumably identifiable variable is responsible for the different results." In a similar vein, Dulany (1962, p. 103) has observed that, with respect to verbal conditioning, "a turn through thesis microfilms and a little hearsay scholarship will show an appreciable second literature, distinguished in the main by better control, negative results and lack of publication."

Although Matarazzo *et al.* failed to replicate Greenspoon's findings with plural nouns, they succeeded in two additional studies in conditioning the response class, *humans*—i.e., "any word which clearly and unambiguously designated a person." Moreover, the very same experimenters who were unable to increase subjects' rate of emission of plurals, successfully induced subjects from the same population to give more *humans* responses. What differences between *plurals* and *humans* led to the failure to condition the former response class and the successful conditioning of the latter?

The most plausible answer to this question is provided in the data presented by Matarazzo *et al.* concerning the awareness of their subjects of the purpose of the experiment. They evaluated "level of awareness" by means of responses to a *written* questionnaire that each subject filled out after the conclusion of an extinction period. This questionnaire consisted of a single page on which there were two open-ended questions. At the top of the page was the statement, "The purpose of the experiment was:"; in the middle of the page was the statement, "My evidence for this is:." Each subject's written responses to these questions were rated on a four-point scale for degree of conscious awareness by two judges, who had no contact with the subjects nor any information about their performance on the conditioning task. The judges' ratings of levels of awareness were found to be highly reliable in both the *plurals* and the *humans* studies.

In the two studies in which humans were reinforced, the subjects were rated as expressing a significantly higher level of awareness of the response-reinforcement contingency than that indicated by the subjects in the studies in which plurals were reinforced. Furthermore, Matarazzo *et al.* (1960, p. 201) noted, "In many cases, the written responses clearly indicated S's awareness of the contingency between E's behavior and changes in his own verbal responses." On the basis of extensive analyses of the relationships between performance on the conditioning task and reports of awareness, Matarazzo *et al.* (1960, p. 202) concluded that:

. . . both the analysis by groups and the analysis by individuals demonstrate that, in the studies here reported, verbal conditioning or its absence was quite clearly associated with S's degree of reported conscious awareness. It is possible, therefore, that one of the reasons for our failure to condition Plural Nouns, while other investigators have succeeded, lies in the differences in awareness levels of our Ss relative to the Ss (and other experimental conditions) employed in these other studies.

The findings of Matarazzo *et al.* clearly demonstrated an empirical relationship between performance on a verbal conditioning task and awareness as defined by responses to a postconditioning written questionnaire. These findings, however, are still subject to interpretation within the alternative theoretical frameworks of descriptive behaviorism and cognitive learning theory. Although Matarazzo *et al.* repeatedly point up the association between awareness and the presence or absence of verbal conditioning effects, and even go so far as to suggest that verbal conditioning may be viewed as a form of concept formation, at other times it would appear that they favor interpreting their findings within the theoretical framework of descriptive behaviorism with its associated epistemological assumptions. This orientation is reflected in their conclusion that awareness is a *concomitant* of performance gains on the conditioning task—e.g., they state, "it can be concluded, especially in the two Humans studies, that conscious awareness, as here defined, was a concomitant of verbal conditioning" (1960, p. 201; see also p. 206). Although this statement may be regarded as simply descriptive of the obtained relationship, the conclusion that awareness is a concomitant of performance gains in verbal conditioning would also seem to imply that *reports of awareness* should be treated as merely complex verbal responses, with the same functional properties as the reinforced response class.

An alternative interpretation of reports of awareness in verbal conditioning experiments would be to regard these as indices of mediating cognitive states. Accordingly, it would be inferred that subjects in the Matarazzo *et al.* experiment who recorded the "correct" response-reinforcement contingency were aware of this contingency during the conditioning period. Guided by their hypotheses, aware subjects may select appropriate responses from their repertoire of verbal behavior and verbalize such responses if they want the experimenter to say "Good." Thus, whereas descriptive behaviorism rejects the possibility that subjects' hypotheses may determine other behaviors, a cognitive approach to verbal conditioning permits, indeed demands, that this possibility be examined. Consistent with a cognitive approach to verbal conditioning, reports of awareness in the experiments reported below were regarded as indices of mediating states, and conditioning data were analyzed as a function of such indices as empirical independent variables.

VERBAL CONDITIONING EXPERIMENTS GUIDED BY COGNITIVE LEARNING THEORY

These studies were carried out in the Duke University and Vanderbilt University psychology laboratories over the past three years.[8] Successive experiments were designed generally to clarify the role of awareness in verbal conditioning and to evaluate specific questions raised in the preceding studies. Awareness was conceptualized as a mediating cognitive state and was assessed through experimental operations appropriate to this conception[9] which yielded indices characterized by a high degree of objectivity and interobserver reliability. Except for the indices of awareness, the experimental procedures utilized in these studies were similar in essential details to the word-naming task developed by Greenspoon (1955) and described earlier.

[8] The assistance of Arthur Berger, Ira H. Bernstein, R. W. Holmstrom, Kay Howard, Kenneth D. Kroupa, and Richard G. Ratliff in the collection and analysis of these data is gratefully acknowledged. I am particularly indebted to L. Douglas DeNike for his collaboration in this research.

[9] The concept of awareness employed herein was considered analogous in its definitional properties to the concept of perception proposed by Garner, Hake, and Eriksen (1956). Accordingly, it is assumed that the *scientific meaning* of awareness resides in all of the operations that converge on the concept and in the network of theoretical and empirical relationships that relate it to other concepts (Dulany, 1962). But, given the multiplicity of operations that have been utilized to provide behavioral definitions (indices) of awareness (Adams, 1957), and the vagueness of the theories in which awareness is conceptualized as a variable, it seems imperative that the *pretheoretical* (common-sense or vernacular) meaning of awareness also be provided in order that one's choice of defining (converging) operations may be better understood. In this sense, awareness refers to the thoughts, ideas, and hypotheses of our subjects as they participated in these experiments.

Experiment I: A Failure to Replicate the Greenspoon Effect.
It may be recalled that in Greenspoon's experiment the awareness
interview was not conducted until the conclusion of a 25-minute
extinction period, and that whether or not his R and NR groups
were initially matched for operant rate was questionable. Therefore, in our first study (Spielberger and DeNike, 1962), we attempted to replicate Greenspoon's findings under conditions in
which reinforced (R) and nonreinforced (NR) groups were carefully matched for operant rate, and the awareness interview was
conducted immediately after the conditioning trials. However, our
procedures differed from Greenspoon's in that (a) a 3-minute practice period, in which none of the subjects received reinforcement,
was utilized to determine operant rate for plurals; (b) the acquisition period was of 15 minutes duration; (c) no extinction trials
were employed; and (d) each subject was interviewed immediately
following acquisition trials according to a detailed schedule[10] by a
second exprimenter, who had no knowledge of the subject's performance on the conditioning task. Otherwise, the procedures were
essentially the same as those employed with Greenspoon's (1955)
Group I in which plural nouns were reinforced with "Mmm-hmm."
The subjects were 32 male undergraduate students enrolled in the
introductory psychology course at Duke University.

In the postconditioning interview, all of the 22 subjects in the
R group reported that they noticed the "Mmm-hmm," but none
were able to verbalize the correct response-reinforcement contingency. However, the data for two subjects who reported correlated contingencies were excluded from the analysis of the
relationship between awareness and conditioning, since the hypotheses of these subjects may have guided them in selecting
plurals. The mean number of plural nouns given by the remaining
subjects of the R group, during the operant period and the five
postoperant time periods, is compared in Figure 3 with the mean

---

[10] The interview schedule has been deposited as Document No. 7405 with
the American Documentation Institute Auxiliary Publications Project, Photoduplication Service, Library of Congress, Washington 25, D. C. A copy may
be secured by citing the document number and by remitting $1.25 for photo-
prints or 35 mm. microfilm. (Advance payment required; checks payable to:
Chief, Photoduplication Service, Library of Congress.)

number of plurals given by the subjects in the NR group. Statistical analyses of these data confirmed the impression gained from an inspection of Figure 3 that the R and NR groups did not differ significantly[11] either in the aggregate output of plural nouns or in the rate of emission of plurals over successive reinforced time periods.

In order to compare the results obtained in this study with Greenspoon's findings, and to determine if initial differences in operant rate tend to persist over time periods, the conditioning

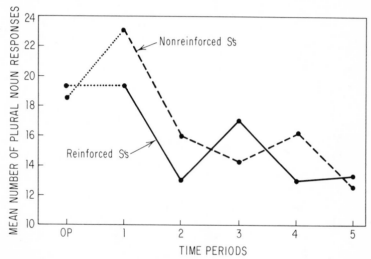

Figure 3 *Number of plural nouns given by reinforced and nonreinforced subjects during an operant period and in 5 post-operant time periods.* From Spielberger and DeNike, *Psychological Reports,* **11**, 1962, p. 359. Reproduced by permission.

data were subjected to further analysis. First, the median operant rate for the total sample was determined to be 10 plural nouns. Next, subjects in the R and NR groups were divided into high-operant and low-operant subgroups, according to whether or not a given subject's operant rate was above or below the median for the total sample. Finally, for the resulting four groups—designated Hi

[11] All findings referred to as "significant" were at or beyond the .05 level of confidence unless it is specifically stated otherwise.

Op-R, Lo Op-R, Hi Op-NR, and Lo Op-NR—the mean per cent plural noun responses given on the conditioning task were compared in Figure 4 with the comparable per cent scores derived for Greenspoon's R and NR groups. The following points may be noted with respect to the conditioning data presented in Figure 4: (1) in the Spielberger and DeNike study (S and D), the conditioning

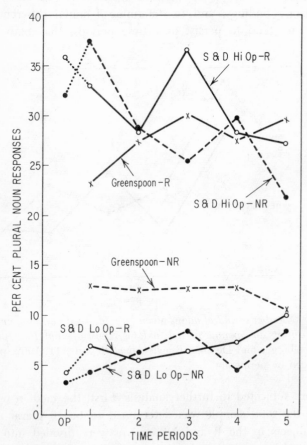

Figure 4 *Percentage of plural nouns given by reinforced (R) and non-reinforced (NR) subjects with high (Hi-Op) and low (Lo-Op) operant rates in the Spielberger-DeNike experiment (S & D) compared with Greenspoon's reinforced and nonreinforced groups.* From Spielberger and DeNike, *Psychological Reports*, **11**, 1962, p. 362. Reproduced by permission.

curves for the high-operant R and NR groups were quite comparable, as were the conditioning curves for the low-operant R and NR groups; (2) the mean per cent plural noun responses emitted over time periods by Greenspoon's R group was not grossly different from that emitted by the two high-operant groups in the present study, and the conditioning curve of his NR group was comparable to that of the low-operant groups in this study; (3) Greenspoon's R group gave over 60 per cent more plural nouns during the first time period than his NR group, and the difference between these groups increased only slightly over the reinforced time periods.

Statistical evaluation of the combined influence of reinforcement and operant rate in this experiment indicated that the reinforcing stimulus did not affect the output of plural nouns. Only the built-in main effect of the control variable, operant rate, was significant. These findings appear to indicate that initial differences in operant rate for plurals persisted over time and that the reinforcing stimulus "Mmm-hmm" had no influence on the emission of plurals, as may be noted in Figures 3 and 4. The only subject in this investigation who gave more plural nouns over time periods was one of the two subjects eliminated from the experiment because he reported a correlated hypothesis.

Although our findings clearly failed to support a theory of automatic strengthening of response by reinforcement, neither did they support the cognitive hypothesis that awareness mediates performance gains in verbal conditioning. The latter interpretation would require, in addition to showing that unaware subjects failed to condition, evidence that subjects who showed performance gains were aware of the correct response-reinforcement contingency. Therefore, in the next study, we attempted to induce awareness in our subjects by manipulating the instructions for the verbal conditioning task.

Experiment II: Induced Awareness in Verbal Conditioning. The goals of this study (DeNike and Spielberger, 1963) were to evaluate the effects of instructions and reinforcement on mediating cognitive states and on performance in verbal conditioning. It was expected that (1) providing subjects with more task-relevant information through instructions would induce more subjects to become aware of the contingency between their verbal behavior and the occurrence of the reinforcing stimulus; and (2) "conditioning" effects would be limited to those subjects who were able to state such contingencies in a postconditioning interview. The conditioning task was similar to that employed in the previous study, except that subjects were required to give a total of 500 words rather than to respond for a fixed period of time. The subjects were 48 female undergraduate students enrolled in the introductory psychology course at Duke University.

Subjects were assigned in equal numbers to *informed, noninformed* and *control* groups. The subjects in each of these groups were told that "a certain way of making up words will be considered correct." The informed group was also told, "You will know you have made up a word correctly by my saying 'Mmm-hmm.'" After a 100-word operant period in which no reinforcement was given, the informed subjects were systematically reinforced with "Mmm-hmm" after each plural noun response. The subjects in the noninformed group were reinforced exactly as were the informed subjects, but they were given no cues as to the presence or meaning of the "Mmm-hmm." The control group was given the same instructions as the noninformed group, and subsequent to the operant word-block, subjects in this group were reinforced for 20 per cent of their responses, according to a predetermined random schedule of reinforcement. Thus, in the control group, subjects were not given any information about the reinforcing stimulus which, moreover, had only a random relation to the words they used.

The subjects were tested individually; each was required to say 400 words subsequent to the operant word-block. Upon completion of the conditioning task, the subject was directed to another room where she was interviewed by a second experimenter, according to a detailed interview schedule similar to that employed in the previous experiment. The experimenter had no knowledge of the experimental group to which the subject was assigned, nor of the subject's performance on the conditioning task.

The mean number of plural noun responses given in the operant word-block and in the four reinforced blocks of 100 words by the informed, noninformed, and control groups is indicated in Figure 5 where it may be noted that *only* the informed group gave an increasing number of plural noun responses over word-blocks. When statistically evaluated, the performance gains of the informed

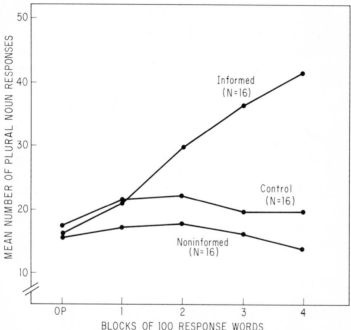

Figure 5 *Number of plural nouns given by informed, noninformed, and control groups during the operant word-block and in 4 post-operant blocks of 100 response words.* From DeNike and Spielberger, *Journal of Verbal Learning and Verbal Behavior*, **1**, 1963, p. 341. Reproduced by permission of the Academic Press, Inc.

group were found to be highly significant, whereas the conditioning curve for the noninformed group was relatively flat and statistically indistinguishable from that of the control group. Thus, only informed subjects showed performance gains. Did the instructions sensitize the informed subjects to the reinforcing stimulus, which then directly and automatically influenced their performance? Or, did informing these subjects of the presence and significance of the reinforcing stimulus help to induce an awareness of the correct response-reinforcement contingency, which permitted them to select plural nouns? These alternatives were evaluated by comparing the performance on the conditioning task of subjects who reported the correct contingency during the postconditioning interview with that of subjects who did not report the correct contingency.

Of the 32 systematically reinforced subjects in the informed and noninformed groups, only 5 verbalized the correct contingency—i.e., stated in the interview that "Mmm-hmm" was contingent upon their giving plural nouns. All five were in the informed group. The performance on the conditioning task of these five aware subjects (aware group) is compared in Figure 6 with that of the subjects in the informed and noninformed groups who failed to verbalize the correct contingency (unaware group[12]), and with the perform-ance of the control group. It may be noted in Figure 6 that only the aware subjects showed performance gains; the systematically reinforced subjects who were unaware of the correct contingency failed to improve. Thus, it would seem reasonable to conclude that (a) the information about the reinforcing stimulus given through instructions to the informed group increased the probability of inducing awareness of the correct contingency in these subjects and (b) awareness of the correct contingency mediated per-formance gains on the conditioning task for those subjects who gave more plural nouns over the reinforced word-blocks.

In this study, the conditioning data were initially arrayed, in Fig-ure 5, solely on the basis of the experimentally manipulated inde-pendent variables. However, this misleadingly appeared to suggest

---

[12] Of the 27 subjects in the unaware group, 19 verbalized correlated hy-potheses—i.e., response-reinforcement contingencies judged to be positively correlated with the correct contingency. The remaining subjects in the un-aware group either failed to verbalize any hypothesis or gave noncorrelated hypotheses. Although the aggregate performance of the subjects with correlated hypotheses was not significantly different from that of the control group, when motivation was taken into account, six subjects with correlated hypotheses, who indicated both that they wanted to receive the reinforcement and that they tried to get it, showed significant performance gains. Neither the subjects with-out correlated hypotheses nor the unmotivated subjects with correlated hy-potheses showed performance gains on the conditioning task.

that the informed group as a whole acquired the reinforced response class. By taking awareness into account as one of the independent variables, and arraying the data as in Figure 6, it may be noted that performance gains were limited essentially to the five subjects with correct hypotheses. The investigator whose theoretical and epistemological assumptions preclude consideration of the possibility that cognitive processes may mediate verbal behavior, if he is to be consistent with his assumptions, cannot go beyond an analy-

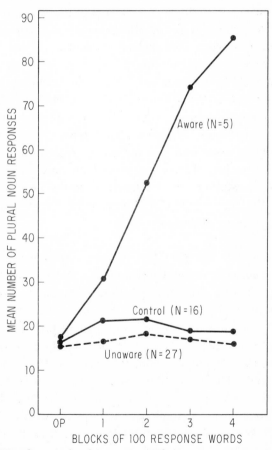

Figure 6 *Number of plural nouns given by aware, unaware, and control groups during the operant word-block and in 4 post-operant blocks of 100 response words.* Adapted from DeNike and Spielberger (1963).

sis of the conditioning data in terms of the manipulated independent variables. The heuristic advantage of an approach to verbal conditioning that incorporates cognitive concepts is clearly demonstrated in the present study, since a larger proportion of the total variance was explained when subjects' awareness was taken into account, as in Figure 6, than when awareness was ignored, as in Figure 5.

Since awareness was inferred in this study from subjects' responses to interview questions asked *after* performance measures had been taken, it could be reasoned that the performance gains of the aware subjects were initially automatically produced by the reinforcement. Subjects who showed performance gains might subsequently have noticed that plural nouns were followed by "Mmm-hmm" and could have responded to this observation by labeling the correct contingency. While this interpretation obviously ignores the failure of unaware subjects to condition, it serves to point up the theoretical significance of the temporal relationship between the development of awareness and the onset of performance gains in verbal conditioning. Therefore, procedural modifications in the evaluation of awareness were introduced in the next study which permitted the investigation of the temporal dependence of performance gains on awareness.

Experiment III: The Temporal Relationship between Awareness and Performance in Verbal Conditioning. DeNike (1963) investigated the temporal relationship between awareness and performance gains in verbal conditioning. For his conditioning task, he employed essentially the same word-naming procedure used by Matarazzo *et al.* (1960), except that his subjects were required to write down their "thoughts about the experiment" during the conditioning trials. DeNike's subjects, 82 female undergraduates enrolled in the introductory psychology course at Duke University, were required to say a total of 300 response words. After each block of 25 words, a light was turned on as a signal for the subject to record her "thoughts." Subjects received no reinforcement during the first two word-blocks, which provided a measure of operant rate for the response class *nouns denoting humans*. Beginning with the third word-block, DeNike's experimental group was reinforced with "Mmm-hmm" for each human noun response, and his control group was reinforced with "Mmm-hmm" according to a predetermined random schedule for 10 per cent of their response words. Awareness of the contingency between human noun responses and "Mmm-hmm" was inferred for subjects in the experimental group from the "thoughts about the experiment" (notes) they recorded during the conditioning trials. On the basis of her notes, each subject was independently rated by four judges as either *aware* or *unaware* of a correct contingency. Agreement between pairs of judges ranged from 90 to 95 per cent. The four judges agreed unanimously in their ratings of 52 of the 61 subjects, and there was at least a 3-to-1 consensus among them with respect to the classification of 59 (96.7 per cent) of the subjects. The notes for the two remaining subjects were submitted to a fifth judge. By this process, 21 of the subjects in the experimental group were classified as aware, and 40 were classified unaware.

The conditioning curves of the aware, unaware, and control subjects are presented in Figure 7, in which it may be noted that the output of human nouns for the aware group increased over the reinforced word-blocks and that the unaware group failed to show any performance gains. Statistical analyses of these data confirmed the impression that the linear trend for the aware group was highly significant and that the performance curve of the unaware group was not distinguishable from that of the randomly reinforced control group. Thus, only subjects who recorded correct contingencies in their notes gave more human nouns over the reinforced word-blocks.

From the conditioning data as presented in Figure 7, it was not possible to determine if the aware subjects manifested performance gains *prior* to the time at which they became aware of a correct contingency. Therefore, in order to evaluate the temporal relationship between performance gains and awareness, DeNike examined the conditioning data as a function of the word-block on which each subject *first* recorded a correct contingency. This word-block was designated the "zero" block, and word-blocks prior to and subsequent to the "zero" block were designated the preawareness and postawareness blocks. The preawareness and postawareness blocks were labeled, respectively, with negative and positive integers, after the practice of Philbrick and Postman (1955). Six aware subjects who recorded correct contingencies in their notes on the first and last reinforced word-blocks were eliminated from this analysis because they had either no preawareness or no postawareness blocks. The "zero" blocks of the 15 aware subjects who re-

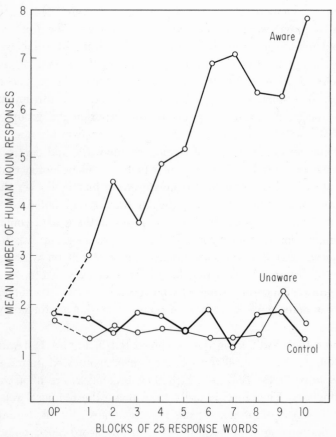

Figure 7 *Number of human nouns given by aware, unaware, and control subjects during operant word-blocks and in 10 post-operant blocks of 25 response words.* From DeNike, unpublished Ph.D. dissertation, Duke University, 1963.

corded the correct contingency in their notes on word-blocks 2–9 were aligned, and the preawareness and postawareness conditioning data of these subjects were separately Vincentized (Munn, 1950). Thus, each aware subject contributed to each preawareness and postawareness word-block.

The Vincentized conditioning curve of DeNike's aware subjects is presented in Figure 8. The performance of these subjects on the

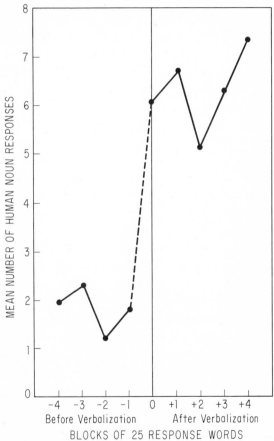

Figure 8   *Number of human nouns given on pre-verbalization and post-verbalization word-blocks for aware subjects who recorded a correct contingency in their notes on the "zero" block.* Adapted from DeNike (1963).

preawareness blocks was essentially the same as during the operant blocks, whereas the mean number of human noun responses given in the "zero" block and in the postawareness blocks was consistently above the operant level. Statistical analyses of these data confirmed the impression that there were no significant performance gains during the preawareness blocks and that the increased output of human noun responses from the "-1" block to the "zero" block was highly significant. The finding that performance gains first occurred on the word-block on which aware subjects first recorded a correct contingency in their notes may be interpreted as evidence that the increased output of human noun responses was consciously mediated. This finding would appear particularly difficult to account for by learning theories that ascribe direct, transsituational, automatic reinforcement effects to verbal stimuli.

The steep rise in the output of humans responses on the "zero" block, which may be noted in Figure 8, contrasts with the conditioning data as presented in Figure 7, in which there was a gradual rise in the mean number of humans given on successive reinforced word-blocks. Since the conditioning curve depicted in Figure 8 clearly indicates that performance gains for aware subjects first occurred on the trial block on which these subjects first recorded a correct contingency, the shape of the conditioning curve for the aware group, as depicted in Figure 7, would appear to be an artifact of averaging the performance of individual subjects who became aware of a correct contingency on different word-blocks.

It was possible for subjects who were aware of the correct contingency in this experiment to give 25 humans responses on each postawareness word-block. However, it may be observed in Figure 8 that the mean number of human nouns given by aware subjects during these blocks did not exceed 8 responses. What limited the aware subjects from acting on their awareness? Analysis of data obtained by DeNike in a postconditioning interview suggested that motivational factors accounted for large individual differences in the performance of aware subjects on the conditioning task. Those who reported that they wanted to receive the reinforcement showed higher levels of performance on the postawareness blocks than did aware subjects who reported that they did not want to receive reinforcement (DeNike, 1963; see figure on p. 100). However, the interview in which motivation to receive reinforcement was determined was not conducted until *after* the conclusion of the conditioning task. Therefore, it was possible that subjects who gave more humans responses simply rationalized this behavior by ascribing to themselves a motivational state consistent with the performance gains they had shown on the conditioning task. In the next study, we attempted, through experimental manipulation of the incentive value of the reinforcing stimulus, to *induce* in all subjects a uniformly high level of motivation to receive reinforcement.

Experiment IV: The Information and Incentive Value of the Reinforcing Stimulus in Verbal Conditioning. The experimental procedures in this study (Spielberger, Bernstein, and Ratliff, unpublished) were essentially the same as those employed by De-Nike (1963), except that during the conditioning task, we attempted to increase the incentive value of the reinforcing stimulus. The subjects, 24 female undergraduates enrolled in the introductory psychology course at Vanderbilt University, were instructed to say words and to record their "thoughts about the experiment" (notes) after each block of 23 response words. For all subjects, there were two nonreinforced word-blocks for determining operant rate and ten reinforced word-blocks.

Subsequent to the operant blocks, each human noun response given by the subject was reinforced with "Mmm-hmm." Between the seventh and eighth word-blocks, each subject was told, "Try to make me say 'Mmm-hmm' as often as you can." It was assumed that these instructions would increase the incentive value of the reinforcing stimulus by inducing in each subject a stronger motivation to receive it. In order to check on the effectiveness of the incentive manipulation, subjects were interviewed immediately after conditioning concerning their motivation to receive reinforcement. The postconditioning interview also provided additional data on subjects' awareness of the correct contingency.

The principal measures of awareness in this study were the notes recorded by each subject during conditioning. These were submitted to two judges who had no contact with the subjects, nor any knowledge of their conditioning performance. The judges agreed perfectly in classifying 15 subjects as aware and 9 as unaware. Of the aware subjects, 7 were judged to have first recorded a correct contingency prior to the incentive-inducing instruction, and 8 were judged to have done so subsequent to this instruction. These subjects were designated, respectively, the aware-pre and aware-post groups. The 9 subjects who failed to record a correct contingency were designated the unaware group. The mean per cent human noun responses given by these three groups in the operant blocks and the reinforced blocks prior to the incentive-inducing instruction are given in Figure 9. The curve for the aware-pre group was based on conditioning data Vincentized as described

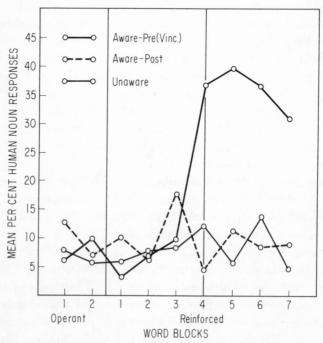

Figure 9 *Percentage of human nouns given by the aware-pre, aware-post, and unaware groups during the operant word-blocks and in the post-operant blocks prior to the incentive-inducing instruction.* From Spielberger, Bernstein, and Ratliff, unpublished study.

in the previous study. For this group, the fourth reinforced word-block was made to correspond with the block on which each subject first recorded a correct contingency in her notes. Word-blocks 1–3 were preawareness blocks and word-blocks 5–7 were postawareness blocks.

Statistical analyses of the data presented in Figure 9 yielded results which indicated that (a) the three groups did not differ during the operant blocks; (b) the performance gains of the aware-pre group first occurred on the word-block on which these subjects first recorded a correct contingency; and (c) the aware-post and unaware groups failed to show performance gains. Thus, in the present study, the findings for the word-blocks prior to the incentive-inducing instruction were completely consistent with those obtained by DeNike in the previous study (see Figures 7 and 8).

Subsequent to the instruction to try to make the experimenter say "Mmm-hmm," the aware-pre, aware-post, and unaware groups all gave more human noun responses than they had given prior to this instruction. The mean per cent human noun responses given by these groups in the three reinforced word-blocks immediately prior to and subsequent to the incentive-inducing instruction is indicated in Figure 10. Improvement from word-block 7 to word-block 8 was highly significant for both the aware-pre and aware-post groups. The marked increase in output of human nouns by the aware-pre group is consistent with the interpretation that the incentive-inducing instruction increased the motivation of these subjects to receive reinforcement, and that their awareness of the correct contingency permitted them to give more human noun responses. The somewhat lower level of performance of the aware-post group appeared to reflect the fact that these subjects had to become aware of a correct contingency before the incentive-inducing instruction could increase their motivation to act on their awareness.

The slight but significant rise in the performance curve for the unaware group subsequent to the incentive-inducing instruction, which may be noted in Figure 10, introduces the possibility that these subjects conditioned without awareness. However, it was also possible that some of them became aware of the correct contingency but failed to record this in their notes. In order to evaluate the latter possibility, the postconditioning interview protocols of the subjects in the unaware group were examined by two judges who had no prior contact with them, nor any knowledge of what they had recorded in their notes. The judges agreed perfectly in rating four subjects aware and five unaware.

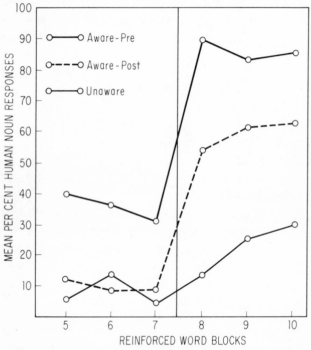

Figure 10 *Percentage of human nouns given by the aware-pre, aware-post, and unaware groups on the word-blocks immediately prior to, and subsequent to, the incentive-inducing instructions.* From Spielberger, Bernstein, and Ratliff, unpublished study.

The performance on the word-blocks subsequent to the incentive-inducing instruction of subjects judged unaware on the basis of their notes but aware on the basis of their interview responses (aware-interview group) is compared in Figure 11 with the performance of subjects rated unaware on the basis of *both* their notes and their interview responses (unaware-interview group). It may be noted that the conditioning curve for the unaware-interview group did not increase, and indeed, by the final word-block, the output of human nouns by this group was below what it had been during the operant blocks (see Figure 9). In contrast, the conditioning curve for the aware-interview group showed a marked rise subsequent to the incentive-inducing instruction, and despite the small number of subjects involved, the improvement in performance

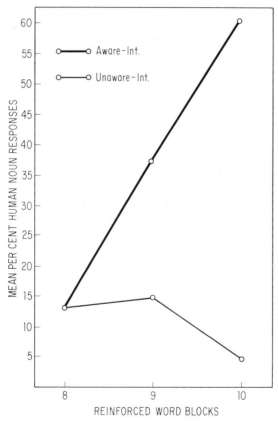

Figure 11 *Percentage of human nouns given by subjects rated unaware from their notes but aware from their interview responses (aware-int.), and subjects rated unaware from both their notes and their interview responses (unaware-int.), in the word-blocks subsequent to the incentive-inducing instruction. From Spielberger, Bernstein, and Ratliff, unpublished study.*

of this group was statistically significant. Furthermore, all of the subjects in the aware-interview group indicated that they became aware of a correct contingency subsequent to the incentive-inducing instruction, and three of them reported that they did not become aware until the final word-block. These findings suggest that subjects who became aware of the correct contingency late in conditioning were reluctant to record their hypotheses in their notes because they did not have sufficient opportunity for testing them.

Data obtained in the postconditioning interview indicated that the instruction to make the experimenter say "Mmm-hmm" increased the incentive value of the reinforcing stimulus. Subjects were asked how much they wanted the experimenter to say "Mmm-hmm" after they first noticed that he was saying it. They were also asked, how much they wanted him to say "Mmm-hmm" after they were instructed to try to make him say it. Only 4 subjects indicated that they "very much" wanted the experimenter to say "Mmm-hmm" prior to the incentive-inducing instruction, whereas 17 subjects indicated that they "very much" wanted him to say it subsequent to this instruction. And, where only a single subject reported that she tried to make the experimenter say "Mmm-hmm" prior to the instruction, 20 indicated that they did so subsequent to this instruction. Furthermore, the shift in the incentive value of the reinforcing stimulus was unrelated to awareness, since almost all of the subjects indicated greater motivation to receive reinforcement subsequent to the incentive-inducing instruction than prior to it. Thus, it would appear that the reinforcing stimulus in this experiment had both incentive and information value, but that performance gains on the conditioning task were limited to subjects who were aware of the information conveyed by the reinforcing stimulus.

Summary of the Findings in Experiments I–IV. There was little evidence in these studies of learning without awareness or of the direct and automatic effects of verbal reinforcement. In Experiment I, none of the subjects were able to verbalize the correct response-reinforcement contingency, and no differences in performance on the conditioning task were found for the reinforced and nonreinforced groups. In Experiment II, performance gains were limited to subjects who were informed about the presence and significance of the reinforcing stimulus and who reported a correct contingency in the postconditioning interview. In Experiment III, in which awareness was evaluated from "thoughts about the experiment" recorded during conditioning, performance gains were limited to subjects who recorded a correct contingency in their notes. Furthermore, the inception of performance gains for aware subjects occurred on the word-block on which they first recorded a correct contingency. In Experiment IV, subjects who had previously recorded a correct contingency in their notes showed performance gains immediately subsequent to being instructed to make the experimenter say "Mmm-hmm." Although this instruction appeared to increase the incentive value of the reinforcing stimulus for most subjects, it facilitated performance on the conditioning task only for those who recorded the correct contingency in their notes or who reported it in the postconditioning interview.

The aggregate findings in these four studies seem to indicate that performance gains in verbal conditioning experiments employing the word-naming procedure are mediated by awareness of a correct response-reinforcement contingency and that motivation to receive reinforcement influences the degree to which aware subjects act on their awareness. Furthermore, this interpretation was also strongly supported by the results of a series of verbal conditioning studies employing the Taffel (1955) sentence-construction procedure carried out by the writer and his colleagues (Spielberger, 1962; Spielberger, Berger, and Howard, 1963; Spielberger, DeNike, and Fink, 1964) in which we found that: (a) Acquisition of reinforced responses was limited essentially to subjects who were able to verbalize correct or correlated hypotheses. (b) Acquisition was *specific* to the reinforced responses for which subjects were aware of response-reinforcement contingencies. (c) Increments in the conditioning curves of aware subjects tended to correspond with the trial-block on which these subjects indicated, during a postconditioning interview, that they first became aware. (d) Providing subjects with more task-relevant information through "learning instructions" increased the number who became aware of a correct contingency. (e) "Learning instructions" also tended to induce more positive attitudes toward the reinforcing stimulus and a stronger motivation to receive it. (f) Subjects who reported stronger motivation to receive reinforcement showed greater acquisition of reinforced responses.

Verbal Conditioning in Retrospect

Since operant conditioning procedures were transferred from the Skinner box to the domain of verbal behavior only a little more than a decade ago, any attempt to evaluate the contribution of verbal conditioning research to psychology or to psycholinguistics is perhaps premature. Nevertheless, it is readily apparent that verbal conditioning has generated considerable empirical interest among psychologists (see Figure 1), along with heated theoretical controversy. Spawned by Skinner's atheoretical descriptive behaviorism, verbal conditioning has been embraced by proponents of S-R learning theories in the traditions of Thorndike and Hull largely because of the apparent support provided for the strong law of effect, and the promise that complex verbal behavior could be explained without recourse to mentalistic concepts. Yet, recent findings strongly suggest that performance gains in verbal conditioning are most parsimoniously interpreted as resulting from the operation of mediating cognitive processes, rather than the automatic effects of reinforcement. When the traditional distinction between learning and performance is made, and methods are employed that permit sensitive evaluations of awareness, the available evidence suggests that "what is learned" in verbal conditioning is awareness of a response-reinforcement contingency. Obviously, one cannot assert on the basis of verbal conditioning findings that learning *cannot* take place without awareness, but these findings would seem to support Adams' (1957) contention that evidence for learning without awareness has not been convincingly demonstrated in the laboratory.

Unfortunately, the methodological consequences of implicit epistemological assumptions associated with the theoretical orientations that have guided verbal conditioning research have deterred the convergence of the findings of verbal conditioning research. As long as investigators with different theoretical orientations continue to employ radically different methods with respect to the evaluation (definition) of awareness, the accumulation of a composite set of facts that will facilitate the convergence of empirical findings will not be possible. What is required is recognition of the methodological consequences of epistemological assumptions associated with different theoretical orientations, and general acceptance of experimental procedures that permit sensitive evaluation of awareness while providing necessary safeguards against biasing or distorting subjects' verbal reports. Otherwise, the role of awareness in verbal conditioning will continue to be obscured by fruitless theoretical controversy generated by noncomparable data.

Perhaps one of the most significant contributions of verbal conditioning research to date has been, paradoxically, the stimulation of interest in concepts such as awareness among psychologists who are inclined to insist that conscious processes are scientifically inaccessible. The descriptive behaviorists, who dictated the basic verbal conditioning methodology, have inadvertently permitted the entry of cognitive concepts into their scientific arenas through their claims that verbal conditioning occurs without awareness. Using the descriptive behaviorists' own conditioning procedures (but more sophisticated methods of assessing awareness), cognitively oriented investigators have been able, substantially, to replicate verbal conditioning findings. More important, however, is the fact that a larger proportion of the total variance in verbal conditioning experiments is accounted for when indices of awareness were employed as independent variables than when reports of awareness were either ignored or treated only as dependent response measures. Thus, although the verbal conditioning game is being played in the ball park of the descriptive behaviorists, the empirical findings in the waning innings seem to favor the visiting, cognitively oriented investigators.

To the layman, the magnitude of the investment of energy by psychologists in verbal conditioning research must seem strange, indeed. At first glance, the demonstration in verbal conditioning that some people (subjects) will do what others (experimenters) wish them to do, provided, of course, they know what is desired of them and want to please, seems quite trivial. The methodological implications of verbal conditioning research, however, are of considerable import if there is active transfer of the procedures developed for the assessment of cognitive processes in verbal conditioning into other research domains. In this regard, present attempts in research on perception to deal *exclusively* with behavior have led Guttman (1963, p. 19) to conclude, "The effort to speak the language of behavior only is just inefficient, and to do so leads to bad experiments on perception, to a truncated set of laws of behavior, and to wide misinterpretation as to what our current knowledge of behavioral laws portends, theoretically and practically." The present status of verbal conditioning research would appear to merit similar conclusions.

Recent concern with awareness in verbal conditioning is perhaps only one palpable landmark in the prevailing Zeitgeist in which other signs of a cognitive renaissance are abundantly evident (e.g., Holt, 1964; Miller, Galanter, and Pribram, 1960). Perhaps, at long last, psychologists will shake off the limiting vestiges of a narrow behaviorism which excludes concepts essential to an understanding of complex human behavior, while retaining the operational rigor essential to fruitful experimental work. And, in the process of questioning their subjects, psychologists shall undoubtedly find, as Farber (1963, p. 197) has suggested, that "subjects or clients will talk, if only to themselves. And, not infrequently, whether relevant or irrelevant, the things people say to themselves determine the rest of the things they do."

Summary

The general goals in this article were to examine theoretical and epistemological assumptions that have guided verbal conditioning research and to evaluate evidence from investigations of verbal conditioning relevant to the claims that learning without awareness has been demonstrated. In pursuing these goals, the principal verbal conditioning techniques were described, present-day empirical interest in verbal conditioning was documented, and the particular stimulus-response and cognitive theoretical frameworks that have guided research in this area were reviewed. Also, the methods and findings of several representative verbal conditioning experiments, carried out within the general frameworks of stimulus-response and cognitive learning theories, were examined in some detail. It was concluded that "what is learned" in verbal conditioning is awareness of a response-reinforcement contingency and that subjects will act on their awareness provided they are motivated to receive reinforcement.

After evaluating theoretical and epistemological issues in verbal conditioning, it was suggested that epistemological assumptions, implicitly associated with the particular stimulus-response and cognitive learning theories that have guided verbal conditioning research, have deterred the convergence of the findings of verbal conditioning experiments and the clarification of verbal conditioning phenomena. Recognition of the methodological consequences of these epistemological assumptions will be required, along with the general acceptance of sensitive operations for assessing awareness, in order to facilitate the convergence of verbal conditioning findings and the establishment of a cumulative body of scientific knowledge with respect to verbal conditioning phenomena.

References

Adams, J. K. "Laboratory studies of behavior without awareness." *Psychol. Bull.*, 1957, **54**, 383–405.

Campbell, D. T. "Operational delineation of 'what is learned' via the transposition experiment." *Psychol. Rev.*, 1954, **61**, 167–174.

———. "Social attitudes and other acquired behavioral dispositions." In S. Koch (ed.). *Psychology: a study of a science*, Vol. 6. New York: McGraw-Hill, 1963, pp. 94–172.

Chomsky, N. "A review of *Verbal Behavior* by B. F. Skinner." *Language*, 1959, **35**, 26–58.

Cohen, B. D., H. I. Kalish, J. R. Thurston, and E. Cohen. "Experimental manipulation of verbal behavior." *J. Exp. Psychol.*, 1954, **47**, 106–110.

DeNike, L. D. "Awareness in verbal conditioning: the assessment of awareness from verbal reports written by subjects during conditioning." Unpublished Ph.D. dissertation, Duke Univ., 1963.

———, and C. D. Spielberger. "Induced mediating states in verbal conditioning." *J. Verbal Learn. Verbal Behav.*, 1963, **1**, 339–345.

Dollard, J., and N. E. Miller. *Personality and psychotherapy.* New York: McGraw-Hill, 1950.

Dulany, D. E. "The place of hypotheses and intentions: an analysis of verbal control in verbal conditioning." *J. Pers.*, 1962, **30**, (Suppl.), 102–129.

———. "How can we speak of awareness and volition as instrumental?" Unpublished paper presented as part of symposium "Awareness as a factor in verbal operant conditioning" at Southeastern Psychological Assoc. meeting, Miami Beach, April 1963.

———. "Hypotheses and habits in verbal 'operant conditioning.'" *J. Abnorm. Soc. Psychol.*, 1961, **63**, 251–263.

Eriksen, C. W. "Discrimination and learning without awareness, a methodological survey and evaluation." *Psychol. Rev.*, 1960, **67**, 279–300.

Farber, I. E. "The things people say to themselves." *Amer. Psychologist*, 1963, **18**, 185–197.

Garner, W. R., H. W. Hake, and C. W. Eriksen. "Operationism and the concept of perception." *Psychol. Rev.*, 1956, **63**, 149–159.

Greenspoon, J. "The effect of verbal and nonverbal stimuli on the frequency of members of two verbal response classes." Unpublished doctoral dissertation, Indiana Univ., 1951.

———. "The reinforcing effect of two spoken sounds on the frequency of two responses." *Amer. J. Psychol.*, 1955, **68**, 409–416.

———. "Verbal conditioning and clinical psychology." In A. J. Bachrach (ed.). *Experimental foundations of clinical psychology.* New York: Basic Books, 1962, pp. 510–553.

Guttman, N. "Laws of behavior and facts of perception." In S. Koch (ed.). *Psychology: a study of science*, Vol. 5. New York: McGraw-Hill, 1963, pp. 114–178.

Hilgard, E. R. *Theories of learning.* New York: Appleton-Century-Crofts, 1956.

Holt, R. R. "Imagery: the return of the ostracized." *Amer. Psychologist*, 1964, **19**, 254–265.

Kanfer, F. H., and A. R. Marston. "Verbal conditioning, ambiguity and psychotherapy." *Psychol. Rep.*, 1961, **9**, 461–475.

———, and ———. "The effect of task-relevant information on verbal conditioning." *J. Psychol.*, 1962, **53**, 29–36.

———, and J. F. McBrearty. "Verbal conditioning: discrimination and awareness." *J. Psychol.*, 1961, **52**, 115–124.

Krasner, L. "Studies of the conditioning of verbal behavior." *Psychol. Bull.*, 1958, **55**, 148–170.

———. "The therapist as a social reinforcement machine." In H. Strupp, and L. Luborsky (eds.). *Research in psychotherapy*, Vol. II. Washington, D. C.: American Psychological Association, 1962, pp. 61–94.

Krieckhaus, E. E., and C. W. Eriksen. "A study of awareness and its effect on learning and generalization." *J. Pers.*, 1960, **28**, 503–517.

Levin, S. M. "The effects of awareness on verbal conditioning." *J. Exp. Psychol.*, 1961, **61**, 67–75.

Matarazzo, J. D., G. Saslow, and E. N. Pareis. "Verbal conditioning of two response classes: Some methodological considerations." *J. Abnorm. Soc. Psychol.*, 1960, **61**, 190–206.

Miller, G. A., E. Galanter, and K. H. Pribram. *Plans and the structure of behavior*. New York: Holt, Dryden, 1960.

Munn, N. L. *Handbook of psychological research on the rat: an introduction to animal psychology*. Boston: Houghton Mifflin, 1950.

Osgood, C. E. "Psycholinguistics." In S. Koch (ed.). *Psychology: a study of a science*, Vol. 6. New York: McGraw-Hill, 1963, pp. 244–316.

Philbrick, E. B., and L. Postman. "A further analysis of 'learning without awareness.' " *Amer. J. Psychol.*, 1955, **68**, 417–424.

Postman, L., and J. M. Sassenrath. "The automatic action of verbal rewards and punishments." *J. Gen. Psychol.*, 1961, **65**, 109–136.

Salzinger, K. "Experimental manipulation of verbal behavior." *J. Gen. Psychol.*, 1959, **61**, 65–94.

Skinner, B. F. "Are theories of learning necessary?" *Psychol. Rev.*, 1950, **57**, 193–216.

———. *Verbal behavior*. New York: Appleton-Century-Crofts, 1957.

Spielberger, C. D. "The role of awareness in verbal conditioning." In C. W. Eriksen (ed.). *Behavior and awareness*. Durham: Duke Univ. Press, 1962, pp. 73–101.

———, A. Berger, and Kay Howard. "Conditioning of verbal behavior as a function of awareness, need for social approval, and motivation to receive reinforcement." *J. Abnorm. Soc. Psychol.*, 1963, **67**, 241–246.

———, and L. D. DeNike. "Operant conditioning of plural nouns: A failure to replicate the Greenspoon effect." *Psychol. Rep.*, 1962, **11**, 355–366.

———, and ———. "Implicit epistemological bias and the problem of awareness in verbal conditioning: a reply to Greenspoon." *Psychol. Rep.*, 1963, **12**, 103–106.

———, ———, and L. S. Fink. "Anxiety and verbal conditioning." *J. Abnorm. Soc. Psychol.*, 1964, in press.

———, and S. M. Levin. "What is learned in verbal conditioning?" *J. Verbal Learn. Verbal Behav.*, 1962, **1**, 125–132.

———, ———, and M. Shepard. "The effects of awareness and attitude toward reinforcement on the operant conditioning of verbal behavior." *J. Pers.*, 1962, **30**, 106–121.

Taffel, C. "Anxiety and the conditioning of verbal behavior." *J. Abnorm. Soc. Psychol.*, 1955, **51**, 496–501.

Tatz, S. J. "Symbolic activity in 'learning without awareness.'" *Amer. J. Psychol.*, 1960, **73**, 239–247.

Thorndike, E. L. *The fundamentals of learning.* New York: Bureau of Publications, Teachers Coll., Columbia University, 1932.

———, and R. T. Rock. "Learning without awareness of what is being learned or intent to learn it." *J. Exp. Psychol.*, 1934, **17**, 1–9.

Whorf, B. L. "Science and linguistics." In Sol Saporta (ed.), *Psycholinguistics.* New York: Holt, Rinehart and Winston, 1961, pp. 460–468.

V

INDIVIDUAL
DIFFERENCES
IN VERBAL
BEHAVIOR

INDIVIDUAL
DIFFERENCES
IN WORD USAGE

Jum C. Nunnally

In this article I hope to argue persuasively that individual differences in word usage relate importantly to individual differences in learning, perception, and personality. In stating this position, I am sure that I will fall into the trap that most theorists do and attempt to explain too much with a few simple principles. Hopefully, the principles will serve to explain at least some phenomena that hitherto have not been explainable and will provide a better explanation than previously has been available for some other phenomena.

For two reasons the article will be more concerned with theory than with experimental evidence. First, the theory that will be stated requires for its validation a considerable amount of evidence that has not yet been obtained. Second, the relevant experimental evidence that is available is too large to be discussed in detail here. Several experiments will be discussed in detail later to indicate the fruitfulness of the theory and to show the types of experiments that follow from the theory. The theory and related evidence have been described by the author and his colleagues in a number

203

of other papers (Nunnally and Flaugher, 1963*a* and 1963*b;* Nunnally, Flaugher, and Hodges, 1963). The purpose here will be to refine and extend the theory and to present new experimental evidence bearing on it.

As a prelude to the exposition to follow, it might be useful to pick apart the title in order to see what ground is intended to be covered. The term "individual differences" is used more broadly than is customary. Customarily the term is used to denote reliable differences among people that are relatively stable over time. In addition to employing the term for that class of behaviors, a second usage will be to denote differences in central tendency among groups of people, which are not necessarily reflected in individual differences within those groups—such as differences in word usage by children and adults and by deaf and normal Ss. A third usage will be to denote experimentally induced differences in word-usage between groups of Ss.

Looking further at the title, it is important to distinguish between the phenomena of word usage and broader phenomena having to do with individual differences in language behavior in general. Important individual differences may be found with respect to many aspects of language behavior, including grammatical style, rate and kinds of information transmitted, speech intonations, and many others. Here we will be concerned only with individual differences in the words that people use.

Any theory that attempts to account for behavioral variables in terms of language variables necessarily should pay tribute to the Whorf-Sapir (Carroll, 1956) concept of linguistic relativism. In essence, linguistic relativism is a very broad hypothesis that says that differences in language behavior reflect differences in the way people think. It was noted, for example, that the Navahos have no words concerning simultaneous happenings in distant places, and perhaps as a consequence, they have difficulty in discussing what is happening in a remote village without taking account of the time that it would take to go "from here to there." Another observation was that the Eskimos have no single word for snow, but rather, they have a variety of related words: one for wet snow, another for blowing snow, another for packed snow, and others. This suggests that, as might be expected, Eskimos spend more time thinking about snow than do natives of, say, Atlanta, and they probably would be more capable of making fine discriminations about snow conditions.

Although the theory presented here does indeed owe a debt to linguistic relativism, it differs in several important ways. Linguistic relativism does not lend itself to neat experiments because it principally concerns cross-cultural correlations of language behaviors with other important forms of behavior. Of course, there are many uncontrolled variables that tend to make the interpretation of such cross-cultural comparisons quite difficult. Here we will be concerned with differences in word usage within cultures rather than between cultures.

Linguistic relativism is such a broad hypothesis that it is difficult to decide how to test it. The theory that will be presented here leads rather directly to experimental investigation. Many of the supposed differences in language behavior envisioned by linguistic relativism are so abstract and complex that it is difficult to know how they should be measured. Here we will be concerned with aspects of word usage that are directly susceptible to conventional methods of psychological measurement.

Word Usage Related to Problem-Solving, Conditioning, and Instrumental Activity

Our theoretical discourse will start with two questions, ones that will be considered either quite superficial or quite profound, depending on your interpretation of what I mean. The questions are (a) why do people learn particular words, and (b) once particular words are learned, what effects do they have on behavior in general? I will attempt some partial answers to these two questions in terms of well-known psychological principles, and these in turn will suggest some rather novel approaches to investigating the effects of individual differences in word usage.

Children learn words partly to solve problems. The child learns to say "water" because this will provide the required form of reinforcement more rapidly than will crying, random motions, or the use of any other words. Such problem-solving behavior follows the principles that pertain to problem-solving in general. More appropriate responses (words) gain habit strength, and inappropriate responses lose habit strength. Thus, if the child wants milk but refers to all liquids as "water," the resulting delays in reinforcement will lead to learning the more quickly reinforced word "milk." Gradually in this way children learn to solve problems by accurately employing those words that more quickly result in relevant reinforcements.

In addition to words being learned as aids to problem-solving, words probably also are, in part, learned through direct conditioning. Such conditioning takes several forms. In one form, an external stimulus pattern conditions the use of a particular word or words. For example, after many instances in which parents say "no, no" when a child attempts a forbidden act, the child often will say "no, no" himself when he starts to perform the act. (If one is inclined to do so, he can extrapolate this process to give a partial account of the development of adult conscience.) In another type of conditioning, word usage is directly conditioned to particular "internal states" of felt need and emotion. A mother frequently responds to indications of pain or discomfort on the part of the child by saying, "Does your stomach hurt?" Eventually this leads the child to say, "My stomach hurts," when in fact some other part of the body is causing the discomfort. The use of the word "stomach" has become conditioned to states of internal discomfort in general.

Once words are accurately assimilated into the child's repertoire of potential responses, then, among other things, they serve as instrumental responses. Examples of such instrumental responses are (a) "Give me a dime" to obtain money, (b) "Thank you" in order to incur the good graces of someone, and (c) "You look lovely tonight" to obtain the favor of a charming lady. Such instrumental responses are analogous to those of the instrumental activity of a rat in bar-pressing or the instrumental activity of the family dog in barking for his nightly meal. One advantage of considering word usage as a form of instrumental response is that it leads us to inquire about the types of reinforcements that particular types of words do obtain or, for the cognitive theorist, are thought to be obtained. Another advantage of this way of thinking about word usage is that it suggests that conventional paradigms of operant learning can be used to investigate alterations in the rate of production of words of particular kinds. Of course, this is what has been done in the burgeoning field of verbal conditioning as evidenced in the work of Greenspoon (1955), Taffel (1955), Dulany (1962), Spielberger (1962), and others.

After particular words have been learned (in the several senses of problem-solving, conditioning, and instrumental behavior), the rate of production of such words is governed by the state of needs in the individual. Drive states typically occasion heightened activity. To some extent that activity is random and, in that sense, not obviously related to drive reduction. To the extent to which previously acquired classes of responses are capable of obtaining relevant reinforcement, the heightened behavior is less random. If words of particular kinds will facilitate the reduction of a drive, the probability is increased that those words will be uttered. This follows because such words have been learned as agents in problem-solving and because, subsequently, the words have served as instrumental acts. Even if the drive cannot be consummated by the use of particular words and/or by responses of the skeletal muscles, the heightened drive state itself will increase the probability that certain drive-related words will be uttered. This is due to the direct conditioning of certain words to the drive state.

The principles above can be illustrated with a hungry child who previously has learned that one way to satisfy the hunger drive is to use words related to food—e.g., "I'm hungry," "Give me a sandwich," and "I want to eat." Increased hunger drive increases the probability that words concerning food will be employed in temporally related utterances. Even if no food is available, and in consequence, the instrumental activity itself would be expected to extinguish over a period of hours, the child still uses words relating to food. This is because food-related words have previously been conditioned to the drive itself. As has been shown to be true in fasting adults, the increased habit strength of food-related words under conditions of heightened drive erupts in fantasy. In one experiment a blank screen was seen as picturing food of various kinds (McClelland and Atkinson, 1948).

Many other things being equal, the more different drives with which a word has been associated, the higher is the probability that the word will be used in situations in general. This is why the word "please" is used so frequently: it tends to serve as an instrumental response for obtaining many different types of reinforcement.

Frequency of Word-usage

What has previously been said about how words are acquired and used should have implications for how words in general are used by people in general. It would be expected that people would use words more frequently that had been (a) conditioned to more drive states, (b) served successfully to solve problems, and (c) more frequently and more effectively used as instrumental responses. In other words, frequency of word usage by people in general should reflect the nature, relative strength, and typical resolution of needs in general. If so, it should be revealing to perform content analyses of the frequency with which different words are used by people in general. Although entirely satisfactory norms for word usage are not available, the Thorndike-Lorge (1944) word list (henceforth referred to as the T-L list) is a useful approximation to such a set of norms. As was shown by the work of Underwood and Schulz (1960), Noble (1963), and others, frequency of usage as indicated in the T-L list correlates substantially with other aspects of usage, including Noble's meaningfulness measure, and ratings of familiarity and pronunciability.

Although I know of no careful content analysis to compare words of high T-L frequency with words of low T-L frequency, an inspection of the two types of words suggests some interesting differences. As a number of investigators have documented, pleasant words occur more frequently than do unpleasant words. Not only are there many more pleasant than unpleasant words in English, but pleasant words are used much more frequently. This probably is because pleasant words generally are more effective agents of successful drive reduction than are unpleasant words, because, as the saying has it, "Sugar will catch more flies than vinegar."

Another obvious difference between low-frequency and higher-frequency words is that the former are structurally more complex. They are longer, have more syllables, and are more difficult to pronounce. These, then, are more difficult responses to make. Typically in instrumental activity, simpler responses gain ascendancy over more complex responses. This is why the average person tries to gain the good will of others by saying "Thanks" rather than "Your benevolence is highly appreciated." The latter would be a more difficult response for the average person, and because it might not be understood by the other person, the desired effect might not be obtained. Of course, there are situations where relatively infrequent words are more effective in obtaining reinforcements. Otherwise, one would wonder why such words are in the language at all. Also, there are important individual differences in the extent to which people use words at different levels of the T-L list. These two matters will be discussed in a later section.

Word frequency for people in general, such as is evidenced in the T-L list, may be thought of as representing a very general habit hierarchy. It is assumed that the list represents an approximate rank-ordering of words in terms of their probabilities of being emitted by people in general in situations in general. Thus, in any randomly selected segment of discourse, the probability is higher that the word "pretty" will be used than that the word "exquisite" will be used.

In situations where specific kinds of reinforcement are sought and where the class of successful instrumental responses is relatively clear, very general habit hierarchies are displaced by habit hierarchies directly relevant to the situation. Thus, when one is hungry, sexually aroused, or seeking social approval, response hierarchies directly related to those needs come into play, and consequently probabilities for various words being uttered shift drastically from those suggested by the T-L list.

It is important in this discussion to keep clearly in mind the separate distinctions between (a) kinds of word hierarchies and (b) group norms and individual differences. Almost all would agree that it is fruitful to think in terms of different group norms for word usage in general and word usage appropriate to particular situations. One of the major points of this article is that it also is fruitful to think in terms of individual differences in word usage in terms of both differences in the general hierarchy of word usage and differences in word hierarchies that are appropriate to particular situations. Thus, for each individual we are postulating a very general habit hierarchy, much like a separate T-L count for each person. In addition, we are postulating that each individual has more specific hierarchies that come into play in particular situations. Although both general and specific hierarchies for the individual must overlap considerably with those for group norms for people in general, differences in these regards are thought to be important for explaining individual differences in numerous forms of behavior.

One would expect that very general habit hierarchies, such as represented by the T-L list, would come into play only when response cues are relatively unclear. In other words, one would expect a higher correspondence between T-L frequency and frequency of actual word usage in situations where (a) the individual is highly activated but is not sure which drive is heightened, (b) the drive state is clear but the individual has not yet developed a hierarchy in terms of successful instrumental responses, or (c) the cues are unclear as to which categories of instrumental response are required to obtain reinforcement. To put it more simply, general verbal hierarchies are important when the individual (a) does not know what he wants, (b) has not acquired the skills to get what he wants, or (c) lacks cues as to the specific obstacles that must be overcome to get what he knows he wants. As the projective testers would say, generalized verbal habit hierarchies become more important when the situation is highly unstructured.

In numerous experiments, both general hierarchies of word usage and more specific hierarchies of word usage have shown relations with learning, perception, and emotional behavior. Only several outstanding examples will be mentioned in order to refresh the reader's memory of the multitude of these relations.

Word frequency has a marked effect on visual duration threshold, high-frequency words having a lower threshold than low-frequency words. The relation holds when the two types of words are equated for length, number of syllables, and other aspects of morphological complexity (Solomon and Postman, 1952). High-frequency words are more quickly learned in rote memory experiments. The relation holds for paired-associate learning, serial learning, and free recall (Underwood and Schulz, 1960).

Frequency of usage relates in a number of ways to the results obtained by the classical method of association. Flaugher (1963) used the response words given in the Russell and Jenkins (1954) association norms as clues in a detection game. The response words for each stimulus word were serially presented to each S. After each response word, Ss were asked to guess what stimulus word elicited that response. Among other interesting findings, Flaugher found that the T-L frequency of the stimulus word had a strong positive relationship to how easily stimulus words could be detected.

There is some evidence to suggest that heightened drive states increase the probability of high-frequency words being employed by Ss. Osgood and Walker (1959) performed a content analysis of suicide notes and compared those with personal letters and other documents. They reasoned that people who are preparing to commit suicide are in a very heightened state of generalized drive and, consequently, that the heightened drive should affect the nature of the words used. Among other corroborative findings, it was found that suicide notes had higher-frequency words on the average than did documents written by other people in less emotional circumstances. The occurrence of high-frequency words in situations that provoke strong emotions should follow from the principle that increased drive tends to increase the response potential of responses near the top of the habit hierarchy more than responses further down in the hierarchy. Thus, if the T-L list represents a generalized verbal hierarchy, the relation between the occurrence of states of heightened emotion and the use of high-frequency words should hold. In an oblique way this principle may help explain why high-anxious Ss are relatively more efficient at learning simple rather than complex verbal material.

Individual Differences in Word Usage

So far we have considered principles that are thought to govern word usage for people in general. Principles were discussed regarding how people in general learn words, how words are used after they are learned, how such learning and use result in frequency-of-usage hierarchies, and how such hierarchies are important for learning, perception, and emotional behavior. Up to this point no explicit principles have been given with respect to individual differences in word usage.

The central assumption here is that *wherever general norms for word usage relate to group trends in some other form of behavior, individual differences in word usage may help explain individual differences in that form of behavior.* Thus, if group norms for frequency of usage affect group norms for perceptual recognition, then individual differences in frequency of usage of particular types of words may correlate with individual differences in perceptual recognition of those words. If frequency of usage affects rote verbal learning, then individual differences in frequency of usage of different kinds of words may correlate with the rate of learning those types of words. If words of particular kinds tend to be conditioned to internal states of particular kinds, then existing individual differences in word usage may correlate with the kinds of emotional learning that the individual previously has undergone. If different types of words are used to obtain different types of reinforcements, then the words that people more frequently use may relate to their stronger needs. If words tend to reflect the types of learning environments, or social situations, that people have encountered, then individual differences in word usage may relate to differences in prior social experiences.

The simple principle stated above opens a flood of ideas for investigating the relations between individual differences in word usage and individual differences in learning, perception, and personality. Some of the more salient possibilities will be discussed.

PERCEPTION

The potential effects of individual differences in word usage on perception can be illustrated by a simple example. If one person more frequently used the word "cow" than the word "dog," then his perceptual threshold will be lower for "cow." If another person more frequently uses the word "dog" than the word "cow," then he will have a lower threshold for "dog." Later, experiments will be described that provide evidence for this point of view.

If individual differences in word usage do correlate with individual differences in perceptual recognition, what processes are at work? In part, the effect may be due to individual differences in general hierarchies of word usage. Thus, for one of the individuals in the example above, in any segment of discourse the probability is higher that the word "cow" will be used than that the word "dog" will be used. However, the sheer differences in probabilities of occurrence in general probably are not sufficient to account for the size of the effects. Thus, if in the perceptual recognition experiment Ss randomly drew words from inside themselves, there would be a slight edge in probability for the occurrence of the word "cow" rather than the word "dog." But since the probability of any particular word occurring in any small segment of discourse is very low in an absolute sense, differences in probability of occurrence of words also are very small in an absolute sense. What may occur is that the early stages of the perceptual recognition task serve to shift the Ss "guesses" from the general hierarchy to relatively specific hierarchies. For example, before the S can accurately detect the complete word, he may see that the word begins with "G." Then, the relatively specific hierarchy concerning all words beginning with the letter "G" replaces the general hierarchy in determining the probabilities of responses. In this way, differences in probability of response that actually are very small in terms of the frequencies indicated in the T-L list become magnified as a function of the successive particularization of hierarchies that go on while the experiment is in progress.

Individual differences in word usage may offer a more parsimonious explanation of experimental results that have been explained in other ways. A now classic study was that of Postman, Bruner, and McGinnies (1948), which indicated that individual differences in values, as evidenced on the Allport-Vernon Study of Values, correlated with individual differences in the perceptual recognition of words relating to those values. This finding was taken by many to support a motivational theory of perception. Another interpretation is that corresponding to differences in values are differences in frequency of usage of words relating to those values. Such differences in word usage then correlate with differences in perceptual recognition. Later some evidence will be presented to suggest that this is the case.

If I correctly sense the trend, there is a movement toward the interpretation of supposed motivational effects on recognition threshold in terms of motivational effects on word usage. A decade or so ago there were studies that suggested that taboo words had higher thresholds than ordinary words (McGinnies, 1949), which was taken by some to indicate a process of perceptual repression. Later evidence indicated that Ss were embarrassed to use the taboo words, that they saw them perfectly well but were not willing to say them. In another experiment (Postman, Bronson, and Gropper, 1953), when Ss were told that some taboo words would be presented and were urged not to be embarrassed to say them, the difference in perceptual recognition disappeared. In other words, it was not a matter of perception *per se* but rather of word usage. Ss would not say the taboo words because this was thought to be a poor instrumental strategy, one that would lead to embarrassment rather than to any form of positive reinforcement. When the instrumental response (using taboo words) was made to lead to the positive reinforcement of being correct in the experimental situation, the instrumental activity was resumed.

More recently, cleaner experiments have been undertaken to investigate the supposed motivational components of perceptual recognition. Two processes have been investigated: (a) perceptual defense, which supposedly results in a raising of thresholds for punished words, and (b) perceptual vigilance, which supposedly results in a lowering of thresholds for words that previously have been instrumental in avoiding punishment. Although the many studies in this area do not agree with one another, and apparently there have been many sets of negative results, I hold to an explanation of defense and vigilance in terms of variables relating to word usage. Of course, this idea is not original with me. It is introduced in order to round out the theoretical ideas here. My contention is that conditions of punishment and avoidance of punishment cause the S to consciously shift his use of words from those that result in punishment to those that result in avoidance of punishment.

An experiment by Goldiamond and Hawkins (1958) shows in a striking way the impact that variables concerning word usage can have on experiments concerning perceptual recognition. Outwardly their experiment resembled others in which prior familiarization training with nonsense syllables shows an effect on perceptual recognition. However, one aspect of their experimental procedure threw interesting light on the effects of verbal behavior on perceptual recognition studies. In the first part of the study, each S was given familiarization training with five nonsense syllables. Five different levels of familiarization were employed in order to generate a continuum along which the nonsense syllables ranged in terms of familiarity. In the perceptual recognition task, none of the nonsense syllables were shown; rather in their place were shown Rorschach inkblots. Ss were asked to identify the "words" being presented. Of course, in this situation Ss were only guessing, but the frequency with which a particular nonsense syllable was guessed to be present corresponded closely with the amount of prior familiarization training given with respect to that nonsense syllable. In other words, Goldiamond and Hawkins reproduced the often found relationship between frequency of usage and perceptual recognition without employing any words at all in the perceptual recognition task. This is strong evidence that word hierarchies sometimes have an artifactual effect on perceptual recognition experiments. The results suggest that some results that previously have been attributable to perceptual processes *per se* are entirely explainable in terms of variables concerning word usage.

In discussing the possible effects of word usage in perceptual studies, it is important to make a clear distinction between studies of recognition threshold and studies of other perceptual processes. The claim here is that many of the supposed effects of motivation on recognition threshold can better be explained by the effect of motivation on word usage. Of course, there are perceptual studies in which Ss make no verbal responses at all yet the effects of motivation are clear. These are best illustrated by studies of selective attention, where, for example, it has been shown that "value" influences eye movements and pupillary response.

In spite of the many possibilities for investigating relations between individual differences in word usage and individual differences in perception, only a few related studies have appeared in the literature. A study by Daston (1957) illustrates the potential power of such investigations. He obtained perceptual thresholds for words that patients used frequently in therapeutic interviews. Individual lists were made for each patient containing their own frequently used words. Thresholds for such words were compared with thresholds for control words. The control words were matched on T-L frequency of usage with each patient's own words. Thresholds were lower for the individual's own frequently used words. Obviously, similar experiments could be undertaken for *any* category of words where there are consistent individual differences in usage or where there are differences in usage between different types of Ss.

In studying the effects of individual differences in word usage on perceptual threshold, two hypotheses follow from what was said earlier about the effects of word hierarchies on behavior. First, it should follow that individual differences in word usage should have the most effect on perceptual recognition when the words being displayed are clearly below threshold. Then all the S can do is to rely on word hierarchies rather than on actual perceptual cues. The influence of word hierarchies should play relatively little part as the duration of presentation grows longer and longer. At the higher levels of duration, veridical cues begin to dominate the

Ss behavior, and, consequently, prior word hierarchies have relatively little influence. A second and related hypothesis is that word hierarchies should be strongly manifested in the incorrect guesses made on words at all levels of exposure. When the individual is unsure, his guessing behavior should be more representative of word hierarchies in general and his own private hierarchy of word usage. A recent experiment by Bernstein (1963) suggests this to be the case. So-called perceptual vigilance and defense were manifested only in the Ss' guessing behavior.

VERBAL LEARNING

Numerous pieces of evidence indicate that individual differences in frequency of usage of, or familiarity with, particular words correlate with individual differences in the rate at which those words are acquired in paired-associate learning. Johnson and Watson (1962) found that the number of associates that Ss gave to particular words correlated positively with the rate at which those words were learned. Other studies show that when Ss are given prior familiarization training with nonsense syllables to be used as the response words in paired-associate learning, they learn more rapidly than do members of a control group who receive no familiarization training (see summary of experiments in Hakes, 1961). In other words, when familiarization (or usage) is experimentally induced rather than "natural," it also facilitates rote learning. Although most of the evidence presently comes from experiments on verbal memory, particularly paired-associate memory, word hierarchies may prove to have important effects on more complex types of learning including concept formation and problem-solving.

By what mechanisms do word hierarchies influence verbal learning? I suggest that the mechanisms are much what they are for relations with perception, as previously described. On the first anticipation trial in paired-associate learning, before the S has seen stimulus words paired with correct response words, probabilities for emitting particular words are determined by over-all frequency of usage (T-L list) and by individual differences in over-all frequency of usage. The first trial serves partly to reduce the range of words in which frequency of usage plays a part. The S sees that the response words are all English nouns or all three-letter nonsense syllables. If they are English nouns, they may all be categorizable by the S as pertaining, respectively, to barnyard animals, insects, and types of people. If they are nonsense syllables, they are allocated to categories of word usage in terms of the closeness of their morphological appearance and their "sounds" to real words. Successive anticipation trials serve to consolidate word categories and to reduce their number. Gradually such categories are narrowed to contain only the response words themselves.

Admittedly much is unknown about the process whereby the general hierarchy of word usage gradually is supplanted by particular hierarchies relevant to the list of words being investigated; but the issue is eminently researchable. In one type of experiment Ss could be given prior information about relevant categories of some or all of the words employed in rote memory experiments. For example, in a free recall situation, Ss could be told that the words, respectively, concern insects, barnyard animals, and kitchen objects. Predictable shifts should occur in the rate at which such words are learned from those suggested by the T-L list to those suggested by the probabilities of particular words occurring within categories. The hypothesized effect can be illustrated with the word "bee," which is shown to be a very infrequent word by the T-L list. If the S knew that one category of words was insects, this should considerably increase the probability of "bee" being emitted, and thus in the experiment "bee" would be learned far more rapidly than suggested by the T-L list.

PERSONALITY

In discussing the potential effects of individual difference in word usage on personality, the word "personality" will be used in a broad sense to include persistent needs, characteristic styles of interaction, moods, interests, and attitudes. In this broad domain, there is a wealth of direct and circumstantial evidence to indicate the importance of individual differences in word usage. Dating back to the early work of Carl Jung (1918) is the effort to correlate individual difference in association with "complexes" and other aspects of personality. In the same tradition, more recent investigations by Jenkins (1960) and others of individual differences in association indicate that people who give highly common associations tend to differ in personality from people who tend to give uncommon associations.

Foley and Macmillan (1943) found that people in particular occupations had a greater tendency to interpret homophones as words related to their own occupational interests than to other people's occupational interests. For example, to the stimulus word *administer*, medical students tended to associate such words as *dosage*, *stick*, and *attend*. Students of law tended to associate words like *estate, govern,* and *justice*. Havron and Cofer (1957) found that Ss with strong religious values were better able to learn paired-associates where the response words related to religion than where the response words related to politicoeconomic values; the reverse was true for students with strong politicoeconomic values. Other studies (Dunn, Bliss, and Siipola, 1958; Foley and Macmillan, 1943) have shown relations between individual differences in word usage and individual differences in masculinity, leadership ability, mental illness, and many other aspects of personality. In a later section, recent results obtained by the author and his colleagues will be summarized that show definite relations between individual differences in word usage and individual differences in personality characteristics.

Although the ins and outs of how personality characteristics come to be reflected in word usage may be complex, the basic mechanisms are, I think, rather straightforward. As was previously stated, the particular words that people acquire are, in part, due to the particular environments they have experienced. The child with a hypochondriacal mother, or who himself has been forced to adopt hypochondriacal mechanisms, would be expected to learn and use more words relating to health and illness. The individual with a strong interest in baseball or aviation is likely to talk and read about such topics, and know and frequently employ words relating to those topics. The individual who has adopted a life style of pleasing others rather than showing aggression toward others is likely to employ pleasant words more frequently than unpleasant words. Thus it is for the other means by which individual differences in word usage become related to personality traits—such correlations are generated by (a) types of learning environments (b) conditioned responses to drive states, and (c) different types of instrumental activity.

Three Illustrative Experiments

What has been said so far about the potential importance of word usage would be of little avail if it did not lead directly to interesting new experiments. To show that interesting experiments do follow, an illustrative experiment will be described for each of the areas of learning, perception, and personality.

VERBAL ABILITY AND DURATION THRESHOLD

A recent experiment by Spielberger and Denny (1963) neatly underlines the potential importance of individual differences in word usage for studies of perceptual recognition. They compared recognition thresholds for a group of Ss with high verbal ability with those for a group with low verbal ability. Ss were divided into groups on the basis of a test of verbal ability. All perceptual stimuli were real English words, in three groups, respectively, of high, medium, and low frequency of usage as indicated by the T-L list. Duration thresholds were obtained separately for each S on each word. The results are shown in Figure 1. As they hypothesized, Ss of high verbal ability had lower thresholds on the average for infrequent words than did Ss of low verbal ability. For words of medium frequency of usage, differences between the two groups of Ss were nil. For high-frequency words, Ss of low verbal ability had a small advantage.

Among the possible interpretations of the results by Spielberger and Denny, there is an obvious one that fits in with what has been said about the importance of word usage in perceptual recognition experiments. Ss with high verbal ability are more familiar with infrequent words than are Ss with low verbal ability; they probably use them more frequently, and in that sense the so-called infrequent words are not so infrequent for Ss who are high in verbal ability. If Ss of both high and low verbal ability have the same total amount of experience with words in daily life (which may

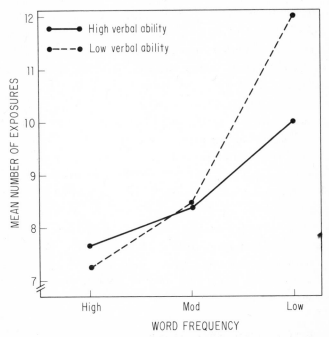

Figure 1 *The mean number of exposures required for the recognition of high, moderate, and low frequency words by Ss of high and low verbal ability.* From C. D. Spielberger and J. P. Denny, *Journal of Experimental Psychology,* **65,** 1963, p. 600. Reproduced by permission of the authors and The American Psychological Association.

not be strictly so), then the failure of Ss with low verbal ability to use so-called infrequent words frequently necessarily requires that they use some words at other levels of the T-L list more frequently than do Ss of high ability. This is what these results suggest. People with low verbal ability may use high-frequency words more frequently than do people of high verbal ability, which in turn is evidenced in the lower thresholds for those words for people of low verbal ability.

Of course, the effect shown by Spielberger and Denny has immense importance for all investigations of tachistoscopic recognition. For one thing, the results indicate that Ss of relatively low verbal ability have a larger standard deviation of threshold levels for words at different levels of T-L list frequency than do Ss of high verbal ability. In turn this indicates that more sensitive experiments can be undertaken with respect to over-all frequency of usage by employing Ss of relatively low verbal ability. Because the experiment dealt with students at Duke University, who as a group are rather high in verbal ability, a more correct interpretation is that more variance in threshold is manifested by students of average to slightly above average verbal ability.

As far as I know, in no previous investigation has level of verbal ability been systematically treated, nor have efforts been made to control that variable by selecting Ss from a narrow band of the continuum of verbal ability. Consequently, *all* previous results of investigations of tachistoscopic recognition may have been clearer if verbal ability had been treated as a systematic effect. As the principles embodied in this article suggest, there may be other dimensions of word usage that interact importantly with perceptual recognition.

ASSOCIATION AND VERBAL LEARNING

A recently completed experiment by me and my colleagues (Nunnally, Koplin, Blanton, and Shaw, 1964) will be used to illustrate the potential importance of individual differences in word usage for verbal learning. The independent variables in the experiment concerned the kinds of associations that Ss give in the classical method of association. It has frequently been found that responses to particular words in the association experiment can readily be learned in paired-associate rote memory. Thus, because *table* is frequently given as a response to the stimulus word *chair*, the pair *chair-table* could rather rapidly be learned in a paired-associate learning experiment. In contrast, it would be relatively more difficult to learn a combination such as *chair-flower*, *flower* not being a response typically given to *chair* in the association experiment. Beyond the differences in learning rates between associates and nonassociates, very little is apparently known about differential effects on learning of different types of associative relations. The experiment to be described was intended to throw light on one such variable.

In the experiment we essentially wanted to learn whether or not the individual's own associates promote paired-associate learning as much or more than do other people's associates, even when the associates given by other people occur with the same frequency in the population as a whole. The major independent variable can be illustrated by looking at a typical hierarchy of responses given in the association experiment. The norms by Russell and Jenkins (1954) indicate that approximately 49 per cent of the Ss gave the response word *table* to the stimulus word *chair*. Next in the hierarchy of response words was *sit*, which was given by approximately 20 per cent of the Ss. We asked questions such as these about the relative positions of response words in association hierarchies. Because *table* is given by almost twice as many people as give *sit* as a response, would people in general more quickly learn the pair *chair-table* than the pair *chair-sit?* Does it make a difference which of these two responses the individual gave? In other words, if a particular individual gave the response *sit*, would this be evidenced in relatively more rapid learning of the pair *chair-sit* than *chair-table?* Conversely, if the individual gave the response *table*, would he more rapidly learn the pair *chair-table* than the pair *chair-sit?* An experiment was undertaken to answer these questions.

In the first stage of the experiment the association task was administered to 72 students enrolled in a class in introductory psychology. Associations were obtained over a month prior to the paired-associate learning phase of the experiment. A 20-pair PA (paired-associate) list was prepared for each S based upon his own responses to the WAT (word association test) according to the following procedure. For each S the Russell and Jenkins normative frequencies for the responses to all 100 stimulus words were recorded. Each S's responses were then ranked from low to high in terms of their normative frequency. Using this list the S's eight responses with the highest normative frequency were selected. Likewise the eight responses with the lowest normative frequencies were obtained.

The eight high-frequency responses (referred to as popular or P responses) were divided into two groups. The odd-numbered ranks were left unchanged. The four pairs formed by these responses and their stimulus words are referred to as the P-P group— i.e., S gave a popular response and it was left unchanged for PA learning. The even-ranked responses were replaced by low-frequency responses from the norms (0.2 per cent level). These four new responses with the appropriate stimulus words form the P-NP pairs; S gave a popular response to a stimulus word and was asked to learn a nonpopular response to that same word.

This procedure was repeated with the responses of low normative frequency. The four odd-ranked responses were left unchanged and with the appropriate stimulus words formed the NP-NP pairs. The four even-ranked responses were replaced by the primary response for each stimulus word. These formed the NP-P pairs.

Four control pairs were constructed by selecting eight words from eight different response hierarchies in the norms. No one of the eight words appeared in the other seven hierarchies involved. These words were arranged in four pairs so that the stimulus and response members of each pair were as formally dissimilar as possible.

At this point all 20 pairs were carefully reviewed in order to eliminate interfering words. No response word was used that appeared in the hierarchy of any other stimulus word in the list. In cases where there was obvious interference (boy-girl and girl-boy both selected for a given S) one of the interfering pairs was replaced by the next choice on the ranked responses for that S.

In addition to having tailor-made lists for each S, it was necessary to construct three random orderings of each list for use in different trials of the learning experiment. The experiment probably would have been done long ago were it not for the large amount of work involved.

The results of the experiment are shown in Figure 2. The curve labeled P-P shows the learning rate for pairs where the S gave the popular response and we used the popular response. The curves labeled NP-NP, NP-P, and P-NP show learning rates for the other three combinations of popular and nonpopular responses. The

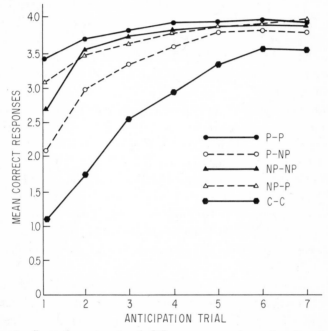

Figure 2 *Learning rates for 5 different types of word pairs, showing the relative effects of "own" and "other peoples'" associations on paired-associate learning.* From Nunnally, Koplin, Blanton, and Shaw, unpublished study, 1964.

curve labeled C-C shows the learning rate for the control pairs. The ordinate of the graph shows the average number of correct anticipations. The abscissa shows the anticipation trials.

Clear differences are shown among the learning rates for the different types of word pairs. The most striking finding is that the four control pairs are learned much more slowly than are stimulus and response words that are found in association. This reaffirms previous findings that words given in association to one another can be learned more quickly than can words that are not given in association to one another.

The next most obvious finding, and the one most important for the discussion here, is that the individual's own associates are learned more quickly than are other people's associates. This is shown by averaging the curves for the P-P and the NP-NP words and comparing this with the average of the P-NP and the NP-curves. The difference between these two averaged curves is marked for anticipation trials 1 and 2, and begins to disappear thereafter.

In addition to showing the power of the individuals own associations for subsequent learning, the results show that frequency of response in the association task for people in general has an effect. This is shown by adding together the P-P and NP-P curves and comparing that with the average of the P-NP and NP-NP curves. Significant differences are found between the two averaged curves, showing a superiority in learning rates for popular response words as compared with nonpopular response words.

The major implication of the experiment for the discussion here is that individual differences in association are not just flukes that have no importance for cognitive processes generally. The results clearly show that individual differences in association (and perhaps individual differences in word usage in general) have effects on verbal learning. This finding opens up many possible experiments linking individual differences in word usage with individual differences in verbal learning.

EVALUATION AND PERSONALITY

To illustrate the importance of word usage for personality traits, some research performed by my colleagues and me will be described. For some time we have employed forced-choice association techniques for the investigation of dimensions of word usage. In a typical item, the S is presented with the stimulus word *orange* and required to choose between the response words *fruit* and *sweet*. The response words are structured in such a way as to measure the tendency to employ different types of associates. From item analyses of such responses, a number of scales have been constructed. Here we will summarize some of the results obtained for two of the scales.

Two of our scales concern respectively, the tendencies to use pleasant words and unpleasant words. Pleasant words are such as sweet, pretty, and friendly; unpleasant words are such as bitter, ugly, and mean. In each of the corresponding scales, pleasant and unpleasant response words are employed in combination with other types of verbal responses. A person is given scores corresponding to the number of pleasant and unpleasant associations chosen on the scales. Correlations between the two scales average about .40 over numerous studies, indicating that there is an over-all tendency to use evaluative responses.

We gave rather common-sense interpretations to these two scales—i.e., that people who use pleasant words tend to be pleasant people and that people who use unpleasant words tend to be unpleasant people. The common ground between the two scales was thought to some extent to be an indicator of over-all emotionality. Numerous small but consistent relations between the scales and other variables tend to bear out our contentions (Nunnally and Flaugher, 1963a). The tendency to give pleasant associations correlates positively with inventory measures of extraversion and negatively with inventory measures of neuroticism. The tendency to give unpleasant associations correlates negatively with extraversion and positively with neuroticism. Also, number of negative associations correlates positively with Taylor Manifest Anxiety Test scores.

Additional evidence is obtained by comparing the average scores from different groups of Ss. Women give more evaluative responses than men, particularly more pleasant associations, which fits in with the widely held notion that women are more emotional than men. Deaf Ss give fewer evaluative responses, both pleasant and unpleasant. Generally the deaf as a group are considered to be rather bland. Schizophrenics give much fewer evaluative responses than normal Ss, which fits in with the contention that schizophrenia is typified by flattened affect. These and other findings with this collection of scales point to the potential importance of word usage for the study of personality.

Methodology

In this section it would be appropriate to state some cautions regarding investigations of individual differences in word usage and to venture some suggestions as to how such investigation can be most profitably undertaken.

TYPES OF WORDS

So far we have talked about words in a general sense without stopping to talk about different types of words. My hunch is that individual differences in three types of words will prove to be most important in relation to cognitive and affective processes. Nouns probably are important to investigate because they relate to the cognitive process of identification. Nouns concerning either concrete or abstract things signify agents of reinforcement—e.g., sandwich, milk, girl, and money. Adjectives (and other classes of words that act like adjectives) are important because they signify personal reactions to objects, or putting it another way, they indicate the kinds and amounts of reinforcement related to particular things —e.g., stale sandwich, fresh milk, pretty girl, and needed money. Verbs are important because they signify the actions that are required in problem-solving situations, and they depict types of instrumental activity—e.g., buy sandwich, drink milk, kiss girl, and borrow money. Probably of lesser importance for cognitive processes are conjunctions, articles, prepositions, and the common pronouns.

WHERE TO STUDY WORD USAGE

Investigations of word usage conceivably could be undertaken in four ways. First, as has been done in a number of studies, word usage can be experimentally induced rather than natural. In a typical study an individual is given familiarization training with some nonsense syllables, and experimental results with these are compared with those for which no familiarization training has been given.

There are three arenas in which "natural" individual differences in word usage can be investigated. First, either with people's consent, or unknown to them, recordings can be made of free conversation in daily life. Content analyses can be made of individual differences in the use of different types of words. Second, content analyses can be made of written material, either material such as personal letters that was written for some other purpose, or material that is written specially for research purposes. Third, word usage can be investigated in a more restrictive setting, in which the individual is supplied with a list of objects or words relating to objects, activities, and attitudes. For these the S is required to give one or several words that bear a specified relationship to the stimulus word or object, or the S is allowed to select one or more response words from a list of available words. This third approach is typified by the classical method of association and by the forced-choice method of association described previously.

Although some research on individual differences in word usage has been undertaken with free conversation and with written material, for two reasons the volume of this research has been rather small. First, Ss talk about or write about different topics or different aspects of topics; consequently, stimulus situations are somewhat different for Ss. Second, the gathering of written material and recorded conversations is tedious, and the content analysis of the material often is a monstrous undertaking. So far most investigations of "natural" differences in word usage have been undertaken in the types of restrictive situations described above, where the stimuli are specified for all Ss and the kinds and numbers of responses are limited. This provides a relatively high degree of experimental control and supplies data that is readily analyzed. Perhaps after we learn more about word usage obtained from such restrictive situations we gradually can move to investigations of free conversation and written material.

DIMENSIONS OF WORD USAGE

It seems to me that investigations of individual differences in word usage eventually will lead to a dead end unless we are able to specify and measure some of the important dimensions along which individual differences in word usage are important. It is not enough to show that individual differences in word usage are important; it is also necessary to specify the dimensions along which such individual differences occur. Looking back at the experiment on association hierarchies and paired-associate learning will provide an illustration of what is meant. There we showed that the individual's own associations have a prepotency in paired-associate learning over the associations given by other people. However, we did not specify any dimensions along which individual's differed in their associations. Consequently, no general conclusions can be reached other than that individual differences are important. Such research is necessary in the early stages of a new arena of investigation, but eventually it should extend to a dimensional analysis of the ways in which differences in verbal behavior are important. Otherwise, this line of research will only prove vexing to those whose research concentrates on group trends. The research will have the same impact that did much of the work by the early Gestaltists, which showed that much was being missed by existing theories but provided few operational principles in return.

What I am suggesting is that important dimensions of word usage will need to be developed in an analogous way to that of the development of dimensions of human abilities. First, new scores of individual differences must be hypothesized, and psychometric procedures must be used to insure that related collections of items actually hang together. Second, each new measure of word usage should demonstrate its importance in some way in relation to perception, learning, or personality. Third, as such measures of word usage are accrued they should be subjected to factor analysis or related procedures in order to reduce redundancy and to clarify the over-all structure.

During the last three years, the author and his colleagues have performed a considerable amount of research to develop scales of individual differences in word usage. Principally, these scales have employed forced-choice association items of the kinds described previously. A number of scales were proposed, item analyses were performed to determine the amount of homogeneity and to improve the homogeneity, and stability of scores was measured over periods ranging up to one year. Factor analyses of the responses of large samples of college students confirmed the relative independence of three scales developed from previous analyses and added three new scales to our list (Nunnally and Hodges, in press). The three older scales already have proved their importance for cognitive and/or affective processes; the importance of the new scales is currently being investigated.

Summary

The major purpose of this article has been to demonstrate that individual differences in word usage correlate with individual differences in learning, perception, and personality. Words are thought to achieve their importance because they figure prominently in the solution of everyday problems, they become conditioned to drive states, and they serve as instrumental acts for the attainment of many types of reinforcement.

Frequency of usage of words by people in general has been shown to have a powerful effect on learning and perception. Particularly with respect to perception, it is now coming to be recognized that many experimental results that previously were thought to concern perceptual processes *per se* can better be explained by individual differences in word usage or by differences in word usage induced by differences in experimental treatments.

The major point of this article hangs on a simple principle, and that is that if general norms for frequency of word usage are important for predicting group trends in learning, perception, and personality, then it may be that individual differences in frequency of usage of words of particular kinds correlate with individual differences in learning, perception, and personality. Experimental results were summarized to show that the principle has some merit;

some hypotheses were stated relating individual differences in word usage to cognitive and affective processes; and three recent investigations were used to demonstrate the power of the principle. The major principle is supported by theory, by existing experimental evidence, and, more importantly, by common sense. There definitely are important relations between individual differences in word usage and individual differences in learning, perception, and personality.

References

Bernstein, I. H. "Perceptual and verbal behavior under two forms of fear inducing pretraining." Unpublished doctoral dissertation, Vanderbilt Univ., 1963.

Carroll, J. E. (ed.). *Language, thought, and reality: selected writings of Benjamin Lee Whorf.* New York: Wiley, 1956.

Daston, P. G. "Perception of idiosyncratically familiar words." *Percept. Mot. Skills*, 1957, **7**, 3–6.

Dulany, D. E. "The place of hypotheses and intentions: An analysis of verbal control in verbal conditioning." *J. Pers.*, 1962, **30**, (Suppl.), 102–129.

Dunn, S., J. Bliss, and E. Siipola. "Effects of impulsivity, introversion, and individual values upon association under free conditions." *J. Pers.*, 1958, **26**, 61–76.

Flaugher, R. L. "Detection value: a measure of verbal relatedness applied to free-association." Unpublished doctoral dissertation, Vanderbilt Univ., 1963.

Foley, J. P., and Z. L. Macmillan. "Mediated generalization and the interpretation of verbal behavior: V. 'Free association' as related to differences in professional training." *J. Exp. Psychol.*, 1943, **33**, 299–310.

Goldiamond, I., and W. F. Hawkins. "Vexierversuche: The log relationship between word frequency and recognition obtained in the absence of stimulus words." *J. Exp. Psychol.*, 1958, **56**, 457–463.

Goodenough, F. L. "Semantic choice and personality structure." *Science*, 1946, **104**, 451–456.

Greenspoon, J. "The reinforcing effect of two spoken words on the frequency of two responses." *Amer. J. Psychol.*, 1955, **68**, 409–416.

Hakes, D. T. "The role of stimulus and response familiarization in paired-associate learning." Studies in verbal behavior, Report No. 4, University of Minnesota, June 1961.

Jenkins, J. J. "Commonality of association as an indicator of more general patterns of verbal behavior." In T. A. Sebeok (ed.). *Style in language*. New York: Wiley, 1960, pp. 307–329.

Johnson, R. C., and N. Watson. "Individual meaning production as related to amount of verbal learning." *J. Gen. Psychol.*, 1962, **67**, 117–120.

Jung, C. G. *Studies in word association*. (M. D. Eder, trans.) London: Heineman, 1918.

McClelland, D. C., and J. W. Atkinson. "The projective expression of needs: I. The effect of different intensities of the hunger drive on perception." *J. Psychol.*, 1948, **25**, 205–222.

McGinnies, E. "Emotionality and perceptual defense." *Psychol. Rev.*, 1949, **56**, 244–251.

Noble, C. E. "Meaningfulness and familiarity." In C. N. Cofer and Barbara S. Musgrave (eds.). *Verbal behavior and learning*. New York: McGraw-Hill, 1963, pp. 76–157.

Nunnally, J. C., and R. L. Flaugher. "Correlates of semantic habits." *J. Pers.*, 1963a, **31**, 192–202.

———, and ———. "Psychological implications of word usage." *Science* 1963b, **40**, 775–781.

———, ———, and W. F. Hodges. "Measurement of semantic habits." *Educ. Psychol. Measmt*, 1963, **23**, 419–434.

———, and W. F. Hodges. "Some dimensions of individual differences in word association." *J. Verbal Learn. Verbal Behav.*, in press.

———, J. H. Koplin, R. L. Blanton, and R. E. Shaw. "Individual differences in word association in relation to paired-associate learning." Unpublished study, Vanderbilt Univ., 1964.

Osgood, C. E., and E. G. Walker. "Motivation and language behavior: a content analysis of suicide notes." *J. Abnorm. Soc. Psychol.*, 1959, **59**, 58–67.

Postman, L., Wanda C. Bronson, and G. L. Gropper. "Is there a mechanism of perceptual defense?" *J. Abnorm. Soc. Psychol.*, 1953, **48**, 215–224.

———, J. S. Bruner, and E. McGinnies. "Personal values as selective factors in perception." *J. Abnorm. Soc. Psychol.*, 1948, **43**, 142–154.

Russell, W. A., and J. J. Jenkins. "The complete Minnesota norms for responses to 100 words from the Kent-Rosanoff word association test." Tech. Rep. No. 11, Univ. Minnesota, 1954.

Solomon, R. L., and L. Postman. "Frequency of usage as a determinant of recognition thresholds for words." *J. Exp. Psychol.*, 1952, **43**, 195–201.

Spielberger, C. D. "The role of awareness in verbal conditioning." *J. Pers.* 1962, **30**, (Suppl.), 73–101.

———, and J. P. Denny. "Visual recognition thresholds as a function of verbal ability and word frequency." *J. Exp. Psychol.*, 1963, **65**, 597–602.

Taffel, C. "Anxiety and the conditioning of verbal behavior." *Amer. J. Psychol.*, 1955, **51**, 496–501.

Thorndike, E. L., and I. Lorge. *The teacher's word book of 30,000 words*. New York: Columbia Univ. Press, 1944.

Underwood, B. J., and R. W. Schulz. *Meaningfulness and verbal learning*. New York: Lippincott, 1960.

VI

PSYCHOLINGUISTICS AND LANGUAGE PATHOLOGY

LANGUAGE:
A PERSPECTIVE FROM
THE STUDY OF APHASIA[1]

Lyle V. Jones
Joseph M. Wepman

Aphasia is a disorder, resulting from organic impairment of the central nervous system, of the abilities necessary to formulate or comprehend verbal symbols (Wepman and Jones, 1961a, p. 74). Aphasia is considered to result from disruption of a central integrative function. Language problems resulting from sensory disorders, the agnosias, and motor disorders, the apraxias, are excluded in this discussion from the aphasias.

The premise of this presentation is that the study of aphasia yields sizable dividends in the form of general principles of language organization. By determining the communication processes

[1] Research upon which this paper is based has been performed with support from PHS research grants No. M-1849 and No. M-1876 from the National Institutes of Health, Public Health Service. The present report is a modification and extension of papers presented by the first author in December 1961 at the University of Illinois Psychology Colloquium and in November 1962 to the Psychology Colloquium at Pennsylvania State University. The authors are grateful to Dr. W. Grant Dahlstrom, of the University of North Carolina, to Dr. Jerzy Konorski, of the Nencki Institute of Experimental Biology in Warsaw, Poland, and to Dr. Edward Zigler, of Yale University, for helpful criticisms of an earlier draft.

that are differentially affected by brain damage, we become aware
of language processes that must contribute to the language skills
of the normally functioning person.

In pursuing research on aphasia, we have followed two main
lines of investigation. First, data were collected from a specially
designed battery of tests in which language behavior was called
for under highly restricted conditions of stimulation, with structured
response alternatives. Second, with only loosely controlled contextual conditions free speech samples were selected from aphasia
patients (as well as from nonafflicted adults) and are being subjected to grammatical analysis. Based upon findings from both
these avenues of research and upon consideration of the course of
development of language skills in normal children we wish to discuss a conceptual model in the form of a schematic diagram of
language processing units inferred to be necessary in a normal,
brain-intact individual.

Factor Analysis of Test Performance by Aphasic Patients

One source of evidence concerning distinguishable language
processes comes from a factor analysis of performance of aphasic
patients on an extensive battery of specially prepared test items.
The items were those of the Language Modalities Test for Aphasia
(Wepman and Jones, 1961b). They include tasks presented visually
and aurally, for which oral, graphic, or matching responses are
required. Stimuli are presented on film strip, with blank frames
being shown while the examiner is presenting auditory stimuli.

Both forms of an experimental version of this test were administered to a total of 168 aphasic patients, selected from hospitals
throughout the northeastern United States. In order to be included
in the sample, it was necessary that their neurological record
clearly attested to brain damage, that their hospital record showed
diagnosis of language disability consequent to brain damage, and
also that, in a screening test and interview, they demonstrated
sufficient residual language skills to follow test instructions and to
produce some coherent speech sounds. Of the 168 patients, 130 had

suffered cerebrovascular accidents, while for 38 brain damage was due to other factors, primarily external trauma.

In an attempt to determine "dimensions" of aphasia, several factor analyses and analyses of variance were performed. Before performing such analyses, it was first necessary to quantify observed qualitative differences among patients' responses to the test items. A number of such qualitative differences were noted among responses produced. A spoken word, for example, might differ from a correct response in a variety of ways. The response might differ from a correct one only as a result of inadequate articulation. Or it might be a well-pronounced word, but a "wrong" word. The response might be completely unintelligible, or it might be an automatic phrase repeatedly used by the subject. The subject might refuse to produce any response.

It is not reasonable to force a set of a priori "weights" upon these response categories to represent the degree of error. Rather, we may turn to an empirical analysis to scale the categories, to transform qualitative response differences into quantitative form. The method is attributable to Fisher (1938); it has become known as the method of optimal scaling (Bock, 1960). The principle by which scale values are assigned to response categories is a familiar one in other contexts. It is desired to assign these numbers so that, for a given class of language tasks, between-individual differences are maximized relative to within-individual variability. Assuming that patients do have characteristic levels of performance, and that their responses to a set of replicated items are dependent upon their performance level, these scale values which achieve optimal discrimination among individuals also measure adequacy of the responses.

Utilizing such scale values, product-moment correlations were obtained among 35 subtests of the test battery, and the age and educational levels of subjects. Several criteria agreed in attesting to six significant principal axes factors, and these were rotated to a varimax solution (Kaiser, 1958). (For a complete report, see Jones and Wepman, 1961.)

Each of four factors was clearly defined by a set of tasks homogeneous in terms of the stimulus and response modalities they involved (see Table 1). Thus factor A was defined by all items demanding oral response to printed stimuli, factor B by all items demanding oral response to auditory stimuli, factor C by all items involving written response to printed stimuli, and factor D by all items involving written response to auditory stimuli. The fifth factor, factor E, was defined by all matching items—items requiring matching of words or sentences, presented either visually or aurally, to alternate-choice pictures. All such items measure ability

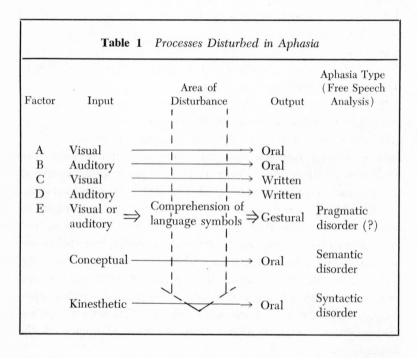

Table 1 *Processes Disturbed in Aphasia*

to *comprehend* language symbols as contrasted with ability to reproduce the symbols. It might be noted that age of patient is represented on this comprehension factor; older patients are more likely than younger patients to suffer disruption of comprehension.

A small sixth factor is defined by performance on simple arithmetic tasks and by educational level. Brain-injured adults with considerable schooling seem less likely to lose their arithmetic skill than those whose education was less.

From these results, it is clear that performance of aphasic sub-

jects may be distinguished in terms of the stimulus-response transmission channels demanded by language tasks. Our test sampled
four such transmission channels—from visual stimuli to oral response,
from auditory stimuli to oral response, from visual stimuli to
written response, and from auditory stimuli to written response. In
addition, a well-defined fifth process was distinguished, that defined by subtests which demanded comprehension of verbal stimuli
as contrasted to reproduction of symbols. From this evidence, we
might postulate at least five distinct dimensions of aphasic disorder,
in terms of which difficulties of a given patient can be characterized.

Somewhat parenthetically, it may be noted that our attempt at
constructing a comprehensive test for aphasia included many potential "dimensions" that were *not* empirically verified. A good
example is provided by the range of words presented as stimuli.
Words were classified by part of speech, by concrete versus abstract reference, by number of syllables, and by expected frequency
of occurrence as evidenced by Thorndike-Lorge counts. In no case
did these distinctions serve to differentiate among aphasic patients.
While several of these variables contribute to the general difficulty
of items, they fail to contribute differentially to the definition of
factors underlying performance of the aphasic patients.

Free Speech of Aphasic Patients

While administration of a structured test to aphasic patients
seems a reasonable means to gather data concerning their language
disorders, it is not the only such means. There is no reason to believe that what one learns from observing a patient's behavior under
test conditions always mirrors the impression one would obtain
from the patient's free speech. Another source of data bearing upon
the organization of language abilities is, then, the free speech of
aphasic patients. For convenience, and to assure somewhat standard conditions of stimulation from one patient to the next, we have
adopted the method of recording patients' responses to the 20 pictures of the Thematic Apperception Test. To characterize the style
of speech of each subject from such data has been and remains a
major problem. An initial approach to the problem involves the

classification of each spoken word into a part-of-speech category (Jones, Goodman, and Wepman, 1963). The speech of individuals then may be contrasted, one with another, in terms of the relative use of various parts of speech. Recently completed at Chapel Hill is a computer program for the Univac 1105, one which will accept English texts and perform a partial grammatical classification in accordance with dictionary look-up procedures. Stored within the computer is a dictionary of 402 English words that occur with high frequency and are unambiguous with respect to grammatical class for TAT stories of normal speakers. Evidence from preliminary analysis of 27 normal speakers (from a total of 56 currently being processed), shows that this list of 402 words accounts for an average of more than 83 per cent of word occurrences in stories to the 20 TAT pictures. The most frequently appearing 34 words account for 50 per cent of word occurrences (Wepman and Jones, 1964b).

Our previous work with free-speech transcripts necessitated word-by-word classification into parts of speech performed by linguistically trained judges, using a computer only subsequent to the classification to obtain summary statistics for each speaker (Fillenbaum, Jones, and Wepman, 1961). We now propose to utilize the computer program for grammatical classification of the bulk of words, employing a postediting scheme to handle the remainder.

It must be remembered that the aim here is one of grammatical analysis of speech, not printed text, from aphasia patients, not from normal speakers. The structure of such speech typically departs sharply from that of orderly English-language communication. Thus a system for analysis that is dependent upon "correct" grammatical structure, or that must utilize contextual cues, is doomed to failure. An instructive approach might be one of generating a grammar appropriate to each individual aphasic speaker. Initially we have chosen a less ambitious aim, that of describing the speech of an aphasic patient by contrasting relative frequency of use of various parts of speech with relative frequencies observed among normal speakers.

Measures of relative frequency of use of various parts of speech do serve sharply to distinguish among aphasic patients (Fillenbaum, Jones, and Wepman, 1961; Wepman, Bock, Jones, and Van Pelt, 1956) and to distinguish, to a lesser degree, among normal speakers. Based upon analysis of free speech from brain-damaged patients, we have come to distinguish three forms of aphasic disorder, highly reminiscent of the three basic characteristics of natural language proposed by Morris (1938). These Morris called the "semantical" property, the relations of signs to objects or events; the "syntactical" function, the relations of signs to signs; and the "pragmatical" property, the relations of signs to interpreters. For aphasic patients who retain sufficient verbal behavior to allow morphemic analysis, we have found useful a description of language behavior in terms of the constructs stated by Morris. Patients have been studied who show differential language disturbances in the power of semantic selection, in the use of syntax, and in the pragmatic ability of the speaker to interpret signs as they relate to the objects or events they represent.

The disturbance we would call semantic aphasia is marked by the inability of a patient to call forth signs that represent given objects, actions, or events. The loss of the ability to nominate specific symbols is described by Jackson (1931) as "propositionalizing" disability, by Jakobson (1956) as "similarity disorder," and by Luria (1958) as "loss of ability to communicate ideas." Word usage by patients with this disorder tends to be limited to the more frequent words of the language (Wepman, Bock, Jones, and Van Pelt, 1956). Notably, there is retention of some grammatical form and function. Speech is frequently interrupted by pauses, word-finding attempts, and circumlocutions.

The attempt of a typical semantic aphasic patient to respond to a TAT picture illustrates the problem:

Well she doesn't feel very good, or she feels better maybe, or no, she . . . I can't remember these words out loud, I'm sorry. . . . I don't know what, she's feeling sad about somebody, but I don't know what.

In the syntactic aphasic patient, the ability to nominate at least some of the substantive symbols of the language remains relatively intact, but he displays a loss of the grammatical functions of language. Thus there tends to be a reduction from the expected number of occurrences of at least some of the highly frequent function words of the language. Syntactic aphasic patients tend toward a telegraphic style of speech (Luria, 1958). Jakobson (1956) refers to such patients as those who retain normal word selection and substitution but who display a contiguity disorder.

For comparative purposes, observe the conversational pattern of a typical syntactic aphasic patient. In response to the same TAT picture he spoke as follows:

> Sad . . . bed . . . weeping . . . crying. That's a family . . . yeah . . . crying, its ah . . . picture.

These same syntactic patients also may fail to properly use inflection, tense, or gender (Goodglass and Berko, 1960; Goodglass and Mayer, 1958; Wepman and Jones, 1961a). Lack of syntactic refinement in communication thus marks the speech of these patients; despite these difficulties, it should be noted that the syntactic disorder may not seriously interfere with the ability to communicate meaningfully and effectively.

A third disturbance of language skills, called pragmatic aphasia, is one less often noted in the literature. Perhaps the disability is closest to that which Luria describes as "breakdown in the regulatory function of speech connections" (1958). In pragmatic aphasia there is disruption of the ability of the individual to obtain meaning from a stimulus and use it as a basis for symbol formulation. Analysis of the speech of pragmatic patients suggests only slight constriction of vocabulary. However, words and neologisms apparently unrelated to the stimulating situation are commonly found. Meaning of the patient's utterance typically is severely disturbed.

Pragmatic patients show usually a retention of all of the phonological properties of language. They speak with well-retained intonational patterns; there is a flow of words, but with no apparent self-criticism. Word groups convey little or no meaning; yet there appears on the part of the patient no recognition of his failure to communicate.

The brief example that follows represents one such patient's attempt to describe the same TAT picture as that of the previous two examples.

Well, now, what would you call that? That's a blashker. He's plays here. Somebody's come to there's he's, through of haystrue . . . in desert over something, as work, or, . . . course there's too much lecture for him and she's fortunate.

So far we have indicated two alternate sets of constructs applicable to the description of aphasic behavior, one set derived from factor analysis of test responses, one set obtained from consideration of patients' free speech. A question naturally arises concerning whether the two sets of constructs are empirically related. Several studies aimed at assessing such relations between free speech and test performance have met with only very limited success (Ross, 1960; Spiegel, 1960). At best, there is only partial overlap between the two sets of constructs, and no clear one-to-one relationship between categories of one set and those of the other. There is some indication that the pragmatic aphasic patient is likely to perform poorly on comprehension tasks; tentatively, we might consider the breakdown of the process responsible for language comprehension to produce speech of this pragmatic sort.

The three aphasic disorders noted above, semantic, syntactic, and pragmatic, are listed in the final column of Table 1.

Observation of Postoperative Lesion Patients

All of the above evidence has been derived from the study of aphasic patients who have suffered rather diffuse brain damage, most frequently induced by cerebrovascular accident—i.e., by "stroke." It would be instructive to compare with such evidence that which results from observations of patients with specific, localized brain lesions. Such patients have been extensively studied by Dr. Jerzy Konorski, of the Nencki Institute of Experimental Biology in Warsaw, Poland. From discussion and written communication with Dr. Konorski comes this third source of evidence concerning the nature of aphasic disorders.

In studying brain-injured patients, Konorski utilizes a variety of behavioral tests to determine the nature of language loss. To estimate *extent* of loss, Konorski presents what he calls a many-signal test, involving a sequence of stimuli to which the patient is asked to respond. Even when correct reactions might be given to single stimuli, failures often are observed in the sequential task. Included are items that require repetition of words spoken to the patient, items that require the patient to indicate the objects named by the examiner, and items that require patients to produce oral explanations of simple concepts spoken by the examiner. None of the tasks presented by Konorski involve printed stimuli, and none demand written responses. Thus, his reports yield no evidence concerning forms of language disorder that depend upon printed stimuli or written responses.

Konorski has been led by his findings to characterize four types of language disorder. Based upon his descriptions of these disorders and upon our discussion of the problem with him, these disorders have been matched to those we earlier had discovered. Konorski's characterizations of the disorders are as follows (Konorski, 1961).

Acoustic-oral transmission disorder "is characterized by more or less selective disability (or impairment) of repetition of heard words." Clearly, it is such a disorder that is responsible for the appearance in the factor analysis of a factor defined by repetition of aurally presented words and sentences, factor B of Table 1.

Acoustic-conceptual aphasia "is characterised by selective impairment of comprehension of the speech heard. This is the so-called Wernicke's 'sensory' aphasia. In this type of speech disorder, just as in the preceding one, both nomination and automatized verbal sequences may be almost unimpaired, which enables the patient to speak quite fluently. . . . Repetition may be also well preserved or less impaired than understanding," showing the difference between the acoustic-oral and acoustic-conceptual systems. This disorder would seem to be that identified from factor analysis as the comprehension factor, factor E of Table 1, also related to the pragmatic impairment of free speech.

Conceptual-oral aphasia "is characterized by selective impairment of nomination with spared repetition, comprehension and automatized verbal series. The speech of these patients has a peculiar character since they chiefly utilize the well-established routine phrases with circumlocution of essential parts of the sentences. . . ."

Clearly, this disorder is equivalent to semantic aphasia, as discovered from analysis of free speech.

The kinesthetic-motor aphasias are characterized by a disturbance of oral expression in which there is "more or less pronounced deterioration of automatized syllabic or verbal sequences. . . . In contradistinction to the nominative aphasia, the speech is 'telegraphic' in style, condensed, but always matter-of-fact." This description matches that independently put forth to characterize syntactic aphasia, as found from patients' free speech.

Now, it should be emphasized that Konorski's methods of observation are very different from those we have employed. Also the etiology of his patients is different from ours. And, of course, the Polish language, the medium in which he tests for speech disorders, differs considerably from English. These differences serve to magnify the importance of the degree to which our findings and those of Konorski appear to agree. Wherever the behavioral tests presented to patients are such as to allow the same language disorders to be discovered, they seem to have been discovered independently in Konorski's laboratory and ours.

Some Postulated Language-Processing Units

As an additional aid to specification of major components of language skills, let us consider mechanisms by which these skills might develop in the young child. The model to be proposed is quite consistent with that of Simon (1957) and Carroll (1961), expressed also by Wepman and Jones (1964a). It draws heavily upon earlier research findings as summarized by McCarthy (1954). The resulting model of language functioning is a modification and extension of one proposed by Konorski (1961); it is closely related to the view of Osgood and Jenkins (1954) on learning of language decoding and encoding behavior, and is consistent with the theory of language learning presented recently by Mowrer (1960).

Noted by many investigators of infant development is the appearance, between the ages of two and four months, of babbling, cooing, or self-initiated vocal "playing." Movements of the mouth and larynx are accompanied by vocalization. Let us postulate the establishment of associations between the processing of particular kinesthetic sensations from the mouth and larynx and the processing of the consequent auditory stimulation. The situation is schematically displayed in Figure 1, where the associations are represented by the double arrow between the "kinesthetic processor" and the "acoustic processor."

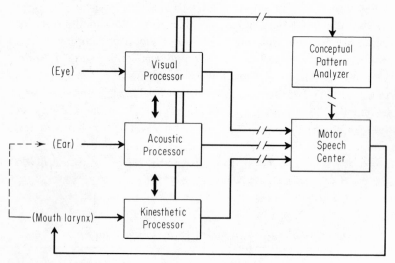

Figure 1 *Major components of a conceptual scheme for language skills involving speech.*

The role of these perceptual processors is not one of abstracting "meaning" from the stimuli, as will soon become more apparent. The processor, in interaction with memory, is thought of more as a stimulus recognizer, its function remaining specific to a given sensory modality. Its psychological function parallels that which is commonly attributed to secondary sensory association areas of the cerebral cortex.

Echolalic behavior appears in infants at an age between 6 and 10 months; the infant is able to repeat or imitate sounds produced by himself and by others. These phenomena provide evidence for associations between the acoustic processor and the motor speech producer, as shown in Figure 1. With acoustic feedback, there is provided a means for monitoring pronunciation, and as the child develops, this repetition skill becomes more and more refined. Then frequent repetition of particular sound sequences leads to their consolidation, to more or less automatic sequencing, dependent upon connections between both acoustic and kinesthetic processors and the motor speech producer.

As early as seven or eight months of age, the infant vocalizes recognition of objects visually presented. A visual processor thus is represented in the system, with connections both with other sensory processors and with the motor speech producer.

The vocalization of humans is not distinguishable from that of other animals—some birds, for example—by the mechanisms discussed so far. In human communication, however, sound compounds serve as symbols for objects, activities, and for "concepts." We postulate a processing system responsible for comprehension of language symbols, a "conceptual pattern analyzer" which, in interaction with memory, integrates the resultants from stimulus processors for all sense modalities. It is postulated that only at this conceptual level do symbols become stripped of their sensory origin. Here, symbols are manipulated in "canonical form," enriched by conceptual associations from memory. Output from the conceptual pattern analyzer then may provide direction to motor speech production.

Findings from research in aphasia are coordinated with this portrayal of language processes in Figure 1. Each "break" in a transmission channel may be matched to a form of disturbance found in aphasic patients, as presented earlier. Represented are (a) the disruption between the visual processor and motor speech production (factor A of Table 1); (b) disruption between the acoustic processor and speech production (factor B of Table 1); (c) disruption between the kinesthetic processor and speech production, the syntactic disorder evidenced by disturbance of oral sequencing; (d) disruption between the conceptual pattern analyzer and speech production, the semantic disorder in which patients are unable to produce particular words representing objects, actions, descriptive characteristics, or concepts; and (e) disruption between sensory processors and the conceptual pattern analyzer, pragmatic aphasia, where comprehension or understanding is disturbed.

Notice that, in this model, disruption of the conceptual process is represented as a unitary disorder, a failure of comprehension that transcends the modality of the stimulus. This is consistent with results from the factor analysis and with other evidence cited earlier.

An analysis can be performed for processes associated with writing parallel to that for speech, and a similar schematic diagram may be constructed (Figure 2). Here, factors C and D of Table

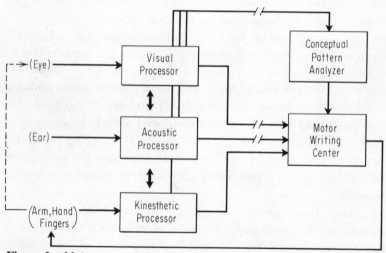

Figure 2 *Major components of a conceptual scheme for language skills involving writing.*

1 provide empirical evidence for two additional forms of disturbance: inability to correctly copy visual stimuli, represented by a disruption between the visual processor and a motor writing producer; and inability to translate language stimuli from auditory to written form, represented by a disruption between the acoustic processor and a motor writing producer. The model presented suggests that we might profitably look further to determine whether

some aphasic patients display an analogue to semantic aphasia when required to compose a text rather than to speak. Disruption between the conceptual pattern analyzer and the motor writing producer would lead to such a disorder. Further, we might search for evidence that disruptions occur between the kinesthetic processor and the motor writing producer. There is no doubt that in normal writing may be observed errors of sequencing, where letters are anticipated or misplaced. Whether such errors typify an aphasic disorder is difficult to determine, since with severe left-hemisphere brain damage, patients' writing skill tends to be so disturbed that graphic production of strings of words is a task they refuse to perform.

Of considerable interest would be a careful survey of studies of infant language behavior in terms of the model presented here. To take explicit account of the stimulus-response transmission channels required for each language task might serve to bring increased order and coherence to our view of the development of communication skills of the child. There is evidence showing that such considerations are pertinent to the differential acquisition of language skills in six- to eight-year-old children (Zigler, Jones, and Kafes, 1964).

Summary

Factor analysis of test results has demonstrated the existence of four stimulus-response transmission factors and a fifth comprehension factor which reflect disturbances of language performance in aphasia patients. From analysis of the free speech of aphasic speakers the comprehension difficulty is again found (pragmatic aphasia), as well as difficulty in word-finding (semantic aphasia) and difficulty in word-sequencing (syntactic aphasia).

Systematic observation of aphasic patients suffering from postoperative lesions has led Konorski to recognize speech syndromes apparently the same as our pragmatic, semantic, and syntactic disorders, and to postulate also an auditory-oral transmission defect. Visual-oral, visual-written, and auditory-written transmission disturbances did not have an opportunity to appear in Konorski's analysis, since no visual tasks nor written responses were studied. These findings from research on aphasia are collated with findings regarding development of language skills in children. A schematic model is described that designates the language processes postulated from these sources of evidence; the specific aphasic disorders that have been discovered are identified as distinct disturbances of processes within the model.

References

Bock, R. D. "Methods and applications of optimal scaling." Univ. North Carolina, Psychometric Lab. Rep. No. 25, May 1960.

Carroll, J. B. "Language development in children." In S. Saporta (ed.). *Psycholinguistics*. New York: Holt, Rinehart and Winston, 1961.

Fillenbaum, S., L. V. Jones, and J. M. Wepman. "Some linguistic features of speech from aphasic patients." *Language and Speech*, 1961, 4, 91–108.

Fisher, R. A. *Statistical methods for research workers*. New York: Hafner, 1938.

Goodglass, H., and J. Berko. "Agrammatism and inflectional morphology in English." *J. Speech and Hearing Res.*, 1960, 3, 257–267.

———, and J. Mayer. "Agrammatism and aphasia." *J. Speech and Hearing Dis.*, 1958, 23, 99–111.

Jackson, H. *Selected writings of J. Hughlings Jackson*. J. Taylor (ed.). London: Hadder and Stoughton, 1931.

Jakobson, R., and M. Halle. *Fundamentals of language*. 'S-Gravenhage: Mouton and Co., 1956.

Jones, L. V., M. F. Goodman, and J. M. Wepman. "The classification of parts of speech for the characterization of aphasia." *Language and Speech*, 1963, 6, 94–107.

———, and J. M. Wepman. "Dimensions of language performance in aphasia." *J. Speech and Hearing Res.*, 1961, 4, 220–232.

Kaiser, H. "The varimax criterion for analytic rotation in factor analysis." *Psychometrika*, 1958, 23, 187–200.

Konorski, J. "Analiza patofizjologiczna róznych rodzajów zaburzen mowy I próba ich klasyfikacju." (Pathophysiological analysis of various forms of speech disorders and an attempt of their classification.) *Rozprawy wydziatu nauk medycznych.*, R. VI-T. II, 9–32, Warsaw, Poland, 1961.

Luria, A. R. "Brain disorders and language analysis." *Language and Speech*, 1958, 1, 14–34.

McCarthy, D. "Language development in children." In L. Carmichael (ed.). *Manual of child psychology*, 2nd ed. New York: Wiley, 1954, 492–630.

Morris, C. "Foundation of the theory of signs." *International Encyclopedia of Unified Science*. In O. Neurath (ed.). Chicago: Univ. Chicago Press, 1938.

Mowrer, O. H. *Learning theory and the symbolic processes*. New York. Wiley, 1960.

Osgood, C. E., and J. J. Jenkins. "A psycholinguistic analysis of decoding and encoding." *Suppl. J. Abnorm. Soc. Psychol.*, 1954, 49, 126–135.

Ross, D. C. "A classification of aphasics." Ph.D. dissertation, Univ. North Carolina, 1960.

Simon, C. T. The development of speech. In L. E. Travis (ed.). *Handbook of Speech Pathology*, New York: Appleton-Century-Crofts, 1957.

Spiegel, D. K. "An investigation of relationships between aberrant test responses and characteristics of free speech samples from aphasia patients." M.A. dissertation, Univ. North Carolina, 1960.

Weisenberg, T., and K. McBride. *Aphasia*. New York: Commonwealth Fund, 1935.

Wepman, J. M. In R. West (ed.). *Proceedings of the Institute on Childhood Aphasia*. San Francisco: California Society for Crippled Children and Adults, 1962.

———, R. D. Bock, L. V. Jones, and D. Van Pelt. "Psycholinguistic study of aphasia: a revision of the concept of anomia." *J. Speech and Hearing Dis.*, 1956, 21, 468–477.

———, and L. V. Jones. *Studies in aphasia: an approach to testing*. Chicago: Univ. Chicago Education-Industry Service, 1961a.

———, and ———. *The language modalities test for aphasia*. Chicago: Univ. Chicago Education-Industry Service, 1961b.

———, and ———. "Five aphasias: a commentary on aphasia as a regressive linguistic phenomenon." *J. Assoc. Res. Nerv. Ment. Dis.*, 1964a, in press.

———, and ———. "Studies in aphasia: psycholinguistic methods and a case study." In V. E. Hall (ed.). *Proceedings of the Conference on Speech, Language and Communication*, 1964b, in press.

Zigler, E., L. V. Jones, and P. Kafes. "The acquisition of language and abilities in first, second, and third grade boys." *Child Development*, 1964, in press.

AUTHOR INDEX

SUBJECT INDEX

259